Making Sense

Seventh Edition

Making Sense

A Student's Guide to
Research and Writing

Geography and Environmental Sciences

Margot Northey
Dianne Draper
David B. Knight

OXFORD
UNIVERSITY PRESS

OXFORD
UNIVERSITY PRESS

Oxford University Press is a department of the University of Oxford.
It furthers the University's objective of excellence in research, scholarship,
and education by publishing worldwide. Oxford is a registered trade mark of
Oxford University Press in the UK and in certain other countries.

Published in Canada by
Oxford University Press
8 Sampson Mews, Suite 204,
Don Mills, Ontario M3C 0H5 Canada

www.oupcanada.com

First Edition published in 1992
Second Edition published in 2001
Third Edition published in 2007
Fourth Edition published in 2009
Fifth Edition published in 2012
Sixth edition published in 2015

Library and Archives Canada Cataloguing in Publication

Northey, Margot, 1940-, author
Making sense in geography and environmental studies : a student's guide to
research and writing / Margot Northey, Dianne Draper, and David B. Knight.

(The making sense series)
Includes bibliographical references and index.
ISBN 978-0-19-902680-7 (softcover)

1. Geography—Authorship. 2. Human ecology—Authorship. 3. English
language—Rhetoric. 4. Report writing. I. Draper, Dianne, 1949-, author
II. Knight, David B., author III. Title. IV. Series: Making sense series

G74.N67 2019   808.06'691   C2018-906698-9

Cover image: © iStock/cgardinerphotos
Cover design: Laurie McGregor
Interior design: Sherill Chapman

Oxford University Press is committed to our environment.
This book is printed on Forest Stewardship Council® certified paper
and comes from responsible sources.

Printed and bound in the United States of America

1 2 3 4 — 22 21 20 19

Contents

Preface

The first edition of this book, published in 1992, clearly addressed a need: it was widely adopted as a supplementary text for students in geography, the environmental sciences, interdisciplinary environmental studies, and other disciplines, including history. The second edition, published in 2001, incorporated changes that had resulted from the remarkable developments in computer technology; reordered the chapters based on student suggestions; and provided an innovative integration of reference styles. An updated second edition, published in 2005, included the newly made revisions to CSE, APA, and MLA referencing guidelines. The third edition, published in 2007, responded to the continuing computerization of academic life, and included new or rewritten sections on plagiarism and cheating, research ethics, annotated bibliographies, preparing a questionnaire, formatting and protecting your work, and GIS-based projects published online. The fourth edition, published in 2009, made many necessary changes, again due to continuing technological developments, such as an expanded discussion of Internet sources and how to critically evaluate and use them. New material on group work was added, as were figures on Baker's funnel/inverse funnel approach to writing and on preparing a proposal. The list of journals was expanded and relocated to a new appendix for easier reference, and the expanded list of pertinent websites also was relocated to an appendix. Similarly, the fifth edition reflected advances in the integration of computer-based research in libraries and online as well as in computer-assisted cartography and GIS.

Changes in the sixth edition included new material on thinking critically and on active listening as well as additional details about poster preparation. Updates relating to the use of computers in research, and additional examples from human geographical research fields were added, as were brief chapter summaries.

In this seventh edition, changes include additional material on peer review (Chapter 1), the use of bibliographic management tools and the growth of Open Access publishing (Chapter 2), and the nature and importance of an abstract in a thesis or Honours paper (Chapter 6). The new revisions to CSE and MLA referencing guidelines have been incorporated (Chapter 7). Suggestions for working effectively on group assignments (Chapter 8), expanded sections on mental maps (Chapter 12), the careful use of language (Chapter 13), and the addition of selected terms to the glossary relating to sustainability also are new in this edition. The previously included list of journals was removed because the many databases now available provide quick and effective keyword search capabilities.

Acknowledgements

The seventh edition of *Making Sense in Geography and Environmental Sciences* continues to build on its earlier editions. For the first edition, Margot Northey kindly gave David Knight permission to create a specialized volume for geography students based on her original *Making Sense*. Dianne Draper became a co-author for the fourth edition. Both authors are grateful to Margot Northey for her inspiration and trust, and to the generations of students and faculty who provided feedback on each edition of this book that helped to continue its development. Both authors previously acknowledged the benefits they derived from their editorial responsibilities with various publications and journals.

David Knight was a professor of geography and a professional editor for over 30 years; now retired from university life, he volunteers with the Alzheimer's Society and performs as the timpanist in symphony orchestras. Dianne Draper, a professor of geography for over 40 years, undertook the revisions for the sixth and seventh editions. She is grateful for David's insights and contributions and wishes him many more years of joyful music making.

The authors are grateful for the expert assistance provided by the fine people at Oxford University Press, including Phyllis Wilson, Lauren Wing, and Liana Spada. We also acknowledge the people whose names appear with their illustrations in this book. Colleagues who assisted us in the preparation of earlier editions were acknowledged therein.

Finally, we sincerely hope the many practical suggestions made throughout this book will contribute to your scholarly competence and performance.

Dianne Draper   David B. Knight
Calgary, Alberta   Elora, Ontario

A Note to the Student

This book is intended to teach students in geography, other environmental sciences, and interdisciplinary environmental and sustainability studies programs how to undertake and successfully complete assignments that involve research and writing.

The book's principal goal is to assist you when you write about your reading, thinking, and research so that others may learn from you. You will also find many practical suggestions for how you can read and listen effectively as you seek to make sense of others' research. As the second chapter in this book notes, research takes many forms. How you report your research will vary from assignment to assignment. This book presents, as simply as possible, hundreds of suggestions that will help you tackle the different types of work that you are expected to do.

On writing assignments

Contrary to many students' belief, good writing does not come naturally; even for the best writers it is mostly hard work, following the old formula of 10 per cent inspiration and 90 per cent perspiration.

Writing in university or college is not fundamentally different from writing elsewhere. Yet each piece of writing has its own special purposes, and these are what determine its shape and tone. *Making Sense in Geography and the Environmental Sciences* examines both the general precepts for effective writing and the special requirements of reporting the research process and findings in the geographical, physical, biological, and social sciences, and in interdisciplinary environmental and sustainability studies programs. It also points out some of the most common errors in student composition and suggests how to avoid or correct them. Written mostly in the form of guidelines rather than strict rules—because few rules are inviolable—this book should help you escape the common pitfalls of student writing and develop your confidence through an understanding of basic principles and a mastery of sound techniques.

Organization

The organization of this book reflects linkages between clusters of chapters, as follows:

- *Chapters 1 and 2* deal with fundamentals of research and writing. These chapters offer critically important information, as well as providing many useful tips for when you search for sources, evaluate them, and make use of them in your written work. These chapters also discuss ethical issues and the importance of doing your research ethically.
- *Chapter 3* has numerous tips on how to write notes on your readings and lectures (which will form the foundation of your studies).
- *Chapters 4 to 6* consider the principal types of writing you will do based on research: writing a report on a book or an article; writing an essay; and writing a proposal, research paper, and thesis.
- *Chapter 7* demonstrates how to incorporate quotations into your written work and discusses the major documentation systems, one or more of which you will have to use in your written work.
- *Chapters 8 to 11* identify practical things you can do to get the most out of a small-group experience, such as a discussion group or seminar, including making use of visual aids; suggesting how to handle being in a group project; outlining the essentials of a lab report; giving tips for how to prepare for and take various types of examinations; and providing practical suggestions for doing field work.
- *Chapter 12* explores illustrative material: maps, tables, equations, and graphs.
- *Chapters 13 to 18* focus on the fundamentals of writing, starting with a discussion of the importance of words and then considering basic issues—writing with style; common errors in grammar and usage; punctuation; frequently misused words and phrases; and an extended consideration of pertinent definitions, many of which are directly related to your studies in geography and other environmental disciplines.
- Useful information on weights, measures, and notation can be found in *Appendix I* (pp. 330–1), while *Appendix II* (pp. 332–4) identifies websites pertinent to geographers and others concerned with geographical, sustainability, and environmental issues. Finally, the *Index* beginning on page 335 will help you to find the specific information you want within the text.

1

Thinking and Writing

In this chapter, we examine

- your role and how to see yourself within the learning process; and
- basic issues you must consider for all your written work.

Introduction

Thinking and writing are the most basic skills you need to complete your college or university education successfully. As you begin to use this book, consider your role in the learning process, as outlined below.

- The instructor *offers* (readings, lectures, seminars, discussion groups, lab and field work assignments, etc.), *shares* (by imparting new knowledge and identifying research methods), *provokes* (by raising questions and providing insights), *responds* (to questions), and *evaluates* (assignments and examinations).
- You *listen* (to lectures, webinars), *participate* (in class interactions), *read* (assigned and additional readings), and *do* (lab, field work, and other assignments).
- You, the learner, *take in, think about, mull over, question, analyze, evaluate, integrate, "report back"* (via essays, reports, and examinations), and *"take away"* (all that you gain from a course and, ultimately, all of your courses).

The key message here is that you need to take an active role in the learning process. *You* are the key to *your* education! This book offers many suggestions that will help you make sense of what you are asked to do and will enhance your skills as you seek to do your best with different types of assignments in your courses, whether they are in physical and human geography, agriculture, biology, geology, landscape architecture, environmental history, other environmental sciences, or interdisciplinary sustainability or environmental studies. To start, this chapter highlights thinking and writing.

Writing is a process of many stages, every one of which involves thinking. You are not likely to produce clear writing in the final copy of your assignment unless you have first done some clear thinking, and clear thinking can't be hurried. It follows that the most important step you can take is to leave yourself enough time to think.

Among the other steps that the writing process requires—long before you complete your final paper for submission—are selecting the topic; framing your work within the context of the discipline and course for which it is intended; posing a key question, developing a thesis statement (concise expression of your paper's main argument), or examining a hypothesis; drafting; and revising and editing. This chapter discusses all these aspects of the writing process and concludes with some comments on evaluation criteria, plagiarism, and using your computer for preparing assignments.

Using Your Subconscious

You should be aware at the outset of a problem that eventually puzzles all writers, no matter how skilled: that infamous writer's block. You know the symptoms: "What am I going to write about?" "How am I going to write about this?" "How can I write convincingly when I am unsure about the purpose of the essay?" "How do I define what it is I plan to do?" "What is my key question?" "Do I need a hypothesis, or is a simple statement of purpose enough?" "What can I do to make sense of this material?" "Should I use subheadings?" "How am I ever going to come to a conclusion?" Remember that we do not always solve a difficult problem by "putting our mind to it"—by determined reasoning. Sometimes it's best to take a break, turn to something else, perhaps even sleep on it, and let the subconscious or creative part of your brain take over for a while. Very often a period of relaxation will produce a new approach or solution. Leaving time for creative reflection, of course, does not mean sitting around listening to music or watching TV until inspiration strikes out of the blue. Insights that otherwise might escape you may come if you set aside some quiet moments for reflection, away from your books; try going outside and thinking about the assignment on and off as you walk, run, or bicycle and look at the world around you. Invest in yourself! The dividends can be considerable.

Turn off distractions

When trying to think and write in the library or in your room, it is best to do so without distractions. Some people can work well with certain kinds of music playing; others need silence. Turn off your smart phones or similar devices! Do not give in to the temptation to send or receive text messages or e-mails while you are working. In short, keep focused on your key tasks: thinking and writing.

Thinking Critically

Although there is no one definition of critical thinking that encapsulates all that it is, one interesting definition is: *"thinking about your thinking while you're thinking in order to make your thinking better."* [1] Put another way, critical thinking helps us consciously direct our own thinking processes so that we can think more effectively—that is, more rationally, clearly, logically, accurately, and consistently. Instructors will be looking for evidence of critical thinking in your assignments, so it is important to take time to understand what it is and how to apply it.

Thinking critically is not negative thinking or a form of fault-finding. Instead, being a critical thinker generally involves

- being inquisitive, curious, and eager to know things
- asking relevant and pertinent questions
- taking the initiative to question what you read, hear, and observe
- challenging the underlying assumptions of what you are questioning
- analyzing what you question in a reasoned and unbiased way
- remaining open to new ideas and perspectives
- reserving judgment until you have all the facts
- changing your position or opinion on an issue when convinced by the logic of another position
- reflecting constantly on your learning in order to find patterns, linkages, or related elements that could be applied to other problems or issues (UVIC, Cont Studies: http://distance.uvic.ca/students/thinking.htm)

The ability to think critically is an important skill for everyone to develop because it helps each of us assess our beliefs and opinions to make sure they're supported by good reasons. Thinking critically is essential to the learning process and will help you generate ideas to research and write about in your courses. In writing a paper or in assessing an article for a reading assignment, for example, a critical thinker would consistently ask the following types of questions about the elements of their thinking (see Table 1.1, below).

Table 1.1   Thinking critically: Questions using the elements of thought

Elements of thought	Questions using the elements of thought
Purpose: goals and objectives	What am I trying to accomplish? What is my central aim? My purpose?
Questions: problem, issue	What question am I raising or addressing? Am I considering the complexities in the question?
Information: data, facts, observations, experiences	What information am I using in coming to a conclusion? What experience have I had to support this claim? What information do I need to settle the question?
Interpretation and Inference: conclusions, solutions	How did I reach this conclusion? Is there another way to interpret the information?
Concepts: theories, definitions, laws, principles, models	What is the main idea here? Can I explain this idea?
Assumptions: presuppositions, axioms, taking for granted	What am I taking for granted? What assumption led me to that conclusion?
Implications and Consequences	If someone accepted my position, what would be the implications? What am I implying?
Point of view: frames of reference, perspectives	From what point of view am I looking at this issue? Is there another point of view I should consider?

Source: Based on Paul, R. and Elder, L. (2008). *The Miniature Guide to Critical Thinking: Concepts and tools*. Dillon Beach, CA: Foundation for Critical Thinking.

We know that academic documents can be complex and require high levels of concentration to understand the content. Researchers have found that if students read lengthy academic documents in paper format (rather than on screen) they gain a better understanding of the content, can improve their focusing skills and their ability to read deeply and think critically about the text, and gain a deeper sense of knowing. The effects of reading print may also stimulate richer writing skills.[2]

Guidelines for Any Written Work

With almost everything you write there are some basic guidelines that you should keep in mind:

- Think about the purpose and the context of the work you have to produce.
- State clearly what you plan to do.
- Define your terms.
- Include only relevant material.
- Strive for consistency of expression throughout the work.
- Make sure you are accurate in all of your statements, including your analysis and presentation of data.
- Present your information in a logical and effective order.
- Convey your message as simply and clearly as possible.
- Make sure that your work is both coherent and complete.
- Do not draw conclusions that are not clearly based on your evidence.
- Never assume that one draft will do the job; count on writing at least two drafts before producing the final copy.
- Provide documentation for your sources and ensure that your references are complete and accurate. Be sure to include Internet sources, too.
- Be consistent in style throughout the assignment.
- Attend to the small things: give the work a title, select the most appropriate format for subheadings, and number the pages.
- *Always* proofread and make any necessary corrections before submitting the work.
- Remember to include your name and student number, the name of the instructor, the course number, and the (due) date.

Initial Strategies

To write is to make choices. Practice makes decisions easier, but no matter how skilled you become, with each piece of writing you still will have to choose. Even if the instructor indicates what you must write about, you still must take the time to reflect and make choices.

You can narrow the field of choice from the start if you realize that you are *not* writing for anybody, anywhere, for no particular reason. At school (or anywhere else), it is always sound strategy to ask yourself four basic questions:

- "What is the purpose of this piece of writing?"
- "What is the reader like?" Or, to put it other ways, "Who is my audience?" or "Who am I writing for?"
- "What does the reader expect?"
- "What do I expect of myself?"

Your first reaction may be, "Well, I'm writing for my instructor to satisfy a course requirement," but obviously that's an inadequate response. To be useful, your answers have to be precise. Thus, a better answer might be, "I am going to work with data x using methodology y so that I can then write a research report for course z." And keep in mind your personal investment in the assignment: presumably you will always want to do the best work you can.

Think about the purpose

Your purpose may be any one or more of several possibilities:

- to show that you understand certain terms, concepts, or theories
- to establish that you can do independent research
- to indicate that you can apply a particular research method
- to report on a test you have performed
- to apply a specific theory to new material
- to provide information
- to reveal your knowledge of a topic or text
- to present data you have gathered while doing field work
- to demonstrate your ability to evaluate secondary sources
- to illustrate your creativity
- to show that you can think critically

Certainly, an assignment designed to see if you have read and understood specific material calls for a different approach from one that is meant to test your critical thinking or research skills. If you don't determine the exact purpose, you may find yourself working at cross-purposes—and wasting a lot of time.

Think about your approach

Tied to the purpose for any particular assignment is the issue of approach. Doing research means that you have to make choices before you start; different approaches will lead you to pose different types of questions and to use different methods to find the answers. Your approach to any piece of writing depends in part on what course the assignment is for because there are disciplinary (and sub-disciplinary) differences in approaches to research and writing. Here are some points to consider in thinking about your approach:

- How did the instructor describe the purpose of the course at the beginning of classes?
- What are the essential concepts and presuppositions within the course? How does this particular assignment relate to the latter?
- What are the key themes, processes, and methods that you have heard about in lectures, discussion groups, and labs, or read about in assignments?
- How can you bring these various elements together to write something (be it an essay, field report, lab report, or whatever else) that is germane to the course?

The links between research and writing are discussed in the following chapters.

Think about your thesis and hypothesis

For any research or writing, you must have a clear purpose: you must know what it is that you are proposing to do (see Chapter 2). Isolate the key issue and write it down as your statement of purpose. Take the time to work out your purpose statement carefully. You might start by thinking about the key question or set of questions that you want to answer. Then, turn the key question into a statement. Use a complete sentence to express your key question, and make sure that it is

- *limited* (because you are not going to study everything),
- *unified* (so that there is a sense of wholeness to what you propose to do), and
- *exact* (because both you and your reader must be sure about what you intend to do).

Some types of research will require that you formulate a *hypothesis*. A hypothesis is simply an idea about, or a tentative explanation for, an insight you might have into the natural world and how humans relate to their surroundings. You can test and verify (or not!) your concept through additional study. A hypothesis is also a working thesis, an intended line of argument that you are free to change at any stage of your planning—although once you have actually started your research, you should stick to the hypothesis you have chosen. A hypothesis works as a linchpin, holding together your approach to the project, data, and ideas as you organize and do your research. A hypothesis helps you define your intentions and make your research selective. And, as a result of your exploration of a certain set of data, by the time you start to write up your report or essay you will have determined whether or not your working thesis was valid.

Think about your sources

Whatever you write will be based on some kind of research. Doing research and writing about it is not like writing a short story or novel based on personal reflection and imagination: as a researcher, you must get to know and understand your sources.

As you work your way through college or university you will become well acquainted with three kinds of sources:

- primary,
- secondary, and
- tertiary.

The most important *primary sources* for all students of geography, environmental and sustainability studies, and environmental sciences are the earth itself and the people who inhabit it. In your courses you will learn how to "read" and understand the form and content of the earth's surface as modified by natural and human processes, and the ways people perceive, organize, and use their surroundings. Other *primary sources* include direct field observations, questionnaire data, censuses, maps, land records, air photos, satellite images, and the like. Some books also can be primary sources, if they provide direct evidence that is of use to you. Primary sources vary from one discipline (and sub-discipline) to another; thus, one type of study may rely on temperature readings as a source, while others may demand the use of land-registry data, or fishing-licence records, or tree ring analysis.

Secondary sources, by contrast, are books and articles written by authors who have read and reflected upon a specific literature to provide a context for their research or to serve as the basis for certain generalizations. Because some of your research may be based only on secondary sources, it's a good idea to visit the library regularly, so that you become familiar with the books and journals related to your interests. Some secondary sources may be available to you only on the Internet (see Chapter 2).

Tertiary sources provide extended syntheses of previous research and generally do not have as their primary purpose the reporting of new research undertaken by the authors; most textbooks fall into this category.

Suggestions for finding Internet, library, and other sources can be found in Chapter 2. Ways of reporting your findings are discussed in various other chapters, including (for a book report) Chapter 4, (for an essay) Chapter 5, and (for field work) Chapter 11.

Finally, unless your instructor tells you otherwise for a specific assignment, do not rely only on Internet-based searches. It is not enough—indeed, it is unwise—to examine only online material. Take time to explore and use the rich array of materials available to you in the university library (or libraries). Ask your university's librarians about other available resources (such as municipal collections in the city library or documents from specialized libraries in other cities).

Think about illustrations

In many cases some of the material you will use can be mapped, graphed, or put in a table. Think carefully about the appropriateness of the material you have gathered and ask yourself the following questions:

- Do I really need the data to support or expand upon a point or argument presented in my text?
- Would it be more useful if I placed the data in the text, or would a table, map, or graph convey my point most clearly?
- If I decide to use an illustration, what is the most effective form for displaying the data? (See Chapter 12 for some suggestions.)

Illustrations in academic work are not simply nice additions that may look good; they are an integral part of any work. As you write, then, you also must take into account the material you can show in graphic form. Use tables, graphs, maps, photographs, and other illustrations when they clearly and effectively provide the reader with data that are essential to your case. And, of course, as you edit your work, you need to ensure that you have correctly numbered and titled your illustrations and referred to them appropriately (by their numbers) in your text. In some circumstances, you may be able to display your illustrations on a poster (see Chapter 8).

Think about the reader

Thinking about the reader does not mean playing up to the instructor. To convince your reader that your own views are sound, you have to consider his or her way of thinking. If you are writing a paper on the environmental history of a particular place for a geography professor, your analysis and presentation obviously will be different from what they would be if you were writing for a professor in resource economics or landscape architecture. You will need to make specific decisions about

- the basic questions to be asked,
- the terms to be explained,
- the background information to be provided,
- the data to be used, and
- the details necessary to convince that particular reader that your discussion has merit and is valid.

Remember that your reader will approach your work with certain assumptions and questions posed by his or her discipline and circumscribed by the nature and purpose of the course you are taking, so be sure to frame your answer accordingly. Try to anticipate questions that might be raised and seek to answer them. If you don't know who will be reading your paper—your professor, a teaching assistant (TA) who may be a discussion-group leader or lab assistant, or a graduate student marker—just imagine someone intelligent, knowledgeable, and interested, skeptical enough to question your ideas but flexible enough to adopt them if your evidence is convincing.

Think about disciplinary "languages"

Each discipline has its own basic "language." Although many disciplines share some aspects of their language, there usually are some terms or usages that are unique (on jargon, see p. 241). These "languages" will become evident as you listen to lectures and read course texts. To understand some words, you likely will need to look up definitions. But many terms you will hear and read are not covered adequately in common dictionaries (whether printed or online; see pp. 19–20)—if they are covered at all. Hence, you will need to use disciplinary and interdisciplinary dictionaries (see p. 22). In addition, a comprehensive, up-to-date atlas (print or electronic) is a useful, even essential, study aid.

Think about length and value

Before you start writing, you will need to think about the length of your assignment in relation to the time you have available to spend on it. If both the topic and the length are prescribed, it should be fairly easy for you to assess the level of detail required and the amount of research you need to do. If only the length is prescribed, that restriction will help you decide how broad or how narrow a topic you should choose. You also should think about how important the assignment is in relation to the rest of your work for the course. Obviously, a piece of work worth 10 per cent of your final grade will not demand as much attention as one worth 30 per cent.

Starting to Write

Once you have completed the necessary research, you will face what may be the hardest part of any assignment: actually starting to write. Consider the following methods; one of them may help you structure your thoughts.

- Write an opening statement that clearly indicates the purpose of the piece of work. This will help you to focus your thoughts.
- Jot down your title for the assignment and, if possible, a few subheadings; then start to fill in the sections one by one.
- List your thoughts in point form, in random order, as they come to mind. This step may be necessary before you can identify all the subheadings you will need. Then look to see if you can reorder the points so that they outline a logical development to your argument. If you are using a pen and paper, circling key points and linking them with lines to other points may assist you in ordering things. If you are using a computer you will be able to make use of a wide array of formatting

options, including coloured text, highlighting, and cutting or copying and pasting.

- If you become frustrated with one section, turn to another. By the time you have completed it, ideas on the skipped section may come more easily.

Think about tone

In everyday writing, such as in class notes or e-mails to your friends, you probably take a casual tone, but academic writing usually is more formal. The exact degree of formality required depends on the assignment and instructions you have been given. In some cases—say, if your cultural geography professor asks you to express yourself freely and personally in a journal—you may well be able to use an informal tone. Essays, reports, and theses, however, require a formal tone. What kind of style is too informal for most academic work? Here are the main signs:

Use of slang

Although the occasional slang word or phrase may be useful for special effect in informal writing, use of slang generally is unacceptable. The reason is that slang expressions tend to be regional and short-lived: they may mean different things to different groups at different times. (Just think of how widely the meanings of *hot*, *cool*, and *sick* can vary, depending on the circumstances.)

The right words?

Be careful in your choice of words; for more detail, see Chapter 13. If the words you want to use may be harmful or hurtful to others, don't use them.

Excessive use of first-person pronouns

A formal essay is not a personal outpouring, as in a personal letter or e-mail to someone close to you; this means you should keep it from becoming *I*-centred. It's acceptable to use the occasional first-person pronoun if the assignment calls for your opinions—as long as they are backed by evidence. But you should avoid the *I think* or *In my view* approach when the fact or argument speaks for itself. Still, if the choice is between using *I* and creating a tangle of passive constructions, it is almost always better to choose *I*. (Hint: when you do use *I*, it will be less noticeable if you place it in the middle of the sentence rather than at the beginning.)

Use of contractions

Contractions such as *can't* and *isn't* are not suitable for academic writing (except within a quotation), although they may be fine for informal writing (e.g., e-mails to friends, or this handbook). The problem with trying to avoid excessive informality is that you may be tempted to go to the other extreme. If your writing sounds stiff or pompous, you may be using too many high-flown phrases, long words, or passive constructions (see Chapter 14). When in doubt, remember that a more formal style will always be acceptable.

The Editing Stage

Specific types of writing are addressed in later chapters. With everything you write, however, remember that editing your work is an essential stage. It cannot be emphasized enough that, whatever you are writing, you should never accept your first draft as the final product. In fact, your most serious writing may not begin until after you've written your first draft. Read what you have written to identify illogically developed sections, awkward phrasing, incomplete sentences, skimpy arguments, missing references, and questionable conclusions; you may even need to do more research. Once you have redrafted the material, read it again with a critical eye. Don't hesitate to slash unnecessary verbiage, alter sentences, or restructure paragraphs—and when you have done that, check your references again, for facts, style, and completeness. Two, three, or even more drafts may be required before you arrive at the final copy. In short, you must be not only a writer but an editor.

Writing and editing go together, but they are separate processes. In the writing process you will craft something into being; in the editing process you will critically assess and re-craft that work to make it better. A word of caution: as you prepare successive drafts of your work, be sure to number each one (draft 1, draft 2, and so on—both on computer files and on printed copies) so that you will not mix them up and accidentally submit an early draft instead of the final version. Finally, you can help yourself at the editing stage by numbering the pages of each draft.

A few words about appearance

We've all been told not to judge a book by its cover, but the very warning suggests that we have a natural tendency to do so. Readers of essays find the same thing. A well-typed, visually appealing piece of work creates a receptive reader, and, fairly or unfairly, often earns a higher grade. If your instructor provides specific instructions, be sure to follow them. Otherwise, double-space the lines and use a 12-point font such as Times New Roman or Arial. If your instructor asks you to submit your work online, be sure to clearly identify yourself and the course number. If you are to submit a hard copy of your work, leave wide margins on all sides of the text, so that your reader has ample space to write comments. Number each page (although normally the first, or title, page is unnumbered); unless directed otherwise, on the first page, include the title, your name and student number, the name of the instructor, the course title and number, and the date. The appearance of the paper may be improved by using a staple at the top left corner, slanted so that the folded-over pages will not tear. Good looks won't substitute for good thinking, but they certainly will enhance it.

Evaluation criteria

Remember that your work will be evaluated, not literally weighed! Depending on the assignment, your reader will want to see whether you have arrived at the correct answer, or argued your case well. When reading an essay, he or she will want to be challenged by what you write, not stumble over how you write. Reactions will depend to a large degree on how clearly and effectively you communicate. Some work will simply be "right" or "wrong," but other types of writing will evoke varying responses: "Nice reasoning"; "Interesting idea"; "Good point"; "A bit of a bore"; "Wow, this is heavy going"; "You sure know how to waffle"; "Dreadful!" After some effort, you should be able to get the first two or three of these responses to anything you submit—and none of the rest.

Most instructors will look for and consider the following points when evaluating your work:

- a clear statement of purpose (or thesis statement; see pp. 30–1)
- placement of work within a context provided by a review of pertinent literature
- quality and relevance of evidence
- accuracy
- completeness

- imaginative development (especially in an essay)
- logical organization
- clarity of expression
- correctness of grammar, spelling, and punctuation
- pertinence and quality of illustrations (maps, photos, tables, etc.)
- conclusion
- appropriate and accurate citation of sources
- references/bibliography (which you may have to annotate—see p. 78).

Peer review

In academia, evaluation of a scholar's writing about her or his research work and ideas takes place through a peer review process. Prior to publication of a journal article, for instance, a publisher or editor will ask people who are experts in the same field as the author (i.e., peers) to review the article and indicate its suitability for publication. Among other aspects, reviewers consider the author's work in terms of its

- quality (does the article make an original or important contribution to the field?),
- validity (are the author's conclusions supported by the design and execution of the methodology?), and
- level of organization and completeness (does the article explain clearly and fully what was done, and why and how it was done?).

After an assessment, the reviewer makes a recommendation to the editor to accept, reject, or revise the work. The peer review process helps maintain integrity of science and is intended to improve the quality of published papers.

A warning about plagiarism and cheating

Plagiarism is a form of stealing. The intention is to cheat by submitting someone else's material as your own. Other types of cheating also are deemed to be academic offences, such as submitting the same work to different instructors without their prior knowledge and joint consent. Within post-secondary institutions, penalties for *academic misconduct* range from a zero for the work in question to outright expulsion. You should read and take to heart your institution's rules on academic misconduct. It may be in your academic calendar and surely will be online. Do not ignore it! If you do not understand something, ask your professor or a librarian.

You commit plagiarism or otherwise cheat if you commit any of the following actions:

- submit the work of another person, in whole or in part, as your original work, whether purchased or borrowed;
- fail to identify a quotation from someone else's work;
- fail to document the source of many types of material that you have incorporated into your work (for exceptions, see below);
- fraudulently manipulate or submit false lab work, field work observations, or research data; or
- copy someone else's answer to a test, or lab or field study, and pass it off as your own.

Of these issues, the focus here is on being sure that you fairly and correctly identify when you are using someone else's work within your own. The way to avoid plagiarism is to give credit where credit is due. If you use someone else's idea, acknowledge it, even if you have changed the wording or just summarized the main points. Here are some key guidelines to follow:

- If you quote something by copying an author's exact words, use quotation marks and indicate the source and page number.
- If you paraphrase or summarize someone's material, identify the author and indicate the source.
- Use identifiers within your text when you present someone's ideas, observations, or conclusions (e.g., "Best asserts that . . ." or "As Woodward observed . . .") and include the appropriate identification of the source.
- Authoritative or distinctive material should be cited with the source duly noted, whether you use it to argue against or to bolster your own stance.
- Identify sources for anything that is not common knowledge. You do not need to document things like important dates (of, say, World War II), the names of broad-ranging climate zones or soil types, the present population of the country, or the national anthem. Furthermore, you don't have to cite sources to support facts such as "the earth is round" or that "Brian Berry and Audrey Kobayashi are prominent geographers" (although reference to some of their works might be appropriate).

- Do document unfamiliar facts or claims—statistical or otherwise—or any that are open to question.
- Remember that information you find on the Internet must be properly acknowledged. Even though websites are accessible instantly, they are the property of the individual or organization that publishes them. Accordingly, give appropriate citation within your work when you quote from or otherwise refer to such material (see Chapter 7).

Be sure to record in your reading notes when source material you have copied has been directly quoted or summarized (see Chapter 3). As you assemble your work, be careful as you take things (a fact, a sentence, a paragraph, your paraphrase) to include in your work so that you don't inadvertently copy something that is not original to you. As you write, constantly ask yourself if you are using your own words to present your own ideas. If not, record the source in the pertinent location within the body of your work and in the references, using the method appropriate to the course and assignment (again, see Chapter 7).

Don't be afraid that your work will seem weaker if you acknowledge the ideas of others. On the contrary, your work will be all the more convincing: serious academic treatises are almost always built on the work of preceding scholars, and credit is duly given to the earlier work.

Writing with a Computer

The comments provided above pertain to both handwritten and typed work. What follows are some additional thoughts related to using your computer.

Many students are most comfortable typing their ideas on the computer. Others, who don't like to "type and think" at the same time, may work best by first writing the assignment by hand and then typing it. Based on your own study style, you need to think about when you should first write out your thoughts on paper versus when you should work directly on your computer. Your outline of "first thoughts" may be handwritten or typed, but remember: seeing your ideas appear legibly on the screen can be both gratifying and deceiving, for a clean-looking list may hide poor thinking. You need to be self-critical and fully honest with yourself as you read what you have typed. Whether you choose to handwrite or type first, let your outline be your guide as you set to work on your first draft. Don't rely solely on your memory.

Save regularly and back up your files

There is nothing more agonizing than discovering that something has gone wrong and caused you to lose everything you had been working on. It doesn't happen very often, but everyone experiences it at least once, and always unexpectedly. So, be sure to set your computer to automatically save your file while you are working. Then, if the power suddenly goes off, the most you will lose is the typing you have done since your file was last saved.

Don't keep your essential files only on the computer's hard drive; save a backup copy to an external memory device, such as a portable memory card or stick, or external hard drive. And don't keep your file only on an external device: you don't want to learn the hard way what happens when the memory card that contains your only copy is lustily chewed by your dog, or when you accidentally step on your USB stick and break the connecting end! In other words, use of both the hard drive and an external device, with the regular use of a backup system, could spare you a lot of frustration.

Name and number the draft copies and the final version

When drafting your assignment, you'll find it quick and easy to move blocks of text onscreen as you try out new organizational structures. If after reading your text through you don't like the way the new version flows, you can always go back to your original version. Just be wise enough to make separate copies each time you make major changes.

Be sure to give a title and number to each version of your work, both on the first page of each draft and in the name of each file you save. For example, for a project on glacial deposits, you might save your first draft as <Glacial DRAFT 1>, your second draft as <Glacial DRAFT 2>, and so on. When you are satisfied with your final version, save it again, noting that it is the final version, e.g., <Glacial FINAL>.

Proofreading, and grammar and spell checking

You may have trouble gaining a sense of the whole when you read a lengthy paper section by section on screen. Research suggests this difficulty is a reality for some people[3] so you could try printing a hard copy in order to read and edit your work on paper, then make any needed corrections to your digital file. Don't be surprised when you catch something on paper that you've missed onscreen.

Be sure to proofread for overall comprehension as well as for errors in grammar and spelling. Know that your computer's spelling and grammar checkers are useful, but not infallible. The grammar checker may catch such things as a missing comma, but other suggestions, if accepted, could alter your meaning. While the grammar checker can help by raising questions about how you have written a sentence, be cautious of its suggestions; they may be nonsensical in the context of your writing. Don't accept the grammar checker's suggestions without thinking carefully about what *your* intention is, and *don't* set the grammar checker to make changes to your text automatically. Remember that the computer is a tool for you to use—it won't do your thinking for you.

Similarly, be wary of your computer's spell checker. Whether you have set it to "automatically" check your spelling as you type or you do a later spell check, remember that the software can't catch a word that is correctly spelled but incorrectly used (for example, your spell checker will not catch that you have typed "kid" instead of "kind"). Do not rely on it alone. Use a dictionary when in doubt. When using the spell checker on your computer, be sure to turn on the dictionary language setting you want (e.g., English [Canada], English [US], English [UK], or English [Australian]). In fact, "correct" spelling itself can be an issue; see the next section for more.

Using dictionaries and thesauruses

A good dictionary is a wise investment; get into the habit of using one. It will give you not only common meanings but less familiar applications, archaic uses, and derivations, as well as "correct" spelling. The word *correct* is in quotation marks because American English has different spelling and usage from British English. Canadian spelling and usage follow either British or American practices, but usually combine aspects of both. Before you buy a dictionary, check to make sure that it gives these variants.[4]

Be aware that most print dictionaries, and the dictionary found in your computer's word-processing program, are not sensitive to disciplinary definitions. There are many disciplinary and interdisciplinary dictionaries.[5] Words in them may be defined in ways that differ from what you find in general dictionaries.

A thesaurus lists words that are closely related in meaning. Using one can help when you want to avoid repeating yourself or when you find yourself fumbling for a word that's on the tip of your tongue. But it's important to remember the difference between *denotative* and *connotative* meanings. A word's denotation is its primary or "dictionary" meaning. Its connotations are any associations that the word may suggest; connotations may not be as exact as the denotations, but they are part of the impression the word conveys. If you examine a list of "synonyms" in a thesaurus, you will see that even words with similar meanings can have dramatically different connotations. For example, alongside the word *indifferent* your thesaurus may give the following: *neutral, unconcerned, careless, easygoing, unambitious*, and *halfhearted*. Imagine the different impressions you would create if you chose one or the other of those words to complete this sentence: "Questioned about the experiment's chance of success, he was _____ in his response." Remember that a reader may react to the suggestive meaning of a word as much as to its "dictionary" meaning—and that suggestive meanings can change over time (see Chapter 13). These comments also apply to the thesauruses included in computer programs. Unless you are absolutely certain that the word suggested is the one you want, it's best to check in a good dictionary and confirm the meaning of the word.

Working in a Group

While much of your thinking and writing will be solitary, there also will be times when you will work in a group. Teamwork is common in the work world, so this experience is invaluable. Group interaction can be fruitful but it also presents challenges. Teamwork runs the smoothest when each person willingly brings to the table his or her own perspective, set of skills, and approach to problem solving. If someone works poorly with others then the experience can be soured. To be effective, from the outset your group must identify clearly the objectives of any assignment and divide tasks (e.g., experimentation, library research, writing) equitably. It is imperative that the group reaches a consensus at all stages of the assignment, from problem identification to final word processing (see pp. 97–8). The successful group report is one in which all participants have had an equal voice and an equal share in the work.

Professional Practice

Although this book is intended primarily for students, its advice on how to present ideas also will be useful to you in the professional world. Indeed, the ability to convey your thoughts to others in a clear and concise fashion could be the crucial edge you need to obtain and hold a job and to achieve advancement. The contents of this book, then, are *not* just suggestions to help you think, organize, research, and present findings for academic course work: they also are aids to learning skills that will be important later, in whatever field(s) of endeavour you eventually find yourself.

Chapter Summary

In this chapter we have identified how important you (and your brain) are in the thinking that precedes and accompanies the research process. Like any other scientific field, geography and environmental sciences are human activities; so much of the outcomes of our research depend on the way we "see" the world around us, how we think about, collect, and interpret our data, and how we express, in writing, the conclusions we reach.

There are many aspects involved in the thinking and writing processes associated with research. In this chapter we identified some key guidelines that are useful in any written work, and provided information on a range of choices you need to think about as you begin a research project. We also commented on some of the practical challenges associated with the task of writing up your research.

Notes

1. R.W. Paul, *Critical Thinking: What Every Person Needs to Survive in a Rapidly Changing World* (Tomales, CA: The Foundation for Critical Thinking, 2012), 439.
2. While research shows there is little difference between reading print and on screen in terms of speed and comprehension, this article identifies reasons why it may be better to read complex, lengthy academic documents in print form. G. Walsh, "Screen and Paper Reading Research—A Literature Review," *Australian Academic and Research Libraries* 47, no. 3 (2016): 160–73, DOI: 10.1080/00048623.2016.1227661.
3. One interesting summary article about how our reading differs when we use paper or screens is Ferris Jabr, "The reading brain in the digital age: The science of paper versus screens," *Scientific American* (2013), http://www.scientificamerican.com/article.cfm?id=reading-paper-screens.
4. The authoritative multi-volume dictionary of English words, *Oxford English Dictionary*, 2nd ed. (Oxford: Oxford University Press, 1989), plus the Additions Series volumes (various dates) and the 3rd ed. (an ongoing project), available online. *The Concise Oxford English Dictionary*, 12th ed. (Oxford: Oxford University Press, 2011), a single volume, is the most popular dictionary of its kind around the world. Regionally pertinent dictionaries, with localisms, include: *Canadian Oxford Dictionary*, 2nd ed. (Toronto: Oxford University Press, 2004); *New Oxford American Dictionary*, 3rd ed. (New York: Oxford University Press, 2010); *The Penguin Webster Handy College Dictionary*, 3rd ed. (New York: Random House, 2003); *American Heritage Desk Dictionary*, 5th ed. (Boston: Houghton

Mifflin, 2012); *Merriam-Webster's Collegiate Dictionary & Thesaurus* (Springfield, MA; online); *Australian Concise Oxford Dictionary*, 6th ed. (Melbourne: Oxford University Press, 2017); *New Zealand Pocket Oxford Dictionary*, 4th ed. (Auckland: Oxford University Press, 2012); *Oxford South African Concise Dictionary*, 2nd ed. (Cape Town: Oxford University Press, 2010).

5. Pertinent disciplinary and interdisciplinary dictionaries include Susan Mayhew, *A Dictionary of Geography*, 5th ed. (Oxford: Oxford University Press, 2015); Derek Gregory et al., eds., *The Dictionary of Human Geography*, 5th ed. (New York: Wiley, 2009); David Thomas, ed., *The Dictionary of Physical Geography*, 4th ed. (New York: Wiley, 2015); John B. Whittow, *The Penguin Dictionary of Physical Geography*, 2nd ed. (London: Penguin, 2004); Audrey N. Clark, *The Penguin Dictionary of Geography*, 3rd ed. (London: Penguin, 2004); Danny Harrington, *Geography Dictionary and Glossary for Students* (online: www.tuition.com.hk/geography/); M. Kotlyakov and A. Komarova, *Elsevier's Dictionary of Geography in English, Russian, French, Spanish and German* (London: Elsevier, 2007); B. Delijska, comp., *Elsevier's Dictionary of Geographical Information Systems in English, German, French and Russian* (London: Elsevier, 2002); ArcGIS, *GIS Dictionary* (online: http://resources.arcgis.com/glossary); Michael Allaby, *Dictionary of Geology and Earth Sciences*, 4th ed. (Oxford University Press, 2013); Philip Kearey, *The Penguin Dictionary of Geology*, 2nd ed. (London: Penguin, 2001); Andrew Porteous, *Dictionary of Environmental Science and Technology*, 4th ed. (New York: Wiley, 2008); Michael Allaby, *A Dictionary of Plant Sciences*, 3rd ed. (Oxford: Oxford University Press, 2012); Elizabeth Martin and Robert S. Hine, eds., *A Dictionary of Biology*, 7th ed. (Oxford: Oxford University Press, 2015); Michael Allaby, *A Dictionary of Zoology*, 4th ed. (Oxford: Oxford University Press, 2014); Chris Park, *A Dictionary of Environment and Conservation* (New York: Oxford University Press, 2008); and Michael Allaby, *A Dictionary of Ecology*, 4th ed. (Oxford: Oxford University Press, 2010).

2 Searching and Researching

In this chapter, we examine

- the role of searching in the research process;
- ethical issues you must be aware of; and
- online and library sources, and how to find, validate, and use them.

Introduction

When you receive an assignment, you may be tempted to Google some keywords and use whatever you happen to find as the basis of your work. Although you might well come across interesting information, the question will be whether this information is truly pertinent, accurate, and reliable. Rather than merely *searching*, you should be *researching* to find the "best" sources. Doing research obviously involves searching for information, but that searching must be done in an intentional and focused manner. To help you frame your purposeful search for material, this chapter considers many related points: definition of research; asking questions; sources of knowledge; approaches to research, from objective detachment to subjective involvement; and the central question or hypothesis. As a researcher, you need to be aware of *ethical issues*, so these are highlighted. The focus thereafter is on *sources*: how to find the best sources for your work, whether online or on the library shelves, and how to determine their accuracy, validity, and appropriateness.

Research

As a student in geography or a related field it is vitally important that you learn how to *do* research. The *Oxford English Reference Dictionary* defines research as "systematic exploration and study in order to establish facts and reach new conclusions." The research process can take several forms, although typically a synthesis of what is already known leads to the formation of a new question, or set of questions, and perhaps to the advancement of one or more hypotheses.

Then data are obtained and examined using predetermined methods. Based on the data, a conclusion about the initial question or hypothesis is drawn. The nature of the exploration and the results you achieve depend on your particular purpose, topic, data, and methods. In all cases, however, research involves *purposefully* setting out to understand an event, pattern, or process, in which new data, or old data under new circumstances, are examined critically and, perhaps, tested in some manner.

Asking questions

The ability to ask intelligent questions is one of the most important, although often underrated, critical-thinking skills that you can develop for any work, in or out of post-secondary studies. All research is based on questions. Even if you are given explicit instructions by your professor, lab book, or course guide, it's still important to pose questions about what you're doing, how, and why. More independent assignments expect you to ask questions in order to define what you intend to do and how you will go about it.

The scale you select for your study will help you identify the processes to be examined and the kinds of data you will need. For example, a student of fluvial processes will ask different questions about a whole river basin than about a 100-metre stretch of a stream, while a student of ecotourism development will be attentive to variations in wildlife species and their density depending on the size of the area in question. A large-scale (small area) study will lead to different questions, types of data analysis, and insights than will a small-scale (large area) one.

To be useful, any question should be *limited*, *unified*, and *exact*. Students in geography, sustainability studies, and other environmental programs often approach their work through a five- or six-question formula: *what? where? when? why? how?* and, in some instances, *who?* For a project in historical geography, for example, you might ask any number of questions: "What contrasts within settlement system X can be found for the decades 1850, 1860, and 1870? What was the nature of the land before the area was settled? Who were the original inhabitants and who were the settlers? Where did they come from? How did these groups of people perceive, utilize, and organize the land? How was the land affected over time? When did patterns of use, and their effects, change, and why? What sources can I use to answer these questions?"

By contrast, as a student in a soils course you might ask: "What is the soil type in place *Y*? How does its profile contrast with that in place *Z*? What processes were involved in the formation of the soil? How, when, and why did these processes effect change? Was human action involved in disrupting certain parts of the soil profiles? If so, who were the people and what was the level and type of technology involved? What are the consequences of my findings for the area if it is to be used for housing (or an organic farm, or a shopping plaza, etc.)?" The nature of your questions depends in large measure on the specific subject of your work. More broadly, however, the questions you derive will depend on the type of knowledge you draw upon.

Sources of knowledge

Three elementary sources of human knowledge are

- tradition,
- authority, and
- personal experience.

Traditional knowledge is specific to a particular society and is passed from one generation to another. The "truth" accepted as given by a particular *tradition* generally is not universal. Every day we live within our society's culturally based norms and we often take this knowledge for granted. Much of it rarely reaches conscious thought (for example, in Canada it is a culturally based given that we will drive on the right side of the road). A people's cultural traditions, as they are shared and remade through the generations, are central to an understanding of that people's present orientation and are an important aspect of many types of research. For example, the traditional knowledge of Indigenous peoples is centrally significant with respect to land use planning and resource development in parts of Canada and elsewhere.

Like tradition, *authority* usually has a cultural basis. People in positions of authority—experts of various kinds (political, religious, economic, educational, medical, and so on)—often are able to "guide" others to what they see as "the truth." Their expertise frequently goes unchallenged; in some cases it cannot be challenged, or is challenged with difficulty, because of the threat of reprisals. But such authorities are not infallible, especially if their knowledge is based principally or only on personal experience. All academics—students as well as faculty—must examine sources of authority, whether people or institutions, and must be ready to challenge "expert" research, especially if their own work seeks to build on it. In fact, the principle of academic freedom was established in response to the risk taken by researchers who sought understanding and "truth" that put them at odds with "the authorities."

Finally, *personal experience* should not be discounted. Many people have the ability to recognize patterns, to generalize, and to make predictions on the basis of personal observations. Experience, especially "trial and error," can lead to knowledge, even if a "discovery" is simply being made afresh for the millionth time; sometimes, if we reflect on such experience, it can lead to fresh insights. As a means of gaining knowledge, however, trial and error tends to be unsystematic, haphazard, and inefficient. For all practical purposes, personal experience may be inaccessible unless a researcher purposefully and systematically sets out to observe, record, and understand it.

These sources of knowledge—tradition, authority, and personal experience—both reflect and affect people's ways of thinking, perceiving, and doing things, and can themselves become subject matter for students in geography, sustainability studies, and the environmental sciences. At the same time, it is important for all researchers—even those engaged in apparently objective/quantitative research—to be aware of the way their own traditions, authorities, or personal experience may cloud their thinking. The old saying "know thyself" applies here; unless researchers are aware of the impact these elemental sources of knowledge can have, ignorance or unthinking bias may adversely affect the way they approach and carry out their research.

The spectrum of approaches to research

Many researchers who adhere to the Western scientific tradition explicitly seek to avoid relying on tradition, authority, or personal experience as sources of knowledge. Instead, they seek knowledge and understanding by logical reasoning, which can take two contrasting forms:

- induction, and
- deduction.

Induction proceeds from particular cases through an ordering of information to generalization and, ultimately, to universal statements: that is, from specific information to laws, theories, and explanations. The quality of knowledge arrived at through inductive reasoning depends on the representativeness of the specific cases used as the bases for generalization. The reasoning process itself does not include any mechanisms for evaluating the representativeness of the cases considered, and has no built-in checks or controls.

By contrast, *deduction* proceeds from a general *a priori* premise (presented as a hypothesis), through experimentation and verification to explanatory statements about particular events. Deductive reasoning itself is not the source of new information; rather, it is an approach to illuminating relationships as the researcher moves from the general to the specific. Deductive reasoning depends on acceptance of the initial generalizations as the assumed truth. As techniques for solving problems, both inductive and deductive reasoning have limitations. Consequently, most approaches to scientific research involve some combination of the two. One such approach is called the scientific method.

The *scientific method* combines important aspects of deductive and inductive reasoning to create a system for obtaining knowledge. One important feature of the scientific method is that it provides for self-evaluation, using a system of checks and balances to minimize the possibility that the researcher's emotions or biases will affect the conclusions. This systematic approach to inquiry relies on a general set of orderly, disciplined procedures used to acquire dependable and useful information. The researcher progresses logically through a series of steps, according to a pre-established plan:

1. formulating and delimiting the problem
2. thoroughly reviewing the related literature
3. developing a theoretical framework
4. formulating one or more hypotheses
5. selecting a research design
6. specifying the object or population for study
7. developing a plan for data collection
8. conducting a pilot study and making revisions
9. selecting the sample
10. collecting the data
11. preparing the data for analysis

12. analyzing the data
13. interpreting the results
14. sharing the findings with others

The researcher who faithfully follows the scientific method is expected to be a neutral observer who records and analyzes empirical phenomena (for example, a soil's chemical characteristics, a vegetation pattern, the flow of a rock glacier, or the statistical analysis of, say, settlement patterns or traffic flows) according to the tenets of science. Individual phenomena or events are accepted as exemplars of general laws (such as the physical law of gravity, or the gravity model used for measuring the volume of trade between two places, or the laws embedded in central place theory)—laws that are held to be invariable across time and space. Results produced following this approach, emphasizing *a priori* theory, empirically measurable evidence, mathematical modelling, and statistical analysis, are said to be objective. Accordingly, any other researcher should be able to replicate this work (that is, your work, if you are the researcher).

The focus on empiricism in the scientific method means that the person doing the research is removed from the investigation. Many human geographers, and other researchers in the social sciences and humanities, have a strong reaction against this emphasis on detachment. Their work is said to be subjective and may involve a concern for the feelings and attitudes of those being studied. As different ideas have emerged concerning what is "real," human geographers and others involved with environmental and sustainability studies have been exploring a variety of theoretical approaches to research, including *humanism, phenomenology, existentialism, semiotics* and *iconography, Marxism, structuration* and *structuralism, postmodernism, deconstructionism, anti-colonialism, feminism,* and, related to some of the above, *critical geography.* While only two examples are noted here, many worthwhile books offer overviews of the various approaches.[1]

If *empiricism/positivism* lies toward one end of a spectrum, *humanism* lies toward the other end. The humanistic researcher is concerned with the role of human experience and meaning in understanding people's relationships with their geographical environments. The researcher seeks to appreciate, describe, and interpret human awareness and action as they both create and are created by such geographical qualities as space and place, nature and landscape, the built environment, and "geographies of the mind." The humanistic vantage point is generally *not* that of a dispassionate, neutral observer but, as far as possible, that of an insider, one who may be involved in the process itself, who seeks to understand attitudes, values, and perceptions. If you are working from a humanistic perspective, you will be concerned particularly with understanding the three forms of knowledge identified earlier—tradition, authority, and personal experience—and your writing style likely will be a good deal more subjective and personal than it would be for, say, a science lab.

Feminist geographical inquiry—practised by male as well as female researchers—is explicit in its use of qualitative research methods. Here the goal is direct engagement of "real-life" individuals within their "lived reality." Researchers strive to ensure that the research process is beneficial not only to the researcher but to the subject; in fact, the research is expected to contribute to the subject's empowerment. In relating to their subjects, researchers explicitly must address differences in constructions of gender, material circumstances, life experiences, and class, as well as perceived or actual differences in power and knowledge. Writing from a feminist research perspective necessarily will lead you to take a more immediate, or personal, approach than you can when you use the dispassionate scientific method.

As you approach your own research projects, keep in mind that the popular image of science and scientists as being dispassionate and objective continues to be questioned. Because scientists are people, they are subject to personal limitations, peer-group pressures, politics, and other factors that can both influence the questions they ask and bias their research results. The impressions of objectivity associated with the scientific worldview and the scientific method are being tempered through recognition of the humanity and limitations of scientists, and acknowledgement that the sciences are human (not value-free) activities. Growing numbers of researchers understand that there are multiple ways of knowing, and many points of view, and that a sense of humility (that we don't know all the answers) is necessary to counter the scientific arrogance that sometimes has constrained the creative exploration of new questions.[2]

Handling the spectrum of approaches

There are many approaches to research, then, ranging across the spectrum from high objectivity (quantitative) at one end to high subjectivity (qualitative) at the other, with many variations in between. The goal of objectivity in research—through application of the scientific method—is a powerful guide to critical thought. But a strictly objective/quantified method also can be a negative filter if it means ignoring other, more subjective kinds of research and explanation. Valid arguments can be made for research to be undertaken at both ends of the spectrum. How should you deal with the tension between them? By remaining open to the various approaches. Think about the different questions that each approach may raise—and be aware that no single approach necessarily will lead to *the* answer on everything. Different approaches to research are useful at different times and for different types of research. Students in geography, sustainability studies, and other environmental sciences need to become familiar with the range of approaches to research, and with the varying ways of integrating the objective with the subjective. With practice you will learn how to approach a wide range of assignments.

Stating your purpose and developing a central question or a hypothesis

As we pointed out in Chapter 1, you need to develop a clear statement of purpose for all the research and writing you do. In qualitative research this statement often is framed as a central, or principal, question, but in quantitative research it normally takes the form of a hypothesis. A hypothesis is a working thesis that translates your problem statement or question into a prediction of expected outcomes. By identifying the line of argument that you intend to follow, a hypothesis helps to make your research selective. In research structured by the scientific method, you must hold your hypothesis constant throughout the research process.

Whether you start with a question or a hypothesis, you must return to it at the end of your paper: if you started with a question, you must answer it; if you started with a hypothesis, you must state whether your findings did or did not support it. Whatever form your statement of purpose takes, it should be *limited, unified*, and *exact*.

Make it limited

A central question or hypothesis needs to be limited, that is, narrow enough to be workable. Suppose, for example, that your general subject is land-use planning in Canada: you must limit the subject in some way and create a line of argument for which you can supply adequate supporting evidence. Following the analytic questioning process, you might find that you want to restrict it by time. Imagine that you start with a question: "What role did government play in land-use planning from 2005 to 2015?" This question can be changed into a statement: "Government action directly influenced land-use planning during the decade 2005 to 2015." Or you might prefer to limit it more precisely, by theme and location: "Legislation introduced by the government of British Columbia directly influenced land-use planning during the decade 2005 to 2015." In short, make sure your topic and purpose statement are restricted enough for you to explore the issues in the depth required in order to draw supportable conclusions.

Make it unified

To be unified, your paper must have one controlling idea—a hypothesis or key question with which it will both begin and end. Do not be double-headed, as in "During its term of office the governing party introduced many environmental programs, but its downfall was due to its nuclear energy policy." What is the controlling idea here: environmental programs, or the reason for the downfall of the governing party? The essay should focus on one or the other. It is possible to explore two or more related ideas in a paper, but only if one of them is clearly in control, with all other ideas subordinated to it.

Make it exact

It is important to avoid vague terms such as *interesting* and *significant,* as in "Cemeteries are interesting places as sources of data for reconstructing settlement history." Does *interesting* mean *curious* or *good* or *exciting* or *likeable* or *important* or *worthwhile,* or. . .? Cemeteries are *useful* places as sources of data? Yes, they are. They may, *in addition,* be interesting—but it is their usefulness that is important here. Use words that state precisely what you intend to do.

Ethical Issues

Every research approach entails ethical questions that often are central to the research agenda. Why should this be the case? Donald Meinig, a prominent geographer, reminds us that "those who have a deep fascination for the earth . . . must have a special concern for the care of the earth."[3] This "special concern" applies to the way we do research, by cultivating sensitivity for any impact our research may have on the natural environment and the people we are to involve in our research. Two questions are essential: "Why is this research being done?" and "What is its end purpose?" Implicit in these questions, and the answers you give, are ethical issues that you must deal with. In some instances, you must get permission to undertake the research, as noted below. Before proceeding, however, a word of caution: remember that when you are doing research that in any way involves others, you are a representative of your institution, and any lasting impression you may leave could have positive or negative ramifications for the institution and for other researchers who will conduct research after you.

Research ethics committees

Research ethics committees review and approve the conduct of *all* upper-level research involving human and non-human subjects that is undertaken by honours students, graduate students, and faculty. The requirement for ethics review always applies, even if the research is funded by external research agencies. Your institution's policy on ethical conduct for research involving humans and non-humans will follow national standards, set by the three national research funding councils in Canada.[4] Check your institution's policies, which likely will be available to you online. Some research done in the first or second year of your degree also may have to be approved by an ethics committee, so prior to starting a research project check with your professor about this possibility.

At minimum, the proposal you submit to your research ethics committee will address the following points:

- the purpose or rationale for doing the study
- the study site (why there, and who must be approached for approval to work there)
- the type of data to be gathered
- the research methodology
- any possible risks to the people involved, including yourself, to any non-human species, or to the environment
- possible consequences (good and bad) of your research
- anticipated outcomes

Human geography without interviewing people
This heading title implies research on artifacts in the cultural landscape or the use of data obtained by observing people's actions or from examining current

or historical documents. The provisos identified above apply in these instances too. If you are permitted access to property or documents, take care not to change or damage them. Remain true to what is revealed from your observations and by your analysis.

Research involving human subjects

Research involving humans inevitably has a subjective dimension, explicit or implicit. For example, suppose that you intend to develop, apply, and analyze results from a questionnaire using the scientific method. In such a case, you will attempt to "remove" the subjective aspect by making the questions as value-free as possible, using strict sampling methods, and by employing people not involved with the research design and testing to approach the people who will respond to the questions. An "objectively" structured questionnaire may not be appropriate in all cases, however. If you want to find out about people's attitudes, values, and perceptions, an explicitly "subjective" questionnaire, or perhaps open-ended interviewing, with the data being examined using qualitative techniques, may be more appropriate.

By posing a question, you place that question into the mind of someone who may never have thought of it before. Thus, you have to think carefully about the purpose and appropriateness of your questions. Furthermore, no matter what approach you take, realize that the questions you ask inevitably reflect your own attitudes and values. You must be very careful when choosing what it is you truly want to ask because you don't want to unthinkingly bias the respondent. Researchers whose research is fundamentally subjective in nature must be intensely aware of the way their own perspectives may affect their work, and they often invite participants themselves to verify the findings—a step that strict followers of the scientific method may be reluctant to accept.

Some basic principles apply when doing research involving humans:

- Get permission to do any research at a site that is owned or controlled by others, by first being totally open about what you propose to do and why.
- Be open and honest with the people whom you would like to involve in your research; be clear about the purpose and nature of your research so they understand why they are being asked to participate and what you will ask them to do. When appropriate, or as required by your institution's ethics committee(s), give them access to a written description of your research purpose and design.

- Obtain freely given informed consent prior to involving people in your research. This may be done in writing (on a formal consent form, or at the top of the interview questionnaire) or obtained verbally (using a tape recorder, or recorded in your field notes—in which the person's initials may be recorded against your notation that permission to proceed has been granted). In all cases, be sure you also record the date.
- Ensure that each person understands that he or she has the right to withdraw from your study at any time, without explanation or recrimination. If a person does withdraw, identify in advance how you will deal with the information given to you up to that point. Whether you intend to retain and use the information provided, or not, you need to indicate your intention at the time you seek informed consent from your participants.
- Ask your respondents if they wish to remain anonymous. Know in advance, within your research design, how you will deal with the information gained from a person who wishes to remain anonymous. If a person wants to remain anonymous, specify how you plan to identify his or her input, and ask if this is acceptable.
- Inform all of your participants how you plan to use the material gathered (e.g., for an undergraduate essay or a graduate thesis) and who will have access to it (e.g., your supervisor, an examining committee, or, if it is a thesis, anyone who may see the work in the library).
- Treat your research subjects—and the research site—with respect.
- Be sensitive to gender and cultural differences.
- Always be courteous, even when opinions quite contrary to your own are expressed.

If you are required to complete an ethics application for review by a research ethics committee, be sure to build in time for the review to take place. Reviews may require several weeks to complete, including time for the committee to review your application, as well as time for you to respond to any questions the committee may ask, and subsequent follow-up queries from the committee. If in doubt, speak with your faculty adviser.

Physical and biological sciences
When doing your research, be sure to respect the natural environment, including the terrain and all flora and fauna. Ask yourself if there could be

any short- or long-term harmful consequences for the research site from the proposed research. How will you seek to minimize these effects? Can you reformulate your approach to avoid any negative impact? Can you identify long-term benefits from your work? How do the benefits weigh against any possible negative consequences? Be sure to identify these in your research proposal. An environmental research ethics committee may scrutinize your research proposal before you are permitted to proceed.

Determine whether you must get permission from a government, a land-owner, or a First Nation to do the research on their land. Before making an approach to get permission, you must prepare an outline of your research plan in which you highlight what will happen at the site, how you will analyze the data gained, possible outcomes, and how you will share the research findings, so the person or agency responsible for giving permission is fully aware of your plans. If your research involves animals, you should anticipate requesting approval for your project from an animal care committee, at the department or university level.

Sources

Research is a building process: researchers always build on what they and others have done. As the previous chapter noted, there are three kinds of sources: primary, secondary, and tertiary. Primary sources are the sorts of data that you gather for yourself, whether in the field (see Chapter 11) or in the lab (see Chapter 9), although for some types of research your primary material may have been produced by others and published in books, journals, reports, newspapers, letters, or elsewhere. For all of your work, you will need to consult secondary and tertiary sources. The remainder of this chapter provides some suggestions for finding and using sources, whether online or in libraries.

The Internet

The Internet is an expansive, remarkably diverse, and, at times, frustrating resource. It must be used with care if it is to be of value as a research tool. Hundreds of books exist on how best to use the Internet. What follows is a list of summary pointers: a skeleton guide to the Internet, how to do searches, validating your sources, and selected research websites. (For guidelines on citing Internet and other computer-based information, see Chapter 7.)

Google, Bing, and Yahoo Search are examples of popular search engines that enable you to find information on the Internet. Google Scholar searches specifically for scholarly literature and includes mostly articles, as well as some citations to conference papers and other material.

How to search online

No one search engine provides complete coverage; speed, database size, relevancy rankings, search results, features, and commands vary from engine to engine, so you probably will want to use several engines in the course of your search. Even if you use the same keywords, different results will appear from engine to engine. Be aware that some universities block access to sites from which students might download copyrighted materials, and other providers may block on the basis of content. Most search engines have "help" tutorials you can turn to if necessary. The following points cover some common essentials:

- **Use your keywords.** Start your search with the *keywords* you identified when developing your research plan. Use academic, discipline-based terms as much as possible.
- **Use lower-case letters when typing keywords.** Upper-case letters may restrict your search; if you use lower case, most search engines will consider sites that use both upper- and lower-case letters.
- **Use a simple search if you are sure the search words are restrictive.** For instance, if you know that you want information on the *Otago Daily Times*, then that is all you need to enter. But be warned: a simple search using a wide-open term, such as *geography* or *biology*, is likely to give you millions of sites, so be specific and precise.
- **Avoid vague keywords.** Vague terminology will produce large quantities of irrelevant material. For example, just typing the term *territory* in an Internet search will turn up items concerning a particular area (such as the Northwest Territories, or the Northern Territory), international law, personal territory, tourism, terrorism, burials, personal blog posts, and thousands of other things, including advertisements. In other words, it is important to think of additional keywords so you can be precise. Rather than a basic search, try the *advanced search* mode. For example, you might use *territory* and

geography or, if too many items appear, you might refine this as *territory* and *political geography*. If you are interested in the work of a particular researcher, try adding that person's name to the subject keyword.

- **Things you can do in an advanced search.** Advanced searches provide two or more lines in which you can specify both what you want and don't want. You may be permitted to target publications in a particular language, within varying time periods, that have certain usage rights, and with certain types of occurrences. If the user interface is not this friendly, you can still do an advanced search by using the following strategies:

  1. Use *Boolean* operators and syntax, i.e., AND, OR, and NOT (typed in either upper- or lower-case letters) to link your keywords. In some systems, the minus (−) sign can be used as a substitute for NOT and a plus (+) sign as a substitute for AND.

  2. If you use Boolean operators and syntax, use parentheses to group words: for example, you might search for "caves AND (stalactites NOT stalagmites) AND Tennessee."

  3. If your keywords are not finding as wide an array of sources as you had hoped, you can carry out a *controlled language search*. A controlled language search uses *pre-existing subject headings*, such as those listed in the five-volume *Library of Congress Subject Headings*.[5]

- **Try alternate spelling.** To expand a search, try variant spellings of certain words: e.g., *harbour* and *harbor*; *labour* and *labor*; *encyclopedia* and *encyclopaedia*.

- **Check to see if there is a site map, which is like a table of contents.** It may quickly give you an idea of how useful the site will be for your needs.

- **Try the "links" or "other sites like this" section when you find a source that is close to what you need.** Links to other sites can be helpful. Your library's website may have pertinent links for you to try, too. Similarly, disciplinary websites, set up by units such as your academic department, often identify links to other sites of potential interest, and they may well be of use to you.

- **Don't get stuck on fascinating sites that are, at best, tangential to what you need.** You know how easy it is to get sidetracked while surfing the Web. But you can't afford to spend hours browsing when you really need to focus on research for a specific assignment. Be warned! Remain focused!

- **Bookmark particularly useful websites.** When you find a website you plan to visit again, you can store its URL (uniform resource locator) for future reference as a "Favourite" or "Bookmark." This allows you to return quickly and easily to useful sites at a later time. You can create folders into which you save the site information, naming the folders so they make sense for your research needs.

Because all content on the Internet may be moved, or restructured, or deleted, some URLs may not work when you return to them. To help resolve this problem, many scholarly publishers have begun to attach digital object identifiers (DOIs) to journal articles and other documents. Assigned by a registration agency, a DOI is a unique alphanumeric string that provides a permanent link to the Internet location of each item. When a DOI is available (you will find it displayed prominently on the first page of an article), include it instead of the URL in your filed reference (see Chapter 7 for more on documenting your sources). Because the DOI string can be long, you should copy and paste the identifier rather than typing it out.

- **Record the full URL or DOI and the date the site was accessed.** You will need this information for citations within the text of your work and for your list of references.
- **Look for selected directories that may be helpful.** Each directory is selective, so you will need to check several. See, for example, the Virtual Library at http://vlib.org, for which volunteers from various specialties compile lists of key links for their particular areas of expertise.
- **Know when to give up.** Keep in mind the "law of diminishing returns" and try to recognize when enough is enough.
- **Know when not to use the Internet.** Remember that not everything is available online. A great deal of information can be found only in printed sources, so do use the books, journals, and other material in your institution's library (p. 46). When in doubt, seek guidance from your instructor and reference librarians.

Validating your sources

Your biggest challenge when using the Internet is how to determine if a site is reliable. Unlike the library, where most of the material available has been critically reviewed, edited, and published by generally reputable outlets, the Internet is unregulated and there are no quality controls. Anyone can publish material online, and many pages are not updated. You will find some gems, but you will also find junk. How can you differentiate? Just as you must use your critical thinking skills in assessing books and journals, so you must assess the value of everything you find on the Internet. Asking yourself the following questions will help you establish the integrity, validity, timeliness, and authorship of what you find (see Table 2.1 on p. 44).

- **Whose material is it?** Who is the author? Who created it? Is the site published by an academic institution? A government or private research centre? A government department? A business? A news agency? An international organization? A group of people with no professional affiliation? An individual? Even if a website is "signed," qualifications may not be provided. Ownership information generally is identified at the top or the bottom of a site (read the URL carefully), or this information may be displayed on the main page or "About Us" page. If you can't find this information, be suspicious.
- **Why are the URL and the domain important?** You can use the URL and domain information to check on who wrote the page, how current it is, and the author's credentials. Consider this made-up example URL: http://www.example.org. The *domain* here is *example.org*. One way to find out more about a page is to truncate the URL by clicking on the URL in the location box, deleting everything after the domain (e.g., in this fictional example, delete the text after .com in *http://www.whatever. com/notes/file3/other.html*), and hitting *enter*. If the page that loads is a reputable source, there is a good chance the document you found is also reputable. However, even reputable sources can make errors, so this is no guarantee that the information you discover is accurate. Careful reading and critical assessment of each document is required.
- **Does the domain provide clues about the source?** The *top-level domain* is a hierarchical framework used to indicate the location of a

web page on the network. Common domains in North America have included *.org* (non-profit and research organizations), *.com* (commercial endeavours), and *.net* (network-related projects). In June 2008, however, the Internet Corporation for Assigned Names and Numbers (ICANN) eased existing restrictions to allow a much wider range of domain names. Personal names, trademarked brands for major corporations, city names, and many other domain names are now used. Some domain names are in non-Latin characters, including Arabic and Chinese scripts.

- The domain name refers to the initial part of a URL (down to the first "/") and tells you who published the page. Key information will include

  – *country:* e.g., *au* (Australia), *ca* (Canada), *cn* (China), *de* (Germany), *fr* (France), *in* (India), *il* (Israel), *jp* (Japan), *mx* (Mexico), *nl* (Netherlands), *nz* (New Zealand), *ru* (Russia), *sa* (Saudi Arabia), *uk* (UK), and *za* (South Africa). Some country codes are not tightly controlled and are subject to misuse, so be thorough when assessing sites.

  – *type:* education, e.g., *edu* (US), *ac* (UK); government, e.g., *eu* (European Union), *gc* (Canada), *gov* (US, UK, and elsewhere); organizations, e.g., *org, com*, and *net*; and museums, *museum*.

- **Personal pages.** Be wary of personal pages. For example, students may post their own writing on a personal page that is hosted by a university's reputable URL. The URLs of personal pages frequently contain an individual's name (such as *pbrowne*) following a tilde (~), a per cent sign (%), or the words *users, members,* or *people*. No publisher or domain owner vouches for the information in personal pages, which often contain highly biased personal perspectives. While personal pages are not necessarily "bad," you need to investigate each author carefully. Thinking about why a page may have been put on the Web will help you avoid being fooled (and looking foolish in turn) or becoming a victim of fraud. You need to consider what sort of intentions the author might have for putting information online—to inform and give facts or data, to explain or persuade, to sell, or to disclose? What tone does the author use—is it, for example, humorous, exaggerated, or condescending? Are the arguments distorted or overblown?

- **Is the site vanity or self-publishing?** A vanity website means that the material listed has not been through the peer-review process that is intrinsic to scholarship or that it hasn't been disseminated by a trade publisher. Some vanity and short-run, generally privately funded, published works (such as a person's memoirs) may have merit, but this can be determined only by critical evaluation. Many people now put such material on their personal websites. The material may be important only to the author! Even when a site's content seems to be scholarly, as with a person's working papers or information that is derived from a thesis or dissertation, the information may be incomplete—particularly if the site is personal rather than academically affiliated. And, again, some universities permit students to have websites using the institution's address as the first component of the URL; don't be fooled by the domain information into thinking that the source must be sound.

- **Who sponsored the site?** Is the site sponsored, officially or unofficially, by a particular organization (such as an environmental advocacy group), an institution (such as a university or a research unit), a corporation, a government, or a quasi-governmental agency? Is there any evidence of third-party financial or other support or sponsorship? With respect to each of these questions, if they hold true, how might the site's content have been influenced?

- **Is advertising included?** If so, can you determine what impact it may have had on the site's content?

- **Who is the audience?** Try to determine what the purpose of the site is. To whom is the content aimed? Serious researchers? School students? Potential customers? People who enjoy reading the vanity rambling of the particular author?

- **When was the site created, revised, or last updated?** The dates of creation, revision, and last updating generally are given on academically useful sites. Be wary of a site that seems to be great, but which has no dates. Dates alone will not mean the site is credible, but it is important to know them. Be skeptical if such information is missing.

- **Is the site credible?** Has the site been reviewed or been given awards? When a site is recognized and given an award by others, this information will be presented. Who gave the award or otherwise reviewed the site? A scientific group? A private agency? Friend "Joe"?

- **What is the quality of the site and of the information it provides?** To answer this question you must assume the critical-thinking stance of an academic.
  - Is the site well designed and organized?
  - Is it easy to use?
  - Do the icons clearly represent what is intended and can you move around the site with ease?
  - Is the text well written?
  - Is the content convincing?
  - Is it thorough in its coverage of the topic, or is it selective and incomplete?
  - How in-depth is the material provided? Is it shallow or is there substance?
  - Is the material on the page unique? In what way? How does it relate to other sources?
  - Do any graphics convey relevant information? Are sources cited?
- **Is the content sound?** Prepare yourself to be critical of what you find online. Studying your textbook and other reading assignments from your course will help you determine whether what you find online is sound.
- **Is the content biased?** Who wrote the information? Does the information reflect the special interests of a sponsor? Does the material support a single stance, political or otherwise? You can get a sense of balance—and thus better appreciate the significance of any bias—if you look for sites offering contrasting views.
- **Is there an ideological bent to the material presented?** Knowing the source of the material, and its sponsors, may assist you in identifying whether or not the site is intended to get readers to accept a particular line of argument.
- **Can you verify the specific information presented on the website?** Don't accept everything at face value. Question it and, if possible, verify it against other sources using, for instance, library-based research.
- **Is documentation provided?** Are footnotes, endnotes, a list of references, or other forms of citations provided? Do they include print and Internet sources, or just Internet sources? How pertinent are they

to the material presented? If references are included, is there a clear rationale for their inclusion? Are references fully cited? Just as you must carefully consider documentation in books and journals, you should be wary—indeed, very wary—of the kind and form of documentation provided on the Internet. The need for documentation will vary, depending on the source of the material: a governmental agency may not offer any documentation at all, whereas an individual who purports to be a scholar, and wants you to believe everything that he or she presents, may provide more supporting documentation than is strictly necessary. As in all critical evaluations of others' work, it's important to ask whether the documentation is germane and complete. Have the sources been used with care and accuracy? Can you think of any major sources that have been neglected?

- **Are the links relevant and appropriate for the site?** Are the links comprehensive or are they limited? The degree to which links are appropriate, as an expansion of the website's purpose, may give you a clue as to the worthiness of the site itself.

- **Should I be wary of open-source sites?** Yes! For example, Wikipedia has been in existence since 2000 as an online encyclopedia that can be edited by anyone in the world. Users who volunteer to write and edit articles do not need specialized qualifications to contribute: most of the entries can be edited by anyone with access to the Internet. Because of its open nature, where entries are based on what people choose to submit or amend (including problematic content), critics charge that Wikipedia's content lacks authority and accountability, is unreliable, and is subject to vandalism (insertion of false information). Articles do not undergo the same formal, peer-review processes as academic journal articles; Wikipedia warns users that not all of its information is accurate, unbiased, or comprehensive. Many academics and librarians consider Wikipedia to be unsuitable as a reference source; indeed, your instructors may discourage you from using citations from this source in your assignments.

- **Above all, be critical, not gullible!** Don't be fooled into accepting everything you find on the Internet. This also means that you should not take the easy route of basing your research on something that is "there," just because it is.

Table 2.1 An overview for evaluating websites

Questions to ask when:	Points to check:
A. Looking at the URL:	
1. Is this a personal page or site?	• Check for a personal name following a tilde (~), %, or *users, members,* or *people.*
2. What type of domain is this? Is the information on the site appropriate for the domain?	• .edu? .gc? .com? .org? .net? country? • other sources?
3. Who is publishing the page? Is it published by an entity that makes sense? Does it correspond to the name of the site? Have you heard of this entity previously?	• Check the publisher or domain name. • Look for links such as "About Us," "Background," "Who Am I," "Biography," and "Sponsors." • You can place greater reliance on information that is published by the source.
B. Scanning the page perimeter:	
1. Who, or what agency, wrote the page? Can you tell what values they stand for?	• Look for name of author, organization, agency, or institution responsible for the page (someone who claims to be responsible for the content). • Look for links that say "About Us," "Philosophy," "Background," etc. • If you can't find this information, locate the publisher by truncating back the URL (for instructions, see Note at bottom of Table).
2. When was the page last updated? Is it current enough for your purposes?	• A date usually is found at the bottom of a web page (there may be a date in the URL). • Check dates on all pages on the site. • Do not use undated factual or statistical information.
3. What are the author's credentials to write on the subject?	• Check whether the author's purported background or education suggests qualifications sufficient to write on the topic; is the page merely opinion? a distorted perspective? • An e-mail address with no additional information about the author is insufficient to assess credentials.
C. Considering quality of information:	
1. Are the author's sources well documented? Did the author get the information from published scholarly or academic journals and books?	• Look for footnotes and "Links," "Additional Sites," "Related Links," etc. • Explore any footnotes or links that may refer to documentation; are the publications or sites reputable? reliable? scholarly? real? (On the Internet it is possible to provide totally fake references.)
2. Is the information complete? If the site provides second-hand information, is it reproduced in an unaltered state?	• You may need to find the original source to determine whether the copy is complete and not altered (if it's retyped, it could be altered easily). • A legitimate source from a reputable journal or other publication should be accompanied by the copyright statement and/or permission to reprint. (You should be suspicious if it's not present.)

3. Does the author provide links to other resources on the topic?

- Are the links working? Are they well chosen?
- Are there links to other points of view? (Links that offer opposing viewpoints are more likely to be balanced and unbiased than pages offering one view only; be sure to check for bias, particularly when you agree with something!)

D. Checking with others:

1. Who links to the page or site?

- Find other web pages that link to the site.

2. Is the page listed in one or more reputable directories or pages?

- Good directories list a small portion of websites, so inclusion in a directory is significant. (Be sure to read the entry, as the directory may not be totally positive about the site.)

3. What do others say about the author or responsible authoring body?

- Look up the author's name in Google or another search engine.
- See which blogs refer to the site and what they have to say about it (use site name, author, or URL to do this on Google Blog Search).

E. Stepping back and thinking:

1. Why was the page put on the Web? Is it suitable for your purpose?

- To inform? Provide facts and data? Explain? Persuade? Sell? Entice? Share or disclose? Other reasons?
- Be aware of the full range of possible intentions behind web pages.

2. Is the tone of the site ironic? Is it satire or parody?

- It's easy to be fooled; be sensitive to the possibility of becoming a victim!

3. Is the website as good (credible and useful) as the books, journals, and other resources available in print or online through the library?

- Generally, published information is considered to be more reliable than information found on the Web; however, a great many reputable agencies, institutions, societies, publishing houses, news sources, and governments make excellent material available online—take the time to check it out carefully.

Note: To truncate back a URL: in the address bar, delete the end characters of the URL stopping just before each slash (/)—leave the slash in place. Press enter to see if any more information is available about the author or the site providing the page. Continue to truncate, one slash at a time, until you reach the first single slash that is preceded by the domain name portion. This is the website's server or "publisher."

Source: Adapted from The Regents of the University of California. (2012). *Evaluating web pages: Techniques to apply & questions to ask*. http://www.lib.berkeley.edu/TeachingLib/Guides/Internet/Evaluate.html.

Copying material from the Internet

You may elect to copy material directly from a website by highlighting something on a page, copying it, and then pasting it into a word-processing document. If you do this, be sure to identify exactly what has been copied, with full and correct source and page information, and the date you accessed the site. Carelessness in this regard could lead you to inadvertently use the material without including quotation marks or without providing source information. The excuse of carelessness will not save you from a charge of plagiarism.

Remain open to "fringe" information

While you want to be sure your information is sound, it's a good idea to remain open to Internet sources that provide access to "fringe" information. For instance, many newspapers that are neither "mainstream" nor officially "accepted" in their countries of origin are available online, and they may convey information that otherwise would never be released. Similarly, oppressed minorities may use the Internet to get their messages to an international audience. You should be cautious when using such sources, but the insights gained from them sometimes can be invaluable. As always, be sure to cite your sources (see Chapter 7).

Libraries

You must become familiar with your institution's library or libraries. Don't put off going to the main library until near the end of the term; in fact, it's a good idea to renew your acquaintance with it at the start of every academic year. And because you may well be taking courses in different disciplines each term or semester, at the start of each, check to see where the key areas in the library are for the courses in which you are registered. The importance of getting to know your way around the library can't be stressed enough. You don't want to be so overwhelmed by its size and complexity that you either scrimp on required research or waste time and energy trying to find information.

Disciplinary "fact sheets," which highlight key sources and their locations, may be available from the library. If you need help, ask for it. Librarians will be glad to show you the bibliographies and guides to the literature, dictionaries, encyclopedias, directories, atlases, gazetteers, handbooks, databases, CDs, DVDs, videos, and other materials for your field of study. Some of these sources will be available online; others will be found only on the library shelves.

Cataloguing systems

How, specifically, do you locate the sources that are in the library? You will see a *call number* associated with every entry in the catalogue. The principal cataloguing systems are the *Library of Congress* system (used in most university libraries) and the *Dewey Decimal* system (used by many public libraries). Find out which system your institution's library uses. Both systems include many sub-disciplines within each category. When searching for books and journals on the shelves, you will save time if you learn which of the major categories applies most directly to your research needs.

Library of Congress System

A	General Works
B	Philosophy, Psychology, Religion
C	Genealogy
D	History—Europe, Asia, Africa, Oceania
E	History—US General
F	History—US Local, Latin America, Canada
G	Geography, Anthropology, Recreation, Atlases
H	Statistics, Economics, Sociology
J	Political Science
K	Law
L	Education
M	Music
N	Fine Art
P	Languages and Literature
Q	Science
R	Medicine
S	Agriculture
T	Engineering
U	Military Sciences
V	Naval Sciences
Z	Library Science

Dewey Decimal System

011–099	Generalities (including Computing)
100	Philosophy, Psychology
200	Religion
300	Social Sciences
400	Languages
500	Science
600	Technology
700	The Arts
800	Literature
900	Geography, History, Travel
A–Z	(by author) Fiction

Using the catalogue

You can't just stumble into a library or go to its online catalogue and "start." You have to proceed with a plan. The "information sphere" is large, complex, and often confusing, so you need to take time to think calmly and rationally about the information you need. Start by reviewing the elements of thought (see Table 1.1 on p. 4). Next, think about your purpose and what you will need to do to complete the job. Consider writing down the various research steps required. Pose some questions for yourself—in addition to those posed on pages 24–5, think about how many authors you should consider.

Although cataloguing systems vary, as noted above, there are two principal ways to use them to locate sources:

- By using *known specific information*: *author* (with surname first, followed by the given name or the initials), *title* (of a book or a journal), or (if you don't already know the title of the work or its author) *call number*. Such searches can be quick, but you must know precisely what you are seeking.
- By *subject,* using *keywords.* As with using keywords in Internet searches, library catalogue searches using keywords can be done when you know neither the specific authors nor the titles you want (see above, on pp. 36–8).
- Don't confine yourself to your library's catalogue. Go online to a major research university's catalogue and see if what you need is there. If you find something relevant, you can return to your own institution's catalogue to check if the work is in the collection.

Typically, subject searches are not helpful for finding materials in the Government Documents, Special Collections, or Archives sections of the library. To use these sources, ask the help-desk librarian or archivist for assistance. If in doubt about how to use your keywords when searching the catalogue, or how to do an advanced search, check to see if there is an online "Library Education" or "Help" page, or seek assistance from a librarian.

Once you have a list of possible sources, you can rank them from the earliest work to the most recent, or from the most pertinent to the least. Once you have decided which of the sources you wish to use, the next step will be to find them; then you can begin reading and taking notes (see Chapter 3).

Browsing

Take a walk among the library's shelves at some point and see what is there. Learn the cataloguing codes for the subject areas pertinent to your courses and browse those shelves. As you wander, you may spot titles and authors you have heard mentioned in lectures or have read about in texts. *Citation tracing*—looking for items identified in your readings—can be rewarding. A quick glance through the table of contents of a book or a journal will indicate whether there is something in it you should read or that you should at least note for later examination. Don't ignore the special collections located in various parts of the library or in an associated centre.

Special collections

The *Reference* section is a "must-know" area. Often it is located in an easily accessed area on the main floor of the library. Dictionaries, encyclopedias, bibliographies, various versions of *Who's Who* and other biographical sources, and many other publications you can check readily for specific information are located here.

Newspapers are located in a designated area in the library. Some are in hard copy, delivered daily. Older material from these and numerous other newspapers may be available on microfiche (with a lifespan of over 100 years, some agencies feel microfiche is a safer format than digital records). A list of titles held by the library is identified in the catalogue. The library's website likely also includes databases of both current newspapers and historical newspapers, with links you can use to see electronic copies of local, national, and international newspapers. If your work involves historical reconstructions, you may have to go to local, provincial, state, or national archives to see certain newspapers.

Sound recordings, video recordings, and *films* are available to you in another special collections area in the library. You may be able to view or hear some of this material in the library, or you may be able to borrow it, likely on a short-term (such as a two-hour, or one-day) basis. Usually you can borrow items for use in a class presentation, but you must plan ahead to arrange a special loan.

The *Government Documents* section of the library is important for some subjects. Located here are materials—including some "fugitive" (hard-to-find) documents—from national and local governments and quasi-governmental agencies, from many countries. Also located here are documents from such non-governmental agencies as the United Nations and its many parts (including, for example, the Food and Agriculture Organization [FAO], the World Health Organization [WHO], the United Nations Development Programme [UNDP], the United Nations Environment Programme [UNEP], the Economic Commission for Latin America and the Caribbean [ECLAC]), the World Bank, and the Organisation for Economic Co-operation and Development (OECD). Materials usually are arranged alphabetically by country or organization. Only some of the data available here may be available online.

Rare Book and Archival Collections in your institution's library may include old (e.g., early nineteenth century) books, unique papers (including diaries and letters) by or about particular individuals, or collections of documents from specific organizations. Some archival, rare book, map, and photograph library sites are available on the Internet, including

- Archives Canada: archivescanada.ca
- US Library of Congress: loc.gov/rr/rarebook
- British Library: bl.uk

Databases and geographic information systems

Most colleges and universities have amalgamated statistical data resources in a single centre, which may be associated with the main library. Such a centre gives you access to statistical consultations and to myriad data sets, many of which will be available to you online via the library's site. These include a wide variety of governmental and non-governmental statistical data on environmental issues, population, international trade, and much more. Thousands of databases now exist, covering every conceivable topic, including some that are readily adaptable to geographic information systems (GIS). GIS services often are provided by staff in a university data resource centre, which may act as a central repository for GIS data available on campus. Pertinent data also may be located in the Government Documents section or the Maps Division of the library, and in a library or special collection in the Department of Geography.

Using various bibliographic management tools (software applications such as RefWorks, EndNote and EndNoteWeb, Mendeley, or Zotero) will enable you to create a personal online database by importing references from text files or online databases. Also known as citation or reference management tools, these types of software not only help you organize and manage your collection of research sources but also enable you to generate bibliographies in multiple citation formats, an important benefit when your instructor specifies a particular citation style! All these tools include a plug-in for word processing programs so you can create bibliographies, but some of the tools provide a web-based interface, mobile applications, and support for collaboration such as sharing your citations with others and having them add to your collection.

How do you decide which tool will best suit your needs? Think about the following points[6] to help determine which of the programs will work best:

- What are the tasks you might want a software program to perform?
  - Do you want to capture and import information from web pages or databases; search a database; manage your collection of PDFs; work on a tablet or mobile site; work without connecting to the Internet?
- How do the basic features of each of the tools compare?
  - What word processors do they use? Can they create records from PDF files and folders? Are there online storage limits and will it cost you to get more?
- How well does each of the tools manage PDFs?
  - While all tools can attach PDF and Doc files to your collection of sources, can they automatically find and attach PDFs or search through attached PDFs?

Your university or college library likely has site-wide licences to one or more of these bibliographic management tools, and may offer information or training sessions for you. Online learning videos and tutorials also are available.

Books

Books are found in three areas: online, on the new-book shelves (books are changed frequently here), and on the general shelves. Depending on the courses you are taking, you will need to become familiar with a variety of source materials in the geographical, physical, biological, and social sciences, and, for some, the humanities as well. For example, as a student in geography, sustainability, or another environmental field of study, when searching for library books, be aware of the ecology section under biology; historical geography under history and geography; resources and resource management under geography, agriculture, economics, forestry, parks and protected areas, and wildlife; urban issues under geography, economics, sociology, architecture, and history; soils under geography, forestry, agriculture, and engineering; geomorphology under geography and geology; climatology and meteorology under those headings as well as under physics, geography, and agriculture; landscape interpretation under architecture, geography, literature, and art; environmental perception under geography, psychology, and urban planning; and so on. Don't forget to examine the many thematic and regional geography sections in the library, which always are usefully varied in their contents.

You can also consult the many thousands of e-books (electronic books) that now exist. (Many e-books available to you free on the Internet may be incomplete, because some pages are not included due to copyright issues.) Your institution's library catalogue system will have links to e-books covering a wide range of subject areas. Many e-books (and e-journals) are available in full only through the library system due to special agreements. Increasingly, scholarly journal articles, book chapters, and monographs are available as Open Access publications, which are free to access, reuse, and distribute.

Because many books are not refereed by topic experts, you should be careful when you refer to them as possible sources. A refereed book is generally one published by a university press, which means several external readers critically evaluated the book before the press decided to publish it. This does not mean that it is "right," but it does mean that it has passed a test for quality and accuracy. Some commercial presses also publish refereed academic books. It is important to consider the source of any book you might choose to cite.

As suggested above, you can save yourself precious time and pressure during mid- and late-term by visiting the library early in each term, well before assignment deadlines. Don't wait until the last minute to get important library sources: otherwise—horrible thought—you may find that the key work you need has been signed out by someone else or that it is available to you only through an interlibrary loan (meaning you have to wait for it to arrive from a different institution in another city or even another country). Plan ahead, and give yourself enough time not only to use the books, but also to place a hold request on the items in the event that you must wait until they become available.

Journals

Numerous journals are available to you both on your library's shelves and online (e-journals) via your library's website or online catalogue. Shelved journals are usually located in two sections of the library: recent issues (sometimes containing a year's run) and back-runs (often covering all the years since a journal began publication). Your instructors expect you to become acquainted with, and use, literature that appears in learned journals.[7]

What makes these journals different from popular publications? Researchers seek to have their findings published in major refereed journals. A paper is published only if it is deemed to be of value. This is determined by the journal's editor, or editorial team, who seek the reactions of (usually three) leading researchers in a field of study, who anonymously critique a submitted paper and provide a recommendation to publish, reconsider after revisions, or reject (i.e., peer review). Typically, the author's name and the names of the other readers are kept from each reader to reduce the chance of personal biases intruding into the evaluation process. Furthermore, the readers' names are kept from the author; thus, in the acknowledgements an author may include with the article, you will see "anonymous reviewers" being thanked for their input.[8]

The number of Open Access (OA) online journals has increased rapidly. In addition to the benefits noted above, OA publishing democratizes access to science and social science research in low-income countries, contributes to improved education and public enrichment, and enables researchers to publish more of their work, including negative results. Authors usually must pay a fee to publish their research with OA publishers; unfortunately, this way of operating has resulted in the emergence of "predatory" OA publishers whose motivation is financial, rather than advancing knowledge and sharing new findings. Using unscrupulous marketing techniques, these predatory publishers often trick academics into publishing in journals of questionable quality and into attending fake or low-quality conferences. There is widespread concern among academics in Canada (and elsewhere) and a variety of responses are underway to ensure standards, including rigorous peer review and ethics, are upheld.[9] Your institution's library subscribes to online journal services that some commercial publishers host on their *.com* sites. These publishers make selected high-quality, peer-reviewed journal articles available as PDF files that your library's subscription may enable you to download for free. If not, you can pay for articles personally.

While academic libraries increasingly subscribe to electronic journals, the print journals on the library's shelves may be useful to you. Not all journals, nor all volumes, have been digitized; you may find back issues of relevant journals that are available only in print format. Sometimes, too, if you are browsing in the print journals, you may make an unexpected discovery that contributes to your understanding and research.

Whenever you take a course in a new discipline, or sub-discipline, get to know what journals are pertinent and available to you. This way you will know the limits of your library's resources. You may be able to get hard copies of some journal articles from libraries at other institutions; however, because some article delivery systems are restricted to faculty, staff, and graduate students, you may need to consult your instructor or TA for help in this regard.

How do you locate journal articles? One approach is to use Google Scholar (see p. 36). Not all journal articles are available through this service, but many items will appear. For example, a 2018 search using "rock glaciers in Banff" as the keywords identified 6,560 items.

How else can you proceed? First, be aware that it takes time and effort to find out what is available in journals. Even if you know the title of an article you want, you may not find the article listed in the library's catalogue—although you can use the catalogue to determine whether or not the library carries the journal, and, if so, discover the call number. Often, you won't have a specific article title or author to search for. There are several ways to identify journals that are potential sources for pertinent material on specific subjects. Your instructor may guide you to certain journals, as may bibliographies in your textbook or other pertinent publications (including those that appear in notes 1, 10, and 11 at the end of this chapter). If a particular journal is in the library, you can browse through the table of contents of several issues and read the abstracts that may be published with the articles. Such abstracts may appear at the top of the article, under the title, or (perhaps on a back page) in a group of abstracts for all of the articles published in the same issue. Alternatively, you can glance through a journal's annual index, usually published in the last issue of each volume year; note that this may not coincide with the calendar year. However, browsing in this manner is an inefficient way to search for articles on specific topics, especially if you are pressed for time. Another approach is to explore indexes and abstracts that are published in separate volumes or are available online.

If you know the author(s) and title of an article in a professional journal you can go directly to the publisher's online site, for it generally will provide you with full information about the paper: volume number, issue number, year, pages. Sometimes the abstract is provided. The full article may be available too, usually for a fee.

Indexes and abstracts

Indexes and abstracts provide an organized way to find books and, of particular use, research articles published in journals. Some list chapters within edited book collections. Librarians can help you identify the aids most appropriate to your studies, available to you either in the library collection or on the Internet.

Your library may have on its shelves *Geographical Abstracts: Physical Geography*, *Geographical Abstracts: Human Geography*, *Geological Abstracts*, *Ecological Abstracts*, and *International Development Abstracts*. Other compilations include

- *Current Geographical Publications* and *GeoBib* from the American Geographical Society Library
- *Biological Abstracts*
- *Social Science Abstracts*
- *Sociological Abstracts*
- *Humanities Abstracts*
- *Oceanographic Literature Review*
- *EconLit*
- *Readers' Guide Abstracts* and *Readers' Guide to Periodical Literature*
- *PsycINFO*
- *MEDLINE*
- *TOXNET*
- *Web of Science*
- *Century of Science*

Some of these may be available only in hard copy or online, while others will be accessible in both formats. For upper-level studies, you may have occasion to refer to *Dissertation Abstracts* (available online).

Checking on authors

If you want to place a particular work into the broader context of its author's various writings and accomplishments, there are many sources you can use to find biographical information. You can check *Books in Print* for particular authors, as well as your library's catalogue—or the online library catalogues at such major research institutions as the University of Toronto, University of Chicago, and the University of Cambridge. Be sure to use the advanced (Boolean) search function. Other sources include the many national, international, and subject-specific versions of *Who's Who*, the *Dictionary of International Biography* (Cambridge: International Biographical Centre, many editions), specialized dictionaries and encyclopedias,[10] as well as biographies and autobiographies.[11]

Maps as sources

Your institution's map library undoubtedly has many loose-leaf maps, map folios, atlases, air photographs, and satellite images, as well as books on cartography, GIS, and related topics. Help may be required to find some of the material, because certain maps, photographs, and satellite images may not be included in the general catalogue. You may have to refer to a particular catalogue, computerized or not. Some material may be grouped and filed under a general heading, in a map cabinet drawer. Likely you will make use of maps that have been compiled and published from various sources. The following criteria may be of use when you are considering paper copies of maps as sources:[12]

- **Scale.** The scale of the map determines the size of area and amount of detail that can be shown (see Figure 2.1). There are several categories of map scales:
  - *1:1,000–1:2,500* (large scales, small areas; details—lot boundaries, building outlines, road widths, etc., are shown correctly to scale)
  - *1:10,000–1:20,000* (fields, lot lines, and buildings may be shown by conventional symbols, and streets will be named)
  - *1:25,000–1:50,000* (topographical scales, used for surveys of relief—usually shown by contours and spot heights but sometimes by shaded relief)
  - *1:250,000–1:500,000* (progressively more generalized maps of topographic type, with less and less detail)
  - *1:1,000,000 and smaller* (smaller scales, larger areas)
- **Format and media.** Size and layout? Sheet maps? On fiche, or CD or DVD? Blueprints? Hand-drawn? Computer-generated? The answers to these questions will determine whether and how you can use the maps.
- **Currency of the data.** Does the date of the data, and the map, relate to the period you are studying? Be wary of "old" data released in map form years after a survey was done—look for both the date of the data survey and the publication date of the map.
- **Reference structure.** Examine the map for evidence of accuracy. On what reference structure is the map based? Are sources cited? Is the projection named? Is the north arrow shown, and the magnetic variation? Is the scale reference identified?
- **Cartographic symbolism.** Do the symbols selected for the categories into which data are sorted follow a graded pattern (e.g., from lesser to greater intensity), or are they confusing? If, say, settlements

are identified by size, do the point data clearly reflect their relative sizes (small, medium, large)? If the symbols are non-standard, are they explained in a legend? Do geographical names follow standard authorities?

- **Graphic language.** Does the map successfully convey the data, at an appropriate scale, using clear words and symbols? If the mapped data are complex, involving several sets of information (e.g., rivers, road and field boundary lines, settlements by size and type, settlement names, crop patterns, and political boundaries, or, as another example, data on three variables, such as hydrological balance, precipitation, and temperature), how well does the map deal with the overlapping data? Can you read the locational information and the contrasting areal patterns with ease? If you want to use just some of the information, how easy is it to extract exactly what you need? Would a different map, or maps, be better?

Figure 2.1 Map types and scale ranges

Source: Reproduced with permission of the compiler, B. Farrell, from B. Farrell and A. Desbarats, *Guide for a Small Map Collection*, 2nd ed. (Ottawa: Association of Canadian Librarians, 1984), 30.

- **Identification.** Is the map titled? Is it part of a series? Is the compiler identified? Is the source of the data cited? Who and where is the publisher and when was the map published?

Selected websites of interest to geographers and environmental scientists

Because millions of websites exist, determining which are most useful to your studies can be time consuming. A selection of websites pertinent to geography, sustainability, and the environmental sciences is provided in Appendix II (pp. 332–4). Many of the sites provide links to other sites, so be open to trying the links. Be sure to apply the points raised above about how to check the validity of websites.

Chapter Summary

In this chapter we have considered aspects of the research process, including the kinds of questions we ask, the sources of knowledge we can tap into, and the different approaches we might take to conduct our research. We have noted that researchers need to be aware of the ethical issues associated with their research projects and the potential effects that research may have on the natural environment and the people we involve in our research. The chapter also provided some suggestions for finding and using online and library sources, and how to validate and use them.

Conducting research effectively can be challenging, but the opportunity to gain experience in scholarship in a field that you care about, to acquire knowledge and skills that will help you in future jobs or graduate school, and to help solve real problems and create new knowledge in geography, sustainability, and environmental sciences represents an important way to help bring positive change to the world.

Notes

1. For an overarching exploration of the discipline of geography, see Geoffrey J. Martin, *All Possible Worlds: A History of Geographical Ideas*, 4th ed. (New York: Oxford University Press, 2005). For books that explore developments in human geography and various approaches to research see Stuart Aitken and Gill Valentine, eds., *Approaches to Human Geography*, 2nd ed. (Thousand Oaks: Sage Publications Inc., 2015); John Harner, Michael Kuby, and Patricia Gober, *Human Geography in Action*, 6th ed. (New York: Wiley, 2013); Arild Holt-Jensen,

Geography: History and Concepts—A Student's Guide, 4th ed. (London: Sage, 2009); and the many entries in Derek Gregory et al., eds., *The Dictionary of Human Geography*, 5th ed. (New York: Wiley, 2009). Counterparts in physical geography and environmental sciences include Kenneth J. Gregory, *The Changing Nature of Physical Geography* (London: Arnold, 2000); David Thomas and A. Goudie, eds., *The Dictionary of Physical Geography*, 3rd ed. (New York: Wiley, 2000); and Kenneth J. Gregory, *Environmental Sciences: A Student's Companion* (Los Angeles: Sage, 2009). Thematic reviews of some sub-fields, with reference lists, appear regularly in *Progress in Human Geography*, *Progress in Physical Geography*, *Progress in Environmental Science*, and *Progress in Development Studies*. Other works that examine aspects of geography and associated environmental concerns include Ronald J. Johnston and P.J. Cloke, eds., *Spaces of Geographical Thought* (London: Sage, 2005); Paul Cloke et al., *Practising Human Geography* (London: Sage, 2004); Noel Castree, A. Rogers, and D. Sherman, eds., *Questioning Geography: Fundamental Debates* (Oxford: Wiley-Blackwell, 2005); John A. Agnew, Virginie Mamadouh, Anna Secor, and Joanne Sharp, *The Wiley Blackwell Companion to Political Geography* (Hoboken, NJ: Wiley-Blackwell, 2015); James S. Duncan, N.C. Johnson, and R.H. Schein, eds., *A Companion to Cultural Geography* (Oxford: Wiley-Blackwell, 2004); Lise Nelson and J. Seager, eds., *A Companion to Feminist Geography* (Oxford: Wiley-Blackwell, 2005); Paul Cloke, P. Crang, and M. Goodwin, *Introducing Human Geographies*, 3rd ed. (New York: Routledge, 2014); David Atkinson et al., eds., *Cultural Geography: A Critical Dictionary of Key Concepts* (London: I.B. Tauris, 2005); and Harm J. de Blij, *Why Geography Matters* (New York: Oxford University Press, 2007).

2. See, for example, Stanley Aronowitz, *Science as Power: Discourse and Ideology in Modern Society* (Minneapolis: University of Minnesota Press, 1988); Paul Feyerabend, *Farewell to Reason* (New York: Verso, 1987); Rupert Sheldrake, *Science Set Free: 10 Paths to New Discovery* (New York: Random House, 2012).

3. Donald Meinig, "The Life of Learning," in *Geographical Voices: Fourteen Auto-biographical Essays*, Peter Gould and F.R. Pitts, eds. (Syracuse: University of Syracuse Press, 2002), 205.

4. Canada's three federal research agencies are the Canadian Institutes of Health Research, the Natural Sciences and Engineering Research Council of Canada, and the Social Sciences and Humanities Research Council of Canada. The *Tri-Council Policy Statement: Ethical Conduct for Research Involving Humans*, 3rd ed. (2014) is available electronically at http://www.pre.ethics.gc.ca/pdf/eng/tcps2-2014/TCPS_2_FINAL_Web.pdf.

5. The *Library of Congress Subject Headings* volumes ("the big red books") are available in the Reference section of the library. Check with a librarian if you can't find them. How can they be of use? If you are doing research on population issues in China, you might start with broad keywords, such as "China and population." But be prepared to reconsider your keywords if the results are not discriminating enough. For example, using the keywords noted above, a 2018 Google search identified 380 million results, in just 0.78 seconds! A more targeted search engine, Google Scholar, found 4,280,000 results using "China and population," and 4,270,000 results using "China–population." Obviously, further refinement would be necessary for any research on this general topic. It is important to try various words, and combinations of words, when using any search engine.

6. Regents of the University of California, "How to Cite—Tools, Tricks, & Tips for Managing Citations: Citation Software—Compare & Choose," May 14, 2018, https://ucsd.libguides.com/howtocite.

7. In libraries—and academic discussions—scholarly journals are not called magazines. The latter term is reserved for periodic (generally weekly or biweekly) popular titles, such as *Maclean's*, *Time*, and *The Economist*. You will find that some professors will refer to a journal article as a paper.

8. The peer review process is not a perfect system; a useful overview of the benefits and weaknesses in the process may be viewed at: J. Kelly, T. Sadeghieh, and K. Adeli, "Peer Review in Scientific Publications: Benefits, Critiques, & A Survival Guide," *The Journal of the International Federation of Clinical Chemistry and Laboratory Medicine* 25, no. 3 (2014): 227–43.

9. Issues associated with the proliferation of predatory journals have been highlighted in numerous issues of *University Affairs*, a trusted source of information for Canada's academic community since 1959, as well as other sites. Here are some articles related to this concern: Marc Couture, "Steering clear of predatory open access journals: Beyond Beall's List," January 25, 2017; Alex Gillis, "Beware! Academics are getting reeled in by scam journals," January 12, 2017; Alex Gillis, "Poor-quality, predatory conferences prey on academics," March 5, 2018; Sarah E. Eaton, "Tips to avoid predatory journals and conferences," June 19, 2018. See also Sarah E. Eaton, "Avoiding predatory journals and questionable conferences: A resource guide," *Population Health* 3, (2017): 464–72. doi: http://dx.doi.org/10.5072/PRISM/20.

10. See the list of disciplinary and interdisciplinary dictionaries in note 5 of Chapter 1 (p. 22). Pertinent encyclopedias include National Council for Science, *The Environment and the Encyclopedia of Earth* and the Environmental Information Coalition, *The Encyclopedia of Earth* (online: http://www.eoearth.org); John E. Oliver, ed., *Encyclopedia of World Climatology* (New York: Springer, 2005); Tim Forsyth, ed., *Encyclopedia of International Development* (London: Routledge, 2005); Barney L. Warf, ed., *Encyclopedia of Human Geography* (New York: Sage, 2006); Andrew Goudie, ed., *Encyclopedia of Geomorphology* (London: Routledge, 2004); Andrew Goudie and D.J. Cuff, eds., *Encyclopedia of Global Change: Environmental Change and Human Society* (Oxford: Oxford University Press, 2002, e-reference edition, 2005); Paul Robbins, *Encyclopedia of Environment and Society* (Thousand Oaks, CA: Sage, 2007); and K.J. Gregory et al., *Environmental Sciences: A Student's Companion* (Thousand Oaks, CA: Sage, 2009). The *Encyclopedia of Life*, available from http://www.eol.org, began in 2007 with the goal of creating a participatory and accessible online database of information on every species on Earth.

11. For historically important figures see the series produced by the International Geographical Union, Study Group/Commission on the History of Geographical Thought, *Geographers: Biobibliographical Studies* (London: Mansell, 1977) and books such as Harm J. de Blij, *Wartime Encounter with Geography* (Lewes, Sussex: The Book Guild, 2000); Yi-Fu Tuan, *Who Am I?: An Autobiography of Emotion, Mind, and Spirit* (Madison: University of Wisconsin Press, 1999); Peter Gould, *Becoming a Geographer* (Syracuse: Syracuse University Press, 1999); Anne Buttimer, *The Practice of Geography* (London: Longman, 1983); David Lowenthal, *George Perkins Marsh: Prophet of Conservation* (Seattle: University of Washington Press, 2000); Gary S. Dunbar, *A Biographical Dictionary of American Geography in the Twentieth Century* (Baton Rouge, LA: Geoscience Publications, Department of Geography and Anthropology, Louisiana State University, 1992); R.J. Johnston and M. Williams, eds., *A Century of British Geography* (Oxford University Press, 2003); and Peter Gould and Forrest R. Pitts, eds., *Geographical Voices: Fourteen Autobiographical Essays* (Syracuse: Syracuse University Press, 2002).

12. Based on Barbara Farrell, "Map Evaluation," in *World Mapping Today*, B. Parry and C.R. Perkins, eds. (London: Butterworth, 1987), 27–34.

3 Writing and Reading Lecture Notes

In this chapter, we examine

- ways to write and use your notes on readings and lectures; and
- the importance of three-part reviewing.

Introduction

The notes you take in lectures or that you jot down while reading your textbook are for you—not anyone else—to use when you study for examinations, prepare to participate in a class, or write papers. Good notes don't just happen—you need to be systematic in your approach so that you can use them to the fullest possible benefit at a later time. This chapter explains why notes are important and suggests some ways to improve your note-taking skills.

Writing Helps You Remember

As you listen to a lecture, watch an instructional video, participate in a class discussion, work on a lab experiment, read a book or article, or review Power-Point slides from a lecture, keep in mind that you will remember the points raised much more clearly if you take notes. Don't just write them for the moment—write them for your use later.

Taking Notes on Readings

Good, concise notes taken as you read the course readings and materials can be invaluable. Writing notes helps you concentrate while you read, and the act of writing itself helps you remember what you have read. Think carefully about your file-management plan. Use an easily recognizable file name, if you're taking notes on a laptop. Keeping your readings notes on a particular topic in the same folder will help later. Files can be merged and reorganized once you have completed the readings for an assignment. The following suggestions will help you make the most of your notes on course reading material.

- Record the full bibliographic particulars of the work you are reading: author and title information, place of publication, publisher, year of publication, total pages of the work (preliminary pages [e.g., i–xxv], and text pages [e.g., 1–25]), and, if a journal, the volume and issue numbers. Record the library catalogue number in case you need to find the work again. For an online source, record the URL so you can easily go back to it. Nothing is more frustrating than using a piece of information in an essay only to find (perhaps under a severe time constraint) that you aren't sure where it came from or that you have neglected to copy down all of the publishing information.
- On each new file, page, or card on which you intend to record information, start by including a shorthand reference to the source so that you can later link it to the full bibliographic information.
- Don't mix quotations or paraphrases from several sources on the same file, page, or card. Keep everything from one reading together.
- If you take several ideas from one source, put the main bibliographic details about the author and work on one card or page and then use a separate card or page for each particular idea or theory. That way you will be able to shuffle the material later, to help you better organize your thoughts and to put them in the order in which you will use them when you write. If saved as a computer file, you can cut and paste material for reorganizational purposes, but be sure to keep the bibliographic details linked to each entry of the material.
- Concentrate and be selective. Not everything in a chapter or article is equally important, so try to identify the points that are most relevant to the particular assignment and, more generally, the course for which you are reading the material.
- Read critically. Give careful consideration to the author's argument and try to separate opinions from facts.
- Writing out long passages from your readings may not be the best use of your time. Rather, read a section and then make concise notes that highlight the main points. When completed, your notes will reflect the outline and content of the work.

- Underline or highlight important quotations or paraphrases in your notes, or make photocopies of longer passages. When you underline in *your* notes, indicate that the underlining was not in the original. *Never* underline library copies of books and journals. And remember that neither underlining nor photocopying will help you to think in the way that writing your own notes does.
- Use headings that will remind you of details; these may differ from the ones used by the author. Record the author's headings and any of your own in your notes.
- Record page numbers as you make notes, whether for summary points, for your own paraphrasing, or for direct quotations. When a passage runs on for more than one page, it's a good idea to put a short horizontal line in the left margin with the first page number above and the second below; an additional mark within the sentence will indicate exactly where the page break was. Knowing the exact page source will be important if you end up citing only part of the quotation.
- If you are using a laptop, all of these pointers still apply (see sample below). Note the use of a line in the left margin and // to show the location of the page break in the quotation. Be sure to identify your own comments, as suggested (within brackets, *in italics*) in the following sample entry.
- If you decide to copy excerpts from a work, be sure to record the location of any omissions. For instance, if you start a quote in the middle of a sentence, indicate the omission of the earlier material with an *ellipsis*: *three* or, when appropriate, *four* dots or periods (see p. 275).

Selhub, A.M., and Logan, A.C., *Your Brain on Nature: The Science of Nature's Influence on Your Health, Happiness, and Vitality* (Toronto: HarperCollins, 2012). Discussion of "animals and their effects on the brain" (pp. 127–149). In section on animals and mental health care (pp. 131–132).

      "Most telling was that a pet could stave off negative psychological
(131)   reactions . . . to a social rejection experiment. . . . Backing all of
____   this up is a 2011 survey//of over 2000 adults that showed that . . .
(132)   60 per cent of the pet owners surveyed attributed their increased
       personal happiness to having a pet."

[This may be useful in the essay on. . . .]

- Record quotations correctly, word for word, as in the original. If there is a spelling error or a doubtful word or expression, put "[*sic*]" in square brackets immediately after the item, to indicate that your citation is faithful to the original, error and all!

- Always record clearly whether your notes are direct quotations, paraphrases, or your own comments. For exact quotations, use quotation marks. If you paraphrase, use a special mark at the beginning and end for later reference. You don't want to have your instructor point out that you must have "quoted" your own paraphrase!

- If you use abbreviations, be sure you know what they stand for. If you develop your own scheme for abbreviating, keep a record in case you forget what any of your abbreviations mean.

- After you have read a work, write down your personal reactions to it. This record could be useful later if you are asked to comment on the relative worth—for you—of the various assignments, or if you need to write a review or research paper requiring evaluative comments. This record of your reactions also will be helpful at the review stage—by which time you may have developed different insights due to having read or heard other things since the first reading. If that is the case, jot down the new thoughts as well. Later, when you look at these varied insights, you will be able to see a progression in your thoughts. These notes may be of use if you are asked to provide your evaluation and comments on the usefulness of a source in an annotated bibliography.

The reading log

Keep a log of everything you read for each course—as a computer file or as handwritten entries in a notebook or on cards. You will be pleasantly surprised by how easily a glance at a log will trigger memories of what you have read, even before you turn to your more detailed notes. The log should include full referencing information, so that you will have a ready-made list of documented sources on selected course themes and topics. Such a list can be invaluable when compiling bibliographies for other purposes. Cards are flexible because they can be shuffled in many ways for different course needs, but a handwritten notebook log has the benefit of keeping everything read for any particular course together in one place. If you type your log instead, be sure to keep a backup copy in case the file is accidentally erased or corrupted.

Taking Notes During Lectures

Lecture notes—and notes written during other types of classes—can be invaluable. Writing them is a serious business because so much depends on them. The following suggestions will help you write, and thereafter use, good notes.

You may be permitted to take your laptop to the lecture room, or use a laptop during smaller classes, including discussion groups and seminars. Remember, though, that the use of laptops in small class settings can be distracting, to you and others, and as a result some professors may not allow their use.

Preparation

The suggestions below pertain to both forms of note-taking—written on paper and typed on a laptop.

- Begin writing lecture notes *before* the lecture starts. Consult the instructor's course outline to see if the topic of the day is listed. But remember, the instructor may not always stick to his or her own schedule. Read the assigned pre-lecture readings and take notes as you do. This will provide a framework within which you can place the lecture. By reading your assignments *before* the lecture you'll be attentive to any information given in class that does not appear in the assigned readings.
- If you use a laptop, have a separate folder for each course, and keep separate files for each lecture within each folder. Title the files clearly so you can go directly to the one you want at a later time.
- Keep your handwritten or hard copies of computer notes together for each course by using a large binder with separators, or individual small binders. A binder is more useful than a notebook because it allows you to insert any handouts alongside your notes.

Active listening

Be an active listener during lectures. Arrive prepared, pay attention, take good notes, and remain attentive to anything new or different that is being presented. Here are three important points, as a start:

- **Attend lectures!** Don't rely on a friend to take notes for you. Because you may respond differently to the lecture material than your friend, you should be there to listen, write, and think for yourself about what is being said. Even if the instructor provides electronic copies of lecture materials, these do not replace your presence in the classroom. And don't be late: the instructor's first words may be critically important to helping you understand what is to follow. If your instructor has you use a clicker (see p. 69), you must be present from the moment the class starts so that you can participate in all clicker exercises.

- **Listening is an intentional and purposeful act.** Listening is different from hearing. How can you train yourself to listen? Read the assignments in advance and memorize definitions and disciplinary jargon. Go to lectures with the attitude that you intend to learn something new. Think positively, even if you find the lecturer a bit boring. Focus on what the person is saying, not on how it is being said. Pay attention so you don't miss any essential information or genuine "nuggets" that may slip by if you are daydreaming. To help you to stay alert, occasionally move your body, especially your legs and feet, and periodically take some deep breaths. You will find that writing notes will help you to concentrate. The key is to listen carefully so you can best understand what the instructor is saying.

"Cue" words can help alert you to the importance of an idea or topic; use these words to anticipate what information to write down:

words that identify emphasis or importance	*fundamental, essential, crucial, vital, significant*
words that indicate ordering or scope of topics	*first-second-third, initially, finally, an example of this*
words that indicate a shift in direction	*however, nevertheless, in contrast, whereas*

The lecturer's intention and your responsibility

Remember that the lecturer's intention is not to summarize the textbook or other assigned readings but to present some essential points about the topics under consideration. The lecturer may expand on one or more points in the textbook, compare and contrast different sets of material, give examples gained from field or lab research that has not yet been published, outline a con principle, work through a problem, present and discuss a hypothesis, ex particularly complex problems, synthesize seemingly disparate ideas, challenge current thinking about a topic, answer questions from the students, and so on. Your tasks are to listen and then link what you have heard with what you have read so that you can develop a comprehensive understanding of the key issues, appropriately grounded in the basic assumptions and methods of the discipline in question, and to reflect on and question the material.

Online or televised classes

Some courses may be offered to you either online or as televised lectures. You will take notes for these classes just as you do when you are in a room with the lecturer. Televised classes may be easier to follow than live ones because you may be able to replay some or all of the lecture. The downside is that because you do not have live access to the lecturer, direct questioning is not possible. Find out if your instructor uses conferencing software to create a virtual classroom in order to deal with students' questions.

When you're watching an online or televised lecture, be aware of the temptation to break your concentration by getting a beverage, texting a friend, taking a phone call, or responding to other distractions. Try to eliminate the possibility of these disruptions so that you can focus on what is being said— and do take good notes.

Some specific pointers for taking notes

Here are some points to keep in mind as you are taking notes in class:

- Start your note-taking on the very first day of the course; important organizational information may be given that will be useful later.
- Begin the notes for each lecture on a separate sheet of paper or as a new file on your laptop. Record the date and lecture title or topic.
- Pay attention to the organization of the lecture. Your instructor may provide an outline of the day's lecture. If so—and if the lecturer is faithful to the outline—it will be easy for you to jot down the major points, perhaps a key phrase or two, and any references provided. If there is no outline, or if the lecturer is disorganized, you will have to listen even

more attentively; your outline will be especially helpful later, as you reflect on the purpose and content of the lecture.

Don't spend the entire time writing. Stopping your note-taking from time to time to just listen to the instructor can help your overall concentration.

- Listen carefully, think as you listen, and try to understand. Be attentive so that you can hear supporting information and insights as well as the main points.
- Write down definitions given by the instructor because they may differ from the definitions of the same terms given in the course readings. If this is the case, consider the differences.
- Write down key words and phrases, names, places, dates, equations, and numbers.
- Try to record the emphasis that the instructor places on ideas (underline, use asterisks or coloured highlighters).
- If you write down a quotation (given on the blackboard or screen, or read out), use quotation marks and record the name of the author.
- Copy any sketch maps or diagrams that your instructor presents. (If you are using a computer, always make sure to have a few sheets of paper on hand for situations like this. Some, but not all, professors will let you download some of their figures from a course website.)
- If you use abbreviations for things said, be sure to record elsewhere what the abbreviations stand for so you know later what it is that you have written down!
- As the lecture proceeds, if a question pops into your mind, write it down on the left margin or within [brackets], to indicate that it is your thought. You can seek to answer it later, by yourself, or by speaking to the lecturer either at the end of the lecture or during the lecturer's posted office hours.
- Near the end of the lecture, carefully listen for the speaker's conclusions; write them down accurately and concisely.
- If there is a question period after the lecture, listen closely; someone else's question may be just as important as the lecturer's response. Don't be afraid to pose a question, even if you think it's too simple—you may well find that others share your puzzlement and will be grateful to you for speaking up.
- Always leave space to add information and comments to your notes later, after you have reread and reflected on them in relation to other

lectures and readings. This is easy when you use a laptop; however, be careful to distinguish your later comments (using *italics*, or perhaps a different colour of text) from those taken during the lecture.

- To be safe, if your notes are on the hard drive, save them to an external backup device.

Hand-held devices to provide feedback and for tests

Some instructors may ask you (and everyone else in the class) to provide feedback during lectures, using hand-held clickers (or some other numbered keypad). The data received wirelessly by a computer will be aggregated and translated into bar graphs that the instructor may show on a screen. By this means, near-instant feedback from the members of the class is provided. Not only can students see their collective response to a question, but the result may be used by the instructor to modify the lecture. Clickers may be used for in-class testing, so be aware that your responses sometimes must be carefully thought through, for each individual's responses will be tallied and become part of their course grade. Clickers may also be used as a means of keeping track of your attendance, so be sure to arrive on time for all of your classes.

Three-part post-lecture reviews

Immediate post-lecture review

Review your day's notes as soon as possible after each lecture. You don't need to rewrite them, unless they are such a mess that rewriting them is the only way to salvage them or if you like to have typed copies of your handwritten notes. If your notes are on a laptop, print them, so you can study from the hard copy. Don't study using just a computer; many students find they have better retention when they use the printed page (see note 2 in Chapter 1). Jot down any thoughts that come to mind that you wish to have clarified or expanded upon, by seeking assistance from the instructor, the TA, or doing your own reading.

Periodic review

Periodically review clusters of related lecture notes. If a logical break in themes is not evident, create your own. Do such reviews hand-in-hand with your notes on course readings and other pertinent material, such as from the lab or from field work. Because you will be taking several courses at once, stagger the periodic reviews so that you will have only one or two per week. By doing immediate post-lecture and periodic reviews you will develop a richer understanding of and appreciation for the course material.

The full-course review

This task, done just prior to the final examination, will be easier if you have systematically completed the two earlier types of review. If you have to do a last-minute desperate cram it will be because you have failed to do the earlier forms of review.

Two warnings

First, if you miss a lecture, *don't* ask the instructor to lend you his or her lecture notes. The professor's lecture notes are personal notes and may not be in a form that will make sense to another reader because they may just be guides to thought, to be developed as the lecture proceeds. Certainly they will not include comments made spontaneously that are often highly pertinent, nor will they include any questions raised by classmates. If you must borrow notes, get them from a classmate you trust to take good notes covering everything that has taken place in the class.

Second, instructors generally do not permit anyone to tape or otherwise record their lectures or seminar discussions. If you have a particular reason for doing so, as when you have a documented learning disability, you must obtain specific prior permission from your instructor, usually at the start of a semester. Many institutions have established specific procedures to facilitate such a request, so be sure to find out what you need to do before asking your instructor.

Using Your Reading and Lecture Notes

Your notes on readings and lectures will be useful for many purposes: when reviewing for tests; writing research essays, abstracts, or research proposals; creating bibliographies (including annotated bibliographies); preparing for discussion groups, seminars, tutorials, labs, or field work; and, of course, studying for examinations. They also can be of use if you wish to formulate some key questions prior to seeing your instructor or TA in her or his office. Write the questions down so you remember them during such visits. (As a courtesy, you might give the instructor or TA a copy of your questions when you enter the office; this will facilitate the best use of the time available.) Because so much depends on the quality of your notes, you should take the task of writing them seriously. Doing a good job of note-taking right from the start will save you hours of frustration later.

Chapter Summary

Listening actively and creating effective notes from lectures, readings, and other materials are among the most important skills you need for learning on campus. The challenge is to experiment and find what strategies will work for you and your learning style. You can enhance your skills in general by preparing for lectures in advance, by actively listening and taking notes during class, and by reviewing and responding to your notes. You might wish to follow some of the specific suggestions in this chapter.

4 Writing a Report on a Book or an Article

In this chapter, we examine
- how to prepare abstracts, analytic book reports, and literature reviews; and
- how to write an annotated bibliography.

Introduction

The term *book report* covers a variety of writing assignments, including an abstract or summary of the contents of a book or an article, an analytic report containing some evaluation, a sophisticated literature review, and an annotated bibliography. The following guidelines cover all four kinds of reports. Before you begin your assignment, be sure to find out exactly which type of report is expected. Check with your instructor if necessary.

The Abstract, Précis, or Summary

An abstract is a pithy summation of a work. Brevity and clarity are the keys to this kind of summary. If your instructor gives you a word limit, that limit will tell you exactly how many words you have in which to briefly, but accurately, sum up the content of the work in question. An abstract is not evaluative: it does not say anything about your reaction to the work. It simply records, as accurately as possible, in as few words as possible, your understanding of what the author has written.

How can you summarize the contents of a 20-page article or a 300-page book? Given that the word count is vital in an abstract, you will have to be a strong editor. The following pointers may help.

- **Determine the author's purpose.** An author writes an article or book for a reason: to cast some new light on a subject, to propose a new theory, to fill a knowledge gap, or to bring together the existing knowledge in a particular field. Whatever the purpose, you have to discover it if you want to understand what guided the author's selection and arrangement of the material. The best way to gain insight into the author's intent is to check the table of contents, preface, and introduction of a book, or the introduction and headings of an article, and, generally, to skim the work in order to get a quick overview. The details will be much more understandable once you know where the work as a whole is going.

- **Reread carefully and take notes.** A second, more thorough reading will be the basis of your note-taking. Because you already have determined the relative importance that the author gives to various ideas, you can be selective and avoid getting bogged down in a welter of unimportant detail. Just be sure that you don't neglect any crucial passages or controversial claims. When making notes, condense the ideas. Don't take them down word for word, and don't simply paraphrase them. You will have a much firmer grasp of the material if you resist the temptation to quote. Force yourself to interpret and summarize. This approach will also help to make your report concise—remember, you want to be brief as well as clear. Condensing the material as you take notes will ensure that your report is a true summary, not just a string of quotations or paraphrases. You can start your summary in point form.

- **Give the same relative emphasis to each area that the author does.** Do not simply list the topics in the work or the conclusions reached: discriminate between primary ideas and secondary ones.

- **Follow the book's (or article's) order of presentation.** Strictly speaking, a simple summary need not do so, but it usually is safer to follow the author's lead. That way your summary will be a clear reflection of the original.

- **Follow the chain of the arguments.** Do not leave any confusing holes. You won't be able to cover every detail, of course, but you must trace all the main arguments in such a way that they make logical sense.

- **Mention (briefly) the key evidence supporting the author's arguments.** Without some supporting details, your reader will have no way of assessing the strength of the conclusions.

- **Write your first draft.** Using complete sentences, write a comprehensive summary of the contents of the work.
- **Editing, counting, re-editing, and re-counting.** Editing what you have written so that the sentences become tight, with no wasted words, is a difficult task, but with practice you will reduce your abstract to the required number of words. If your sentences seem choppy or disconnected (because you are leaving out so much of the original) you can use linking words and phrases (see pp. 244–5) to help create a flow and give your writing a sense of logical development. After a first editing, don't be dismayed if the word count is still too high. Edit, and edit again, cutting down sentences while keeping all the main points in view. You will be surprised to see how complex ideas can be reduced to fewer and fewer words. In the end you will have a summary that clearly conveys the contents of the work, within the required word limit.
- **Reread for accuracy, comprehensiveness, and mistakes.** Before handing the abstract in to your instructor, check it one more time. Are any major points missing? Have you recorded fairly what is in the work (not what you wish had been in it)? Are there any grammatical or spelling errors?
- **Check for proper identification.** For a book, remember to check that you have included the name of the author or editor, the title of the work, and the full publication information. For a book chapter, include all of the above details plus page numbers. For a journal article, include all of the above details plus volume and issue numbers. See Chapter 7 for more information about how to document your sources. Remember to include your own name and (if called for) student number, the course name and number, and date of submission.

See Table 6.2 for a checklist to help ensure you prepare all the parts of an abstract.

The Analytic Book Report

An analytic book report—sometimes called a book review—not only summarizes the main ideas in a book but at the same time evaluates them. It's best to begin with an introduction, and then follow with the summary and evaluation. Publication details usually are identified at the beginning, but may be placed at the end also.

Writing guidelines

Introduction

You should provide all the background information necessary for a reader who is not familiar with the book. Here are some of the questions you might consider:

- What is the book about?
- What is the book's disciplinary or interdisciplinary focus?
- What is the author's purpose? What kind of audience is he or she writing for? How is the topic limited? Is the central theme or argument explicitly stated, or only implied?
- What documentation is provided to support the central theme or argument? Is the documentation sound? Is it presented clearly, and does the discussion of it develop logically? Does the documentation support the author's contentions and conclusions?
- Do the title and subtitle fairly identify the book's content?
- How has the author divided the book into chapters? Do the chapter titles accurately reflect each chapter's contents?
- How does this book relate to others in the same specific field? To other works in the same broad area?
- What are the author's background and reputation? What else has he or she written?
- Are there any special circumstances connected with the writing of this book? For example, was it funded by or written for a scientific organization, a corporation, an ideologically based think-tank, an advocacy group, or a governmental agency?
- What sources has the author used? Does the list of references (or the bibliography) include both historically important and recent works in the field?

Not all of these questions will be applicable to every book. Nevertheless, an introduction that answers at least some of them will make it easier for your reader to appreciate what you will later state in your evaluation.

Summary

Obviously, you cannot analyze a book without discussing its contents: the basic steps are the same as those outlined above for the abstract or summary. You may choose to present a condensed version of the book's contents as a separate section, to be followed by your evaluation, or you may prefer to integrate the two, assessing the author's arguments as you present them. Again, remember that you are discussing someone else's work: review the book the author actually wrote—not the one you would like him or her to have written. In short, be fair.

Evaluation

In evaluating the book, you might ask some of the following questions to help you provide some critical comments:

- What is the author's stated purpose?
- How is the book organized? Are the divisions useful? Does the author give less attention to certain areas? Is anything left out?
- On what kinds of sources does the author rely?
- What is the nature of the evidence presented? Is the evidence reliable and up to date? Is it presented and analyzed in an appropriate manner? Is it distorted or misrepresented in any way? Does the evidence support the author's ideas? Could the same evidence be used to support a different case? Does the author leave out any important evidence that might weaken his or her case? Is the author's position convincing?
- If maps, graphs, tables, or photographs are used, how effectively do they reveal or convey essential points, or how well do they give support to written statements?
- Is there an inherent ideological basis to the line of argument?
- What kinds of assumptions does the author make in presenting the material? Are they stated or implied? Are they valid?
- Does the book accomplish what the author set out to do? Does the author's position change in the course of the book? Are there any contradictions or weak spots in the arguments? Does the author recognize those weaknesses or omissions? Remember that your job is not only to analyze the contents of the book, but also to indicate its strengths and weaknesses.
- Does the author agree or disagree with other writers who have dealt with the same material or problem? In what respects?

- Is the book written clearly and is it interesting to read? Is the writing repetitious? Too detailed? Not detailed enough? Is the style clear? Or is it plodding, or jargonish, or flippant?
- Does the book raise issues that need further exploration? Does it present any challenges or leave unfinished business for the author or other scholars to pick up?
- To what extent would you recommend this book? What effect has it had on you?
- Finally, don't forget to comment on the essential "trappings." If the book has an index, how good is it? Is there a list of additional readings, or a full-fledged bibliography?

The Literature Review

The literature review can be a stand-alone submission as part of a course requirement, or it might be a portion of a major essay or an honours or graduate thesis. It is not a summary of articles and books you have read. Rather, it is a discursive exploration (or discussion) of themes or trends you have identified in your cited sources. This entails synthesizing and evaluating these sources according to the guiding research question or hypothesis you have posed. In geography, sustainability studies, and the environmental sciences a literature review may conclude with your identification of areas of controversy within the literature being considered. These will help you formulate research questions that deserve attention. Your literary review should stand on its own merits as an attractive piece of writing.

One way to learn how to write an effective literature review is to read good examples. Some disciplinary journals, including *Progress in Human Geography*, *Progress in Physical Geography*, and, on occasion, the *Annals of the Association of American Geographers*, publish overviews of the literature on a given subject. Often literary reviews appear in weekend book review sections of major newspapers such as the *Globe and Mail*, *New York Times*, and *The Times* of London, as well as the *New York Review of Books* and *The Times Literary Supplement*. If you are writing a review chapter for your honours or graduate thesis you may wish to examine theses and dissertations in the library for additional examples. Whatever examples you choose, note the various techniques reviewers use to catch and hold the reader's interest. The basic rule is to reinforce your comments with specific details from the books, article, or reports in question; concrete examples will add authenticity and life to your review.

Annotated Bibliography

An annotated bibliography is simply an alphabetized bibliographic listing of works that includes a very short summary statement about each work. The statement normally is no more than a sentence or two in length. Think carefully about the central purpose of the book or article and its contents and then sum them up as briefly as possible. Generally, also, there will be a brief comment on the relative worth of the publication for the topic you are writing about. For example:

> Fong, Y.T., *Population Growth and Urban Development in China* (Hong Kong: Mei Ling Settlement Research Centre, 2006).

> Using census data and population estimates, Fong explores China's changing population from 1951 to 2001 and identifies the consequences for mid-sized cities. The burgeoning populations in such cities have created a strong demand for new housing stock. This general survey provides a context for my focus on housing needs in the city of Yiphee.

Chapter Summary

In this chapter we have identified some guidelines to help in your writing of four types of reports, namely an abstract, an analytic report, a literature review, and an annotated bibliography. The more you practise your writing, the better you will become at conveying your thoughts accurately and effectively.

5 Writing an Essay

In this chapter, we examine

- how to plan your essay;
- organizational elements to have in mind as you write your essay; and
- the importance of editing your work before you submit it.

Introduction

Writing a good essay requires you to apply your critical thinking skills. If you dread writing an academic essay, you will find that following a few simple planning and organizational steps will make the task easier—and the result better.

The Planning Stage

Some students claim they can write essays without any planning at all. On the rare occasions when they succeed, their writing usually is not as spontaneous as it seems: in fact, they have thought or talked a good deal about the subject in advance, and they come to the task with some ready-made ideas. More often, trying to write a lengthy essay without planning just leads these students to frustration. They get stuck in the middle and don't know how to finish, or they suddenly realize that they're rambling off in all directions.

By contrast, most writers say that the planning, or pre-writing, stage is the most important part of the whole process. Certainly the evidence shows that poor planning usually leads to disorganized writing; in the majority of student essays the single greatest improvement would not be better research or better grammar, but better organization.

The insistence on planning doesn't rule out exploratory writing (see p. 87). Many people find that the act of writing is the best way to generate ideas or overcome writer's block; the hard decisions about organization come after they've put something down on the page. Whether you organize before or after you begin to write, however, at some point you need to plan.

Know your source material

You don't write an essay on "something" out of thin air. You first need to become fully acquainted with the source material you plan to use. Before you start writing, finish analyzing your primary material, if it is from lab or field research, or from the results of statistically manipulated and tested information from a data set. If your writing is to be based on books and journal articles, first develop good notes on your readings so you can draw upon them in a well-organized manner when writing your paper (see Chapter 3). Be aware that some instructors prefer, or will demand, that you use materials other than textbooks. Get to know what is expected of you, and approach your writing accordingly, with appropriate use of sources.

Ask questions

Your essay may be on a topic for which you have done no prior research. Some instructors ask students to choose their topics from a list of suggestions; others simply identify broad subject areas and permit students to develop their own specific topics within them. In the latter case, because a subject area is bound to be too broad for an essay topic, you will have to analyze it in order to find a way of limiting it. The best way of analyzing is to ask questions that will lead to useful answers.

Chapter 2 outlined a formula of six linked questions: *what? where? when? why? how?* and *who?* Posing these five or six questions—*who?* is not relevant in some research areas—will lead you to five or six initial answers that will in turn lead to other questions. Most initial questions, and the answers to them, tend to be too general, but they will stimulate more specific questions that will help you to refine your topic and formulate *the* basic question. The most important question can be posed within your statement of purpose, or transformed into a thesis statement, perhaps as a hypothesis. Remember to make your statement limited, unified, and exact (see p. 7).

Try the Three-C approach

A systematic scheme for analyzing your subject is the three-C approach. It forces you to look at your topic from three different perspectives, asking basic questions about *components*, *change*, and *context*:

Components:
- What parts or categories can you use to break down the subject?
- Can the main divisions be subdivided?

Change:
- What features have changed?
- What temporal and spatial patterns can be observed?
- Is there a trend?
- What caused the change?
- What are the results of the change?

Context:
- What is the larger issue surrounding the subject?
- In what tradition or school of thought does the subject belong?
- How is the subject similar to, and different from, related subjects?

What are the components of the subject?

In other words, how might your topic be broken down into smaller elements? This question forces you to take a close look at the subject and helps you avoid oversimplification. Suppose that your assignment is to discuss the implications for a downtown area related to the construction of a new shopping mall in the suburbs, at an intersection of a major highway that bypasses the town. You might decide that the basic components of the study are (1) the site and situational characteristics of both the downtown and the mall; (2) the types and sizes of stores attracted to the mall versus the types in the downtown; (3) the responses of shoppers; and (4) the responses of retailers in the downtown. If these components seem too broad, you may break them down further. For example, you might wish to sample specific types of stores, such as clothing stores, or perhaps just women's clothing stores.

Similarly, if you are analyzing the landscape imagery in a work of literature, you could ask, "What kinds of images does the author use?" (e.g., similes, metaphors, and allusions). Or you could ask, "What are the content group-ings?" (e.g., urban versus rural images, or images of summer versus winter, and so on).

What features of the subject reflect change?

In all research involving the environment, no matter what the disciplinary focus, there is a concern with *process*, or change from one state to another: how the physical and biological environments came to be as they are and how they continue to change; how varying beliefs, attitudes, values, and actions on the part of humans have led to the creation of different cultural landscapes (that is, landscapes as moulded and modified by human action); and how various future actions could lead to different consequences for the environment.

To return to the mall example, there are several questions we can pose re-garding change. What level of governmental authority permitted this change (i.e., the creation of the suburban mall)? How did downtown retailing land-use patterns change as a result of the mall's creation? Over what period of time did they change? How did shoppers' spatial behaviour change? How did these changes manifest themselves in people's activities? Did these changes affect downtown merchants? How did those merchants respond? Did the merchants propose changes to the downtown to attract shoppers back from the suburban mall? Did the town government support those changes? What were the results?

What is the context of this subject?

Into what particular school of thought or tradition does your research fit? What perspective will you take as you develop your ideas and interpretations— logical positivist? structuralist? humanist? feminist? realist? postmodernist? critical geography? Be aware of the context that your instructor wants you to work within.

Consider the mall example again. The mall itself is a site for study, not a context. The context is different for different researchers:

- Biologists may be concerned with the impact of the mall on local flora and fauna.

- Landscape architects may be interested in the form and function of the mall.
- Geomorphologists may investigate the impact of the mall's expansive ocaled parking lot on surface or subsurface water flows
- Logical positivist geographers may advance and test a hypothesis based on location theory, using data on shopping patterns, movements of people, the value of goods sold, land values, etc.
- Structuralists may be concerned with the ways in which politics influenced the location of the mall.
- Humanistic geographers may be interested in the importance of symbolism in the mall as opposed to the downtown area, or in what people feel and think about the two locales.
- Feminist geographers may be concerned with the societal consequences of the gender distribution of jobs created in the mall and with the lived experiences of those who work or shop in the mall.
- Critical geographers will want to examine how the relations of power have influenced the way the locations have developed, with a concern about social exploitation, and so on.

Whatever the context, it will have to be buttressed by citation and discussion of pertinent literature. In short, the context for your topic will lead you to pose different questions, which in turn will lead to different types of insights. And remember, no single context (and associated approach) is more "correct" than any other! Just be aware that, because there are differences in underlying assumptions and methods, it is essential to determine a clear context for each project you tackle.

Analyzing an assigned topic

Even if the topic of your essay is supplied by your instructor, you will need to analyze it carefully. Try underlining key words to make sure that you don't neglect anything. Distinguish the main focus from subordinate concerns. A common error in dealing with prescribed topics is to emphasize one portion while neglecting another. Give each part its proper due—and make sure that you actually do what the instructions tell you to do. Note that to *discuss* is not the same as to *evaluate* or *trace*. These verbs tell you how to approach the topic; don't confuse them. The following definitions will help you decide how to approach your assignment:

outline state simply, without much development of each point

trace review by looking back—on stages or steps in a process, or on causes of an occurrence

explain show how or why something happens

discuss examine or analyze in an orderly way; this instruction allows you considerable freedom, as long as you take into account contrary evidence or ideas

compare examine differences as well as similarities (see pp. 89–90)

evaluate analyze strengths and weaknesses, to arrive at an overall assessment of worth

Creating an outline

Individual writers differ in their need for a formal plan. Some say that they never have an outline, and others maintain they can't write without one. Some can't write until they have a title, headings, and subheadings, whereas others decide these details only once most of the work is completed. Most writers probably fall somewhere in the middle. Whatever the details of your study, it will be helpful to jot down the main points in outline form. Even if you later find that you have to change the order because the development of your argument has taken you in directions you did not plan, it's important to start out with a reasonable idea of where you are headed. If you have special problems with organizing material, your outline should be formal and in complete sentences. On the other hand, if your mind is naturally logical, you may find it is enough just to jot down a few words on a scrap of paper. For most students, an informal but well-organized outline in point form is the most useful model. (The example below uses the *decimal system* for organizing the sections. For this and other ways to identify the sections of your essay, see Chapter 6.) The headings and subheadings in an outline should be precise enough to give a good idea of what the final work will include. An example, for a political geography assignment, is provided:

HYPOTHESIS: Changes in Botswana's political systems led to structural changes in the settlement system and to changes in use of resources.

1. Pre-colonial political and settlement systems
    - 1.1 Tribal structures and the power of chiefs
        - 1.11 Social systems and the all-encompassing nature of chiefs' powers
        - 1.12 A fluid socio-political system
    - 1.2 Settlement system and the locus of power
        - 1.21 Environmental characteristics
        - 1.22 Three-part settlement system: lands, cattle posts, and villages
        - 1.23 Chiefs' powers and the seasonal utilization of resources

2. Consequences of colonial intrusion
    - 2.1 Freezing of a fluid socio-political system
        - 2.11 Colonial indirect rule
        - 2.12 Changes in the role of chiefs
    - 2.2 Societal changes
        - 2.21 Imposition of the "hut tax" and the need for paid labour
        - 2.22 Labour migrations to South Africa
        - 2.23 Changes in gender roles in resource use and development
    - 2.3 Changes to the settlement system
        - 2.31 The impact of absentee labourers on pastoral and agricultural activities
        - 2.32 Incipient break-up of the three-part settlement system

3. Independence and rapid change
    - 3.1 Tensions between old and new systems
        - 3.11 Chiefs and tradition versus elected "new men"
        - 3.12 "Modernization" of society
    - 3.2 Changed settlement systems and resource use
        - 3.21 Imposition of a modern settlement system and an extractive resource infrastructure

        3.22 Replacement of customary land tenure with the Tribal Grazing Land Policy and the privatization of land

        3.23 Impact on the settlement system of new laws governing use and development of resources

4.   <u>Conclusion</u>

Appendices (if any; see p. 109).

References or bibliography (see Chapter 7).

The guidelines for this kind of outline are simple:

- **Code your categories.** Use different sets of markings, such as the decimal system used in the example above, to establish the relative importance of your entries. Your word-processing program likely is able to format bullets and numbered lists for you. Select the style that is best for your work.
- **Categorize according to importance.** Make sure that only items of equal value are put in equivalent categories. Give major points more weight than minor ones.
- **Check lines of connection.** Make sure that each of the main categories is directly linked to the central thesis; then see that each subcategory is directly linked to the larger category that contains it. Checking these lines of connection is the best way to prevent essay muddle.
- **Be consistent.** In arranging your points, be consistent. You can move from the most important point to the least important, or vice versa, as long as you follow the same order every time.
- **Use parallel wording.** Phrasing each entry in a similar way will make it easier to be consistent in your presentation.
- **Be logical.** In addition to checking for lines of connection and organizational consistency, ensure that the overall development of your work is logical. Does each heading/idea/set of data/discussion flow into the next, leading the reader through your material in the most logical manner?

A final comment: be prepared to change your outline at any time in the writing process. Your initial outline is not meant to put an iron clamp on your thinking but to relieve anxiety about where you're headed. A careful outline prevents frustration and dead ends—that "I'm stuck, where can I go from here?" feeling. But because the very act of writing usually generates new ideas, you should be ready to modify your original plan. Just remember that any new outline must have the consistency and clear connections required for a unified essay.

The Writing Stage

Writing the first draft

Rather than labour for excellence from scratch, most writers find it easier to write the first draft as quickly as possible and then do extensive revisions later. However you begin, you can't expect the first draft to be the final copy. Skilled writers know that revising is a necessary part of the writing process, and that the care taken with revisions makes the difference between a mediocre essay and a good one.

You don't need to write all parts of the essay in the same order in which they are to appear in the final copy. In fact, many students find the introduction the hardest part to write. If you face the first blank page with a growing sense of paralysis, try leaving the introduction until later, and start with the first idea in your outline. Even if you feel so intimidated that you haven't been able to draw up an outline, remember that once you get started, you'll likely find the writing is not as difficult as you thought it would be. The key is to *just get started*: putting down your initial thoughts on a subject will get you writing words on paper! Instead of sharpening pencils or running out for a snack, try to get going. Don't worry about grammar or wording; scratch out pages or throw them away if you must—just start! Perhaps you can write down a key quotation from an important source and then jot down your initial thoughts on its importance. Remember, the object is to get your writing juices flowing.

Of course, you can't expect this kind of exploratory writing to resemble the first draft that follows an outline. You will need to do a great deal of changing and reorganizing, but at least you will have the relief of seeing words on a page with which to work. Many experienced writers—and not only those with writer's block—find this the most productive way to proceed.

Developing your ideas: Some common patterns

The way you develop your ideas depends on your essay topic, and topics can vary enormously. Even so, most essays follow one or another of a handful of basic organizational patterns. Here's how to use each pattern effectively.

Defining

Sometimes a whole essay is an extended definition, explaining the meaning of a term that is complicated, controversial, or simply important to your field of study: for example, *environment* in biology, geography, sustainability, and environmental studies; *monetarism* in economics; or *existentialism* in philosophy. More often, you will begin a detailed discussion of a topic by defining a key term, and then you will shift to a different organizational pattern. In this case, make your definition exact. It should be broad enough to include all the things that belong in the category and at the same time narrow enough to exclude things that don't belong. A good definition builds a kind of verbal fence around a word, herding together all the essential ideas and cutting off all outsiders.

For any discussion of a term that goes beyond a bare definition, it's important to give concrete illustrations or examples; depending on the nature of your essay, these could vary in length from one or two sentences to several paragraphs or even pages. If you are defining *environment*, for instance, you would probably want to discuss at some length the theories of leading geographers, ecologists, and others, because different approaches lead to different definitions. It may be helpful to consult specialized disciplinary dictionaries and encyclopedias (see notes 4 and 5 in Chapter 1 and note 10 in Chapter 2), along with other pertinent literature.

In an extended definition it's also useful to point out the differences between the term in question and other terms that may be connected or confused with it. For instance, if you are defining *environment* you will want to distinguish it from *landscape*; if you are defining *place* you will want to differentiate it from *space*; if you are defining *climate* you will want to distinguish it from *weather*.

Classifying

Classifying means dividing something into parts according to a given principle of selection. The principle or criterion may vary; you could classify crops, for example, according to how they reproduce (e.g., tuberous *versus* seed reproduction), what soils they grow in, how long they take to mature, or what climatic conditions they require; members of a particular population might be classified according to age group, occupation, income, and so on. If you are using a system of classification, remember the following:

- All members of a class must be accounted for. If any are left over, you need to alter or add more categories.

- Categories can be divided into subcategories. You should consider using subcategories if there are significant differences within a category. If, for instance, you are classifying the workforce according to occupation, you might want to create subcategories according to income level or educational background.
- Any subcategory should contain at least two items; otherwise it is simply a unique entry in your classification.

Explaining a process

This kind of organization shows how something works or has worked, whether it's soil erosion, a rock slide, a weather cycle, a migration, or the stages in a military campaign. The important point is to work systematically, to break down the process into a series of stages. Although at times your order will vary, most often it will be chronological, in which case you should see that the sequence is accurate and easy to follow. Whatever the arrangement, generally you can make the process easier to follow if you start a new paragraph for each new stage. Be aware, of course, that any "stage" you identify may be an artificial highlighting within the overall process, that is, unless your data reveal clear divisions. Take this into account as you write.

Tracing causes

A causal analysis is really a particular kind of process discussion, in which certain events are shown to have led to or resulted from other events. Usually you are explaining why something happened. The main warning here is to avoid oversimplifying. If you're tracing causes, distinguish between a direct cause and a contributing cause, between what is a condition for something to happen and what is merely a correlation or coincidence. For example, if you find that in France both the age of the average driver and the number of accidents caused by drunk drivers are increasing, you cannot jump to the conclusion that older drivers are the cause of the increase in drunk-driving accidents. Similarly, you must be sure that the result you mention is a genuine product of a particular event or process.

Comparing

People sometimes forget that comparing things means showing differences as well as similarities—even if the instructions do not say "compare and contrast." The easiest method for comparison, though not always the best, is to discuss the first subject in the comparison thoroughly and then move on to the second:

Subject *X*:   Point 1
               Point 2
               Point 3

Subject *Y*:   Point 1
               Point 2
               Point 3

The problem with this kind of comparison is that it often sounds like two separate essays slapped together. To use this method effectively, you must integrate the two subjects, first in your introduction (by putting them both in a single context) and again in your conclusion, where you should bring together the important points you have made about each. When discussing the second subject, try to refer repeatedly to your findings about the first subject ("unlike *X*, *Y* does such and such"). This method may be the wisest choice if the subjects for comparison seem so different that it is hard to create similar categories in which to discuss them—if the points you are making about *X* are of a different type than the points you are making about *Y*.

If it is possible to find similar criteria or categories for discussing the subjects, however, the comparison will be more effective if you organize it like this:

Category 1: Subject *X*
              Subject *Y*

Category 2: Subject *X*
              Subject *Y*

Category 3: Subject *X*
              Subject *Y*

Because this kind of comparison is integrated more tightly, the reader can see more readily the similarities and differences between the subjects. As a result, the essay is likely to be more forceful. Similarly, if it is applicable to your task, you might first list positive consequences of, say, constructing a factory adjacent to a recreation park. You would follow that list with a list of negative consequences. By this means you'd be able to clearly identify the different potential outcomes and, from them, draw conclusions within the context of the purpose of the paper.

Introductions

The beginning of an essay has a dual purpose:

- to indicate both the topic and your approach to it, and
- to whet your reader's interest in what you have to say.

An effective way to introduce a topic is to place it in a context—to supply a kind of backdrop that will put it in perspective. You go back a step or two and discuss the area into which your topic fits and then gradually lead into your specific field of discussion. Sheridan Baker calls this the funnel approach, where a broad statement at the beginning narrows to the argument that you explain and develop in the body of your essay.[1] For example, suppose your topic is the effect of acid rain on gravestones in a particular cemetery. You would want to open the paper with a general statement about acid rain, including a definition of that term, a brief discussion of key physical and chemical processes and the role of human activities in those processes, and an overview of the spatial patterns of consequences. Only then would you turn to the examination of your case study, drawing on your field observations and measurements of corrosion on the gravestones. A funnel opening is applicable to almost any kind of essay.

It's a good idea to try to catch your reader's interest right from the start—you know from your own reading how a dull beginning can put you off. The fact that your instructor must read on anyway makes no difference. If a reader has to get through 30 or 40 similar essays, it's all the more important for yours to stand out. A funnel opening isn't the only way to catch the reader's attention. Here are three other common approaches to introductions:

- **Lead-in with a quotation.** Your reader's anticipation may be heightened if you include a short, pertinent quotation, either as a stand-alone comment (within quotation marks, with the author identified) before you open your paper, or within your opening paragraph. This approach works especially well when the quotation is taken from the person or work you will be discussing.
- **Lead-in with a question.** Posing a rhetorical question will only annoy the reader if it is commonplace or the answer is obvious, but a thought-provoking question can make a strong opening. Just be sure that you answer the question in your essay.

- **Lead-in with an anecdote or telling fact.** This is the kind of concrete lead that journalists often use to grab their readers' attention. Save it for your least formal essays—and remember that the incident or fact must really highlight the ideas you are going to discuss.

Whatever your lead-in, it must relate to your topic: never sacrifice relevance for originality. Finally, whether your introduction is one paragraph or several, make sure that by the end of it your reader clearly knows the topic and direction you are taking.

Integrating quotations

A quotation can benefit an essay in two ways (see Chapter 7). First, it adds depth and credibility by showing that your position or idea has the support of an authority. Second, it provides stylistic variety and interest, especially if the quotation is colourful or eloquent. The trick to using quotations effectively is to make sure that they are germane to the topic and properly integrated with your discussion. You don't want them either to dominate your ideas, or simply seem to be tacked on, as an interesting side comment. To ensure that a quotation has the desired effect, always refer to the point you want the reader to take from it: don't let a quotation dangle on its own. Usually, the best way to do this is to make the point before the quotation:

> While doing field research in the Himalayas, McKinley had to walk for miles to reach the villages where he was to do the interviews, stating, "It was a devilishly difficult task, carrying all of the gear, walking up the rocky valley floors, and crossing raging streams using very primitive rope bridges; but it was all very exciting."

Sometimes, however, a quotation can precede the explanation. This is a common approach to begin an essay, as noted above. You must be sure, however, to explain the significance of the quotation so that your reader is not left wondering why you have included it.

If a complete sentence precedes the quotation, use a colon at the end of the introductory phrase; otherwise, use a comma:

> Simpson writes authoritatively: "The soils were wet."

(or)

> Simpson stated her conclusion clearly, insisting that "The soils were wet."

If the end of the quotation comes at the end of a sentence, finish with a period—unless the sentence is a question, in which case finish with a question mark *after* the quotation marks:

> Could it be that Simpson was not correct in stating that "The soils were wet"?

The length of a quotation can vary from a short phrase woven into your sentence to a paragraph or more. If you take part of a sentence, be sure to use an *ellipsis* (see p. 275). If the quotation is four lines or longer, you must indent the quotation and not use quotation marks (see pp. 280–2). Just remember, the longer the quotation, the greater the danger that it will overshadow rather than reinforce your own viewpoint. Don't quote any more than you really need.

Conclusions

Endings can be painful—sometimes for the reader as much as for the writer. Too often, the feeling that one ought to say something profound and memorable produces the kind of prose that suggests violins throbbing in the background. You know the sort of thing:

> The tremendous amount of soil erosion in the valley dramatically highlights the awful plight of the poor farmers, who for generations to come will suffer dreadfully from the loss of the very basis for their livelihood.

Why is this embarrassing? Because it is clearly phony—no more than a grab bag of clichés.

Experienced editors often say that many articles and essays would be better without their final paragraphs: in other words, when you've finished what you have to say, the only thing to do is stop. This advice may work for short essays, where you need to keep the central point firmly in the foreground and don't need to remind the reader of it. But for longer pieces, where you have developed a number of ideas or a complex line of argument, you should provide a sense of closure. Readers welcome an ending that helps to tie the ideas together; they don't like to feel they've been left hanging. And because the final impression is often the most lasting, it's in your interest to finish strongly. Simply restating your hypothesis or summarizing what you have done already is not forceful enough. What are the options?

- **The inverse funnel.** The simplest and most basic conclusion is one that restates your hypothesis in different words and then discusses its implications. Baker calls this the inverse funnel approach, as opposed to the funnel approach of the opening paragraph.[2] In this type of conclusion, the specific arguments made in the body of the essay widen to a more inclusive final statement.

  One danger in moving to a wider perspective is that you may try to embrace too much. When a conclusion expands too far, it tends to lose focus and turns into an empty cliché, like the conclusion in the preceding example. It's always better to discuss specific implications than to leap into vague generalities.

- **The new angle.** A variation of the basic inverse funnel approach is to reintroduce your argument with a new twist. Suggesting some fresh angle can add excitement to your ending. Beware of injecting an entirely new idea, though, or one that's only loosely connected to your original argument: the result could be jarring or even off-topic.

- **The full circle.** If your introduction is based on an anecdote, a question, or a startling fact, you can complete the circle by referring to it again in relation to some of the insights revealed in the main body of your essay.

- **The stylistic flourish.** Some of the most successful conclusions end on a strong stylistic note. Try varying the sentence structure: if most of your sentences are long and complex, make the last one short and punchy. Sometimes you can dramatize your idea with a striking phrase or colourful image. When you are writing your essay, keep your eyes open and your ears tuned for fresh ways of putting things, and save the best for the end.

None of these approaches to endings is exclusive, of course. You may even find that several of them can be combined in a single essay. Whichever approach you take, just remember that a conclusion should never refer to facts that have not been cited already in the main body of your essay.

The Editing Stage

Often the best writer in a class is not the one who can dash off a fluent first draft, but the one who is the best editor. To edit your work well you need to see it as the reader will; you have to distinguish between what you meant to say and what is actually on the page. For this reason it's a good idea to leave some time between drafts, so that when you begin to edit you will be looking at the writing with fresh eyes rather than reviewing it from memory. Without this distancing period you can become so involved that it's hard to see your paper objectively. Before you begin the serious task of editing, allow yourself to go to a movie or the gym—do anything that will take your mind off your work. Also, if you are working on a computer, remember that it can be hard to get a sense of the whole when you read your material as it appears on the screen, section by section. Print out a hard copy to edit on—and use a pencil. Reading it aloud to yourself or a willing listener can help give you a sense of where to make changes (i.e., to parts that feel unnatural to read).

Editing doesn't mean simply checking your work for errors in grammar or spelling. It means looking at the piece as a whole to see if the ideas are *well organized*, *well documented*, and *clearly expressed*. This critical assessment helps you to edit and revise your work so that your ideas are communicated clearly and effectively.

Editing may mean adding some paragraphs, deleting others, rewriting sentences or whole passages, and rearranging things. Experienced writers may be able to check several aspects of their work at the same time, but if you are inexperienced or in doubt about your writing, it's best to look at the organization of the ideas before you tackle sentence structure, diction, style, and documentation. And, don't forget to check the "little" things like subheadings, page numbers, numbers for illustrations (on the illustrations and in the text), spelling (and other details) in your illustrations, and the completeness and accuracy of your references. These items often are neglected—but instructors notice them.

What follows is a checklist of questions to ask yourself as you begin editing. Far from all-inclusive, the checklist focuses on the first step: examining the organization. You probably won't want to check through your work separately for each question: you can group some together and overlook others, depending on your own strengths and weaknesses as a writer.

An editing checklist

- Are the purpose and approach of my essay evident from the beginning?
- Are all sections of my paper relevant to the topic?
- Is the organization logical?
- Will the subheadings be meaningful to readers? Do they clearly identify the various sections in my work?
- Do my paragraph divisions give coherence to my ideas? Do I use them to cluster similar ideas and signal changes of idea?
- Do any parts of the essay seem disjointed? Should I add more transitional words or logical indicators to make the sequence of ideas easier to follow?
- Are the ideas sufficiently developed? Is there enough evidence, explanation, and illustration?
- Would an educated person who hasn't read the primary material understand everything I'm saying? Should I clarify some parts or add any explanatory material?
- In presenting my argument, do I take into account opposing arguments or evidence?
- Have I been accurate and fair in my representation of what my sources state?
- Have I cited all the sources I have used? Is the style of in-text citations consistent? (See Chapter 7.)
- Are my illustrations and tables useful? Do they present the data in the clearest, most effective way, or would a different form make a better presentation? (See Chapter 12.) Is my discussion of each one clear and complete?
- Are all my illustrations and tables numbered correctly? Have I identified each of them within the text?
- Are the tables complete and correct, with the source(s) noted?
- Have I checked my illustrations for correct spelling as well as for content? Have I included the source(s)?
- Do my conclusions accurately reflect my argument in the body of the work?
- Are the contents of my appendices useful? Are they complete and accurate?
- Is my reference list (or bibliography, whichever is appropriate) accurate and complete in all publication details?
- Is my title imaginative, informative, and precise?

Another approach would be to devise your own checklist based on the faults of previous assignments. This is particularly useful when you move from the overview to the close focus on sentence structure, diction, punctuation, spelling, and style. If you have a particular weak area—for example, irrelevant evidence, faulty logic, or run-on sentences—you should give it special attention. Keeping a personal checklist will save you from repeating the same mistakes.

As you edit, you should check for spelling errors. As noted in Chapter 1, your word-processing program may do this automatically, or you can initiate a separate check. Remember, however, that it won't identify words that are wrongly used (such as *there* when you mean *their*), and it may not catch numbers accidentally typed into words (e.g., *swi5ft*). Think of a computer spell checker as a useful first check rather than a final one. Similarly, grammar checkers, though considerably better than when they first appeared, are still not reliable. They will pick up common grammar errors and stylistic problems, but they do make mistakes and likely will never equal the judgment of a good editor. Indeed, some of the "corrections" your spelling and grammar checkers offer are quite funny!

Keep in mind, too, that for final editing, most good writers suggest working from the printed page, rather than from the computer screen. This point was made in Chapter 1, but it is worth repeating. In other words, print one draft before your final copy. Your eye will get a better sense of the text by perusing a whole page at a time than by scrolling down the screen line by line.

Formatting Your Essay

As discussed briefly in Chapter 1, a well-typed, proofread and corrected, attractive essay creates a receptive reader and, fairly or unfairly, often gets a higher mark than a sloppy paper (with bad grammar or atrocious spelling errors), which is more difficult to read. Good looks don't substitute for good thinking, but they will certainly enhance it! In other words, take care to prepare the cleanest copy of your work that you can before submitting it.

Unless instructed otherwise, always double space your work and use margins of at least 2.5 centimetres (1 inch) to frame the text in white space and allow room for your reader to write comments. Number each page at the top or bottom right-hand corner or at the top-centre of the page (without including a page number on the first, or title, page), and provide a neat, well-spaced cover page that includes the title of your paper, your name, the names of your instructor and the course, and a date. Make use of the formatting features such as bold and italics for appropriate emphasis, and choose suitable font faces. You will be safe if you use a serif font such as Times New Roman, usually 12-point, for the body of the essay, and a sans serif font such as Arial for the title and headings.

Keep in mind, though, that while a computer can make your work look good, fancy graphics and a slick presentation won't replace intelligent thinking. Read over your work with a critical eye in the knowledge that you can easily change something that is unsatisfactory. Remember that your computer is a tool for you to use—no more than that.

Protecting Your Work

An essay involves a great deal of time and effort. You don't want to find that some or all of your material is "lost" due to a computer error, or one that you caused, such as by accidentally erasing a section of your work, or even a whole file. Lost files are the nightmare of the computer age. Save your files regularly! Keeping at least two copies of your work as you proceed, one on the hard drive and a backup version on a USB key or other memory device, will give you peace of mind. You may be asked to submit a CD or memory stick with your paper saved on it so it can be checked with anti-plagiarism software. Keep the file at least until you have received the grade for the course. And always print an extra copy, for your files, in case the original is lost.

Chapter Summary

This chapter has emphasized the importance of planning your work before you write. Even if they are brief, plans for your essay can remind you of the important points you want to cover and help to ensure that you structure it logically. Organization of your essay—putting all parts of it into some sort of order—helps you write clearly and effectively. Revising and editing your work with a critical eye to strengthening the logic and flow of your arguments, as well as correcting errors in spelling and punctuation, can help turn a good essay into an outstanding one.

Notes

1. Sheridan Baker and Laurence B. Gamache, *The Canadian Practical Stylist*, 4th ed. (Don Mills, ON: Addison-Wesley, 1998).
2. Ibid.

6 Writing a Proposal, Research Paper, and Thesis

In this chapter, we examine

- things to keep in mind as you prepare and write a research proposal;
- essentials when writing a research paper or a thesis; and
- the importance of required supplementary material in your work.

Introduction

All writing requires planning, but when you are to tackle a major work, such as an Honours research paper (sometimes called an undergraduate thesis) or a graduate thesis, the planning stage is formalized. You may have to prepare a proposal to be approved by one or more faculty members before you will be permitted to do the necessary research. In addition, some senior undergraduate courses require the preparation of a research proposal as a graded assignment. And, of course, a report of some kind is required once any research has been done. The structure of research papers and theses generally conforms to standards accepted across all disciplines. This chapter highlights the essential elements of proposals, research papers, and theses.

Before proceeding, review the section on ethical issues in Chapter 2. These issues must be taken into account when you prepare a proposal or undertake research (involving humans and non-human animals) that will result in a research paper or thesis.

Two general comments: first, always double space your work, unless otherwise instructed; and, second, never put anything on the back side of any page in any work you prepare.

Preparing a Proposal

Sometimes referred to as a research design, plan, or prospectus, a research proposal can be thought of as a strategic plan for a research project. A research proposal should logically and systematically identify *what* you propose to do and *how* you propose to do it. Because the development of a research proposal is a cyclical process, you may revise it as often as necessary until it defines the research project that you wish to do and believe you can complete. Figure 6.1 on pages 102–3 illustrates the typical, major steps in developing a research proposal; the double-headed arrows indicate the non-linearity of the process. Often, particularly when you are revising your proposal, it is helpful to work backwards, in other words, begin with the data-collection tools, and then move to the objectives and to the statement of the problem. Doing so enables you to check for consistency throughout your proposal.

Although your preparation will become increasingly comprehensive and focused, preparing to write a proposal is similar to preparing to write an essay. First, you will have to identify the topic, limit it to something workable, determine how to relate it to others' work, know what data you will need, decide what methods of data collection and analysis will be appropriate, and suggest what the outcome of the study might be. You need to lead your reader to the inevitable conclusion that your topic has never been tackled before, or at least not from the perspective you propose.

There are several parts to any proposal:

- **Statement of research problem.** A formal statement of your research problem includes a description of the nature of the problem (e.g., its size, distribution, and severity) and a rationale for conducting the research. The formal statement also needs to **define your study area**. Even if your instructor has pre-selected the study area, you still need to define it and explain why it is an appropriate choice for study of the problem at hand. Similarly, you need to indicate your **approach or viewpoint** in your statement. There are two parts to this section. First, you need to suggest the broader context (disciplinary or interdisciplinary) into which your specific study fits, and the significance of its contribution. For instance, you might indicate that the data from your planned research will help to fill a gap in available information about the topic. Second, you need to indicate the philosophical stance that you intend to take (e.g., will you use a postmodernist approach? will you take a feminist perspective?).

- **Limitations.** Either within the statement of research problem or as a separate entry, identify the limitations of your study. Know in advance what you will *not* do! In addition to specifying areas or issues that you will not research, you need to identify such practical limitations as constraints on time or funds available for the research, field access difficulties, and other challenges that may affect your ability to conduct your proposed research.

- **Literature review.** The relationship between your proposed work and the existing work in the field must be established. You need to convince your faculty advisers that you are familiar with at least the general research background within which your study fits. For undergraduate students, the literature review need not be lengthy, but it should establish that you are aware of the significant current thinking in the subject area and that you have thought about the contributions your research might make to the topic. For tips on how to approach this review, see the section on literary reviews on p. 77.

- **Research objectives.** The objectives of a research project summarize what you hope to achieve by your study and how the results could be used. Both general and specific objectives need to be specified; general objectives indicate what you expect to achieve in general terms, while specific objectives identify the various aspects of your problem and specify what you will do in your research, where, and for what purpose. In terms of **anticipated results**, depending on the nature of your research, it may be appropriate to comment on the areas of application to which you will direct your possible conclusion (e.g., "Findings will be interpreted, in part, in relation to their significance to planning in the rural region.").

- **Research methodology and data acquisition.** This section should indicate succinctly what information/data you will gather, where and when you will do so, the methods by which you will collect your data, and your reasons for choosing those methods (interviews, questionnaires, experiments, mapping, remote sensing, archival material, instrumentation, etc.). Any sampling procedure you propose should be justified in terms of both the material or population to be sampled and the sampling method to be used.

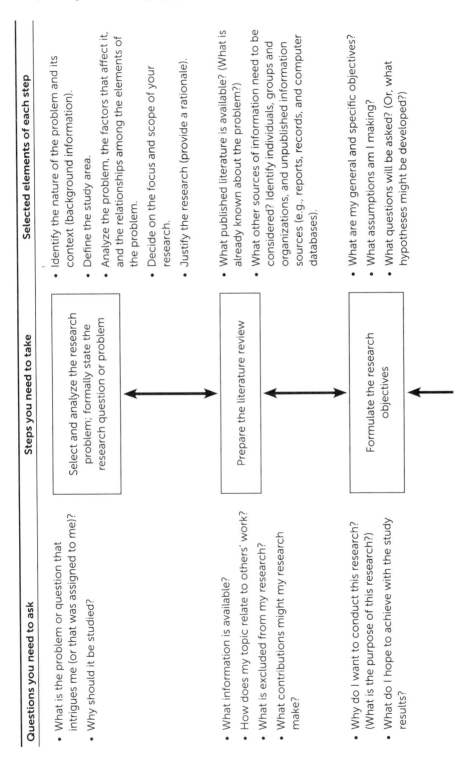

Questions you need to ask	Steps you need to take	Selected elements of each step
• What is the problem or question that intrigues me (or that was assigned to me)? • Why should it be studied?	Select and analyze the research problem; formally state the research question or problem	• Identify the nature of the problem and its context (background information). • Define the study area. • Analyze the problem, the factors that affect it, and the relationships among the elements of the problem. • Decide on the focus and scope of your research. • Justify the research (provide a rationale).
• What information is available? • How does my topic relate to others' work? • What is excluded from my research? • What contributions might my research make?	Prepare the literature review	• What published literature is available? (What is already known about the problem?) • What other sources of information need to be considered? Identify individuals, groups and organizations, and unpublished information sources (e.g., reports, records, and computer databases).
• Why do I want to conduct this research? (What is the purpose of this research?) • What do I hope to achieve with the study results?	Formulate the research objectives	• What are my general and specific objectives? • What assumptions am I making? • What questions will be asked? (Or, what hypotheses might be developed?)

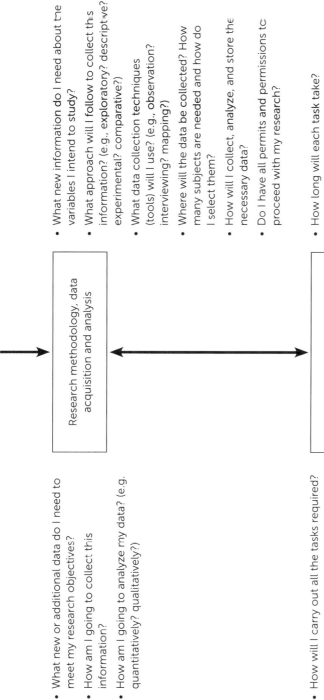

- What new information do I need about the variables I intend to study?
- What approach will I follow to collect this information? (e.g., exploratory? descriptive? experimental? comparative?)
- What data collection techniques (tools) will I use? (e.g., observation? interviewing? mapping?)
- Where will the data be collected? How many subjects are needed and how do I select them?
- How will I collect, analyze, and store the necessary data?
- Do I have all permits and permissions to proceed with my research?

Research methodology, data acquisition and analysis

- How long will each task take?
- What is my timetable? (What is the most appropriate time to carry out the various research tasks?)
- What is my tentative chapter outline?
- Is my bibliography complete and accurate?

Work plan

- What new or additional data do I need to meet my research objectives?
- How am I going to collect this information?
- How am I going to analyze my data? (e.g. quantitatively? qualitatively?)

- How will I carry out all the tasks required?
- When will I collect the data and how long will it take?
- What resources (e.g., equipment, transportation) do I need, and what resources do I have to carry out the project?

Figure 6.1   Typical steps in developing a research process

- **Data analysis.** This section should explain how the information you have acquired is to be evaluated, organized, and analyzed or synthesized. The amount of data and the basic question and/or the nature of the hypothesis will determine how the data ought to be handled. If you will be dealing with large quantities of data that will require computer processing and the use of statistical techniques, these should be identified—and you should be able to defend your choice of techniques. Make sure, as part of your methodology, that you have secured any necessary permissions to proceed with your research; for example, ensure you have permission from the owners to access your selected site, or have obtained written approval of the ethics board at your institution (see pp. 32–5).
- **Work plan.** A work plan or schedule summarizes the different components of your research project and identifies how and when you will perform all the tasks associated with your project. Schedule the dates on which each task should be started and completed. Indicate how long you estimate it will take to do the various sections of the assignment. Be realistic—you're likely to need more time than you think. You can develop a **tentative chapter outline** and identify the anticipated logical order of the sections for the proposed written presentation.
- **Bibliography.** List the most important works you consulted in developing your proposal. Include only the works you cite (and perhaps discuss) in the proposal. Don't "pad" by providing a long list of books, chapters, and journal articles that may relate to the topic, but that you have not yet read.

Identifying sections

Check with your faculty adviser about departmental style preferences. Many departments want sections to be identified with subheadings and/or letters or numbers (see p. 106).

Research Papers and Theses

A research paper prepared during the final year of undergraduate study, or a thesis completed as part of graduate studies requirements, is a long, formally structured essay based on the analysis of some chosen set of data or set of propositions. Findings may be based on primary research, but secondary sources may also be important.

In general, a research paper focuses sharply on a particular issue, whether a body of literature or some specific field or lab research. A thesis is expected to show evidence of originality in one or more aspects of your approach, data or principle, and technique or method; the originality required in a thesis is greater than in a research paper but less than in a doctoral dissertation. Whether your analysis is qualitative or quantitative in nature, the quality of your text always is important.

Your department may have guidelines for the outline and content of senior undergraduate research (Honours) papers and graduate theses. The guidelines for research papers may be similar to those for essays (see Chapter 5), but, as with theses, the structure generally does not allow for much flexibility (see p. 106). Typically, a draft copy of a research paper or thesis is given to your supervisor and your *committee* (composed of other faculty members) for their evaluative comments, after which you will have the opportunity to make changes—from minor corrections in grammar and spelling to major revisions that may require rewriting some chapters or even (dread the thought) the whole work. The final paper is then submitted for examination. The grade is usually based on evaluations of the written work together with an oral defence.

Plan how you will spend your time: doing background reading; formulating your proposal; reading additional material; gathering data; analyzing data; planning the written report; writing the first draft; revising and redrafting; preparing and checking illustrations, submitting the work to your instructor or supervisor (and committee) for evaluation; and (if such is permitted or required) revising as necessary before submitting the final product. To do all this within a period of perhaps only two or three terms (or semesters), you will have to work out a rough schedule in advance. Remember, too, that you should build in some time for yourself—and be prepared to take short breaks when you need them.

Your paper must be structured in a logical manner. Because it will have numerous paragraphs, headings of some sort are not only helpful but required. There are two systems for headings: either written headings/subheadings (A and B in Table 6.1) or some form of numerical differentiation, whether Roman numerals, alphanumerics, or decimals (C, D, and E in Table 6.1). Appropriate headings and subheadings are used with each of the latter three methods (none are shown in the table).

Headings

Headings normally are ranked from most to least important, as in the examples in Table 6.1. Whichever method you choose (or are told to use), be sure to employ equivalent symbols for sections of equivalent importance. And, once you have settled on a style, follow it consistently.

The structure of your work follows a progression, from the title of the project at the start to the references or bibliography at the end. In between is the substance of your work and its supporting apparatus. The outline of your work will have five or sometimes six components, organized as follows:

Table 6.1 Systems for headings

Written headings and subheadings

A.

TITLE OF PROJECT [Centred]

SECTION HEADING [1st order; flush left, all upper case]

Subheading [2nd order; flush left, bold]

Subheading [3rd order; flush left, underlined]

Subheading [4th order; flush left, not underlined, not bold]

B.

TITLE OF PROJECT [Centred]

Section heading [1st order; centred, underlined]

Subheading [2nd order; centred, not underlined, not bold]

Subheading [3rd order; flush left, underlined or bold]

Subheading [4th order; flush left, not underlined, not bold]

Subheading [5th order; indented start to a paragraph, underlined]

Numerical headings and subheadings

C. Roman numeral	D. Alphanumeric	E. Decimal*
I.	A.	1.0
A.	1.	1.1
1.	a.	1.11
2.	b.	1.12
B.	2.	1.2
II.	B.	2.0

* An alternate decimal system places all the numbers at the left margin.

Preliminary material

Numbering the preliminary pages: The preliminary pages (which include the title page, abstract, acknowledgements, list of tables, and list of figures) are numbered with small Roman numerals (e.g., ii, iii, iv) located at the bottom centre of each; however, the number for the title page, which is "i," should not appear. The appropriate Roman numeral for each item in the preliminary pages appears in the table of contents. The number of the first page for each chapter also appears there.

Title page: The title page identifies the title of your work; your name, department or program, and institution; a statement (centred, near the bottom of the page) such as "In partial fulfillment of the requirements for the B.Sc. [or whatever] degree in the Department of Y at the University of Z"; and the year. Your institution likely specifies precise wording for the title page of graduate degrees.

Abstract: A concise and accurate summary of the basic purpose or problem, methods, and major findings of the research contained in your Honours paper or thesis, the abstract is placed on a separate page, following the title page. Although the abstract is brief—usually there is a maximum word count for the abstract—its components mirror your entire research process (see Table 6.2; see also Figure 6.1 and Chapter 4).

Table of contents: On another separate page, list the following items, with the spacing as noted, and with appropriate page numbers located to the right of each heading:

Table of Contents

Abstract
Acknowledgements
List of Tables
List of Figures

CHAPTER
1. Title
2. Title
(repeat for each chapter)

Appendices
1. Title
(repeat for each Appendix)
Bibliography/References

Table 6.2 Components of an Abstract

Abstract Components	Questions to Ask and Write About
Problem statement	What is the problem you are trying to solve? Or what is the main argument of your paper? What is the scale of the issue?
Objective and rationale of the project	What motivated you to undertake this project (why do you care about it)? Why is the problem or topic important or interesting? What effect(s) might the research have?
Approach; methods used	What did you do? How did you go about answering the research questions you identified? What types of evidence did you collect? What methods did you use to collect the data?
Results	What did you find out (overview)? What was the answer to your question (key outcome)? How generalizable are your results? What are the limitations of your results?
Conclusions	What did you learn? What are the implications of your results? What recommendations can you make? What contributions does your project make to knowledge in your field of study?
Keywords	What words and phrases clearly identify the content and focus of your project? (use the words in your abstract)

Sources: University of Southern California. (2018, July 5). Organizing Your Social Sciences Research Paper: 3. The Abstract. Retrieved from https://libguides.usc.edu/writingguide; Koopman, Philip. (1997, October). How to Write an Abstract. Retrieved from http://users.ece.cmu.edu/~koopman/essays/abstract.html.

Acknowledgements: Acknowledge any agency—governmental or not—and your university or department, that financially or otherwise supported your research. Unless they have requested otherwise, remember to name and thank everyone who assisted you, including your supervisor. If some people did not want to be identified by name, you could still thank them in a generic way by saying something like ". . . and those who chose to remain anonymous."

Lists of tables and of figures: Include the number of each item, its title exactly as it appears within the text, and its page number. These lists should appear on one page if each list is short; otherwise each list appears on a separate page, to accommodate the length of the lists. See below under *Illustrations* for the several types of material that are grouped under the term *figure*.

Chapter titles: The list of chapter titles should *not* include subtitles if you are writing a research paper. However, a fully detailed table of contents—including all subtitles—can be useful, and may even be required, in a graduate thesis. If you are unsure of the level of detail to include, ask your supervisor.

Introduction

Your introductory chapter should outline the following, usually with separate headings:

- precise statement of purpose
- definition of terms (if few in number, may be included in text or as footnotes)
- hypothesis/hypotheses or basic question(s), and research objectives
- study area; i.e., the location (in a lab or a field site) where you did the work
- scope of your research
- methodologies (for data collection and analysis)
- limitations (what the research will *not* do)
- researcher's role (in planning and conducting the research)
- researcher's positionality (explicit recognition of relevant assumptions, beliefs and biases the researcher may hold)
- organization of the work (what each chapter contains, to guide the reader)

Substantive report (presented in several chapters)
- extended review of literature
- data: sources and reliability; method(s) of collection and analysis
- presentation of data (which may include illustrations—see p. 110)
- analysis of data (which also may include illustrations—see p. 110)
- summary of findings

Conclusion
- conclusions and, when appropriate, recommendations

Do not introduce new material in your conclusion.

Appendices

Some studies include appendices. Material that supports your discussion in a particular section of the text but is somewhat tangential to its main thrust may be better placed in an appendix. Data too extensive to be included in tables within the main text also may be listed in an appendix. Each appendix is numbered and given a title, and each begins on a new page. Be sure to refer to any appendices in the body of your text—e.g., "(see Appendix 3)"—so the reader knows to look for it at the end of the work. Appendices always appear before the bibliography.

Bibliography or list of references

As in all major works, the final item you have to attend to is the list of books, book chapters, journals, and other items that you have *cited* in your study. Works you may have read in the course of your research but have chosen not to cite are not included. Assembling and checking the accuracy of the nitty-gritty details in your bibliographic list will be a frustrating and time-consuming chore if you didn't record full publication information when you first read the material (see Chapters 4 and 5).

Illustrations

Most research papers and theses are illustrated. An illustration, whether it's a graph, table, map, or photograph, generally appears on the page immediately following the one in which it is identified in the text. It is not acceptable to use the back of the previous page to print your illustrations. If an illustration takes up more than half a page, no text—other than the illustration's title, any very brief comments made about the illustration, and, most important, source information—should appear on the page with it.

Figures include maps, graphs, and photographs. Each is numbered, either from 1 to n—i.e., from the beginning to the end of the main text (any figures in appendices are numbered separately, within each appendix)—or using the decimal system, from beginning to end of each chapter (in which case Fig. 2.1 would refer to the first figure in Chapter 2). *Tables* are numbered in a similar fashion. Always refer to your figures and tables in the text using their identifiers (Figure 5.1; Table 4.3) so the reader knows when to turn to them. And remember to discuss each illustration in your text; otherwise the reader will wonder why it is there. Finally, remember to assign page numbers to all illustrations, in sequence with your text page numbers.

Standards

Just as you are required to meet the highest standards in the conduct of your research, so, too, your writing standards must be high. Aim for a clear and precise style, with proper attention to the fundamentals of grammar, spelling, punctuation, and logical structure. If you struggle with your writing skills, check whether your institution offers in-person or online writing support programs—usually free, such support can help you communicate effectively.

Chapter Summary

This chapter has highlighted the essential elements associated with strategic planning for writing proposals, research papers, and theses. Becoming aware of the typical steps in preparing a proposal or in conducting a research project, and thinking about the organizational and structural aspects of writing up your proposal, paper, or thesis (including supplementary materials), are essential to successfully communicating the results of your research.

7 Quotations and Documentation

In this chapter, we examine

- how to incorporate quotations in your work;
- four basic styles for citing sources in your written work;
- the many types of sources you will cite in your work; and
- when to include endnotes/footnotes and how to prepare your bibliography.

Introduction

Your writing will be enriched by the use of pertinent quotations and appropriate documentation to support arguments. This chapter identifies ways to include quotations in your work, and indicates several styles that are available to you when you include citations to others' work in your own writing. As university codes of conduct and academic integrity identify the importance and necessity of citing the work of another author if you quote, paraphrase, summarize, or otherwise refer to it in your work, learning how to accurately document sources is a vital skill.

Every student is expected to maintain high standards of integrity in his or her coursework and research, and the academic regulations found in university and college calendars reinforce those expectations. What is academic integrity and why does it matter? The International Center for Academic Integrity defines academic integrity as "a commitment, even in the face of adversity, to six fundamental values: honesty, trust, fairness, respect, responsibility, and courage."[1] Consistently applying these values in your academic work, and "doing the right thing" even when it's not easy, brings tangible personal benefits such as enhanced skills in research and writing, and increased self-respect and self-confidence (from knowing you have genuinely earned your degree).

Universities take academic misconduct—including cheating and plagiarism—very seriously. Actions you can take to demonstrate academic integrity include (but are not limited to) the following:

- Complete your own (original) work (don't ask others to complete assignments or write tests for you).
- Don't allow others to use or copy your assignments or tests.
- Cite all sources (including books, articles, reports, web pages, art, images, etc.).
- Give proper credit in acknowledging the work of others.
- Learn how to cite properly and paraphrase effectively.
- Collaborate appropriately (e.g., teamwork may be prohibited).

Quotations

Using quotations effectively can add authority to your writing as well as help you avoid charges of plagiarism. But you should use quotations carefully: never cite a passage just because it sounds impressive. Be sure that it really adds to your discussion, either by expressing an idea with special force or cogency, or by giving substance to a debatable point.

Guidelines for incorporating quotations

1. Integrate the quotation so that it makes sense in the context of your discussion and fits grammatically into a sentence:

   ✗ Whether Bill Gates is a visionary is debatable. "640K ought to be enough for anybody" is now highly ironic.

   ✔ Whether Bill Gates is a visionary is debatable. His 1981 prediction that "640K ought to be enough for anybody" now is considered laughably ironic.

2. Be accurate. Reproduce the exact wording, punctuation, and spelling of the original, including any errors. Identify errors by using *sic* in square brackets—see p. 269. If you italicize or underline part of the quotation for emphasis, add either *my emphasis* or *emphasis added* in square brackets (at the end of the quotation). Note

the placement of the period, inside the quotation marks but outside the brackets:

> "The group's findings were *not* confirmed [my emphasis]."

3. Include as part of your text, enclosed in quotation marks,
   - no more than three or four lines of prose:

   > As Brian Graham has observed, ". . . identity is defined by a multiplicity of often conflicting and variable criteria."[2]

   - no more than four lines of verse. Use a slash (/) to indicate the end of a line:

   > Patrick Duffy, discussing Ireland's "north," quoted from a poem by John Hewitt: "The hospitable Irish / come out to see who passes / bid you sit by the fire / till it is time for mass."[3]

4. A long quotation—normally four or more lines—is usually single spaced and introduced by a colon. If the first line of your block quotation is the first sentence of a new paragraph, indent the first line; otherwise, start flush with the left margin:

   > The environmental determinist Ellen Semple (1863–1932), using a rather florid style, wrote that nature moulded humans:

   > > Man is a product of the earth's surface. This means not merely that he is a child of the earth, dust of her dust; but that the earth has mothered him, fed him, set him tasks, directed his thoughts, confronted him with difficulties that have strengthened his body and sharpened his wits, given him problems of navigation or irrigation, and at the same time whispered hints for their solution.[4]

   For long quotations from poems, write the words line for line as originally written.

5. For a quotation within a quotation, use single quotation marks:

   > Our reporter got this comment from the forester: "I shouted 'timber' as I tried to get out of the way of the falling tree. The tree fell on me, and I screamed 'help' to my mates."

6. If you omit something from the original, use an ellipsis (see p. 275). To omit a full line of a poem, use a full line of single-spaced periods:

> Cedar and jagged fir
> . . . .
> Against the gray
> and cloud-piled sky.

7. If you insert an explanatory comment of your own into a quotation, enclose it in square brackets:

> "The presidents of the two universities [Minnetonka and Mankato] strenuously objected to the government's proposed funding scheme for universities."

Documentation

In any work you do, always fully and accurately record the source of all material—ideas, quotations, diagrams, graphs, maps, etc.—that is not your own. This documentation will give support and substance to your writing and will permit your readers to locate original source material.

There is no one "right" method of documentation: not only do different disciplines follow different conventions, but individual instructors have different preferences and expectations. One may tell you to follow the style in, say, *The Canadian Geographer* or the *Annals of the Association of American Geographers*; another may direct you to a specific style guide. If you are not given specific instructions, you might choose one of the systems outlined below. Whatever you do, remember to follow the one "golden rule" for documentation: always be consistent. Never change systems in midstream.

Basic characteristics

The increasing variety and mobility of texts (i.e., their frequent appearance in different sources), has meant some of the details in the various citation processes have changed. However, the essential elements normally included in all systems of documentation are the following (their ordering and level of detail required is variable):

- Name(s) of author(s). The usual order is surname, other name(s) and/or initials. Do *not* include titles (such as Professor, Colonel, or Reverend), affiliations, or degrees that precede or follow names. *Do* include any prefix (as in "*von* Langenfeld") that is an essential part of a name, or any final element appearing at the end of a name (as in "Blair Mannerly, *Jr.*" or "Angus George, *II*").
- Title of the source. Sources include books, periodical articles, websites, songs and pieces of music, etc.
- Title of the larger entity within which the source is located. Examples of these larger entities include books of short stories, poetry collections, television series, and websites.
- Other contributors. Others who contribute to the source may be credited in citations, including editors, illustrators, translators, and so on.
- Version (or edition) of a work.
- Number. Citations of sources should include, for instance, journal volume, issue number(s), multi-volume book numbers, and other numbered sequences.
- Publisher(s).
- Publication date(s).
- Location. Examples are the page numbers in a journal article or chapter in a book, and the URL of an online work.
- Optional elements. Some citation guides suggest that the inclusion of any information that will help a reader identify the source may be included (such as DOIs, URLs, original publication date, city of publication, and date of access).[5]

Styles

While most disciplines in the physical, biological, and social sciences use (A) *parenthetical references*, some use (B) *notes and a bibliography* or (C) the *citation-name* style. Again, details vary between and even within disciplines.

Because documentation styles vary so widely, this section provides guidelines, not firm rules: check with your instructor or department to make sure you are following the preferred practice. Check with a university librarian if your source doesn't fit the prescribed styles. The basic characteristics of the three styles (A, B, and C) are outlined below, with examples. For documenting cartographic, archival, and architectural records, see section D on *citation-sequence* style.

A. Parenthetical References

This method is followed, with variations, by the Council of Science Editors (CSE), the American Psychological Association (APA), and the Modern Language Association of America (MLA).[6] In this "bare-bones" approach to referencing, citations are given to the authorities/sources used to support or test the development of the case being argued, without any tangential discussions or references. This style has two main features:

- Brief references (termed *citations*) are located at appropriate points in the text.
- At the end of a work, a section entitled *Reference List*, *References*, or *Works Cited* includes the full publication information for those works *directly referred* to in your text; *other works* that you may have consulted but have not referred to directly in your text are *not* listed or are placed in a separate list called Works Consulted or Bibliography.

The CSE's *Scientific Style and Format: The CSE Manual for Authors, Editors, and Publishers* details three variations of the CSE style: the name-year system, the citation-sequence system, and the citation-name system. The following examples illustrate the **name-year citation system**. Should you require additional information, check your campus library or writing centre for a copy of the *Scientific Style and Format*, 8th edition.

In the text

1. The citation often is placed at the end of the sentence in which you refer to the work, with the author's surname and, in most cases, the year of publication in parentheses (note the presence or absence of a comma in the citation); the MLA style does not include the year, but does include the page number whenever possible:

    CSE   . . . main drivers of mining activity in the Arctic (Koivurova, 2015).

    APA   . . . main drivers of mining activity in the Arctic (Koivurova, 2015).

    MLA   . . . main drivers of mining activity in the Arctic (Koivurova 194).

2. A citation provided within a sentence should appear next to the text to which it refers:

CSE, APA   Rautio (2015) examined environmental health in the changing Arctic.

(or)   In 2015, Rautio examined environmental health in the changing Arctic.

MLA   Rautio examined environmental health in the changing Arctic (217).

If you are citing a work that has no declared author, you should provide its full title, or a shortened version of it (e.g., *Cognitive Mapping and What Children See* may be shortened to *Cognitive Mapping*, as long as no other work you are citing is called *Cognitive Mapping*). You may abbreviate a well-known literary work that you are citing repeatedly.

3. If a citation is to an entire work, and the page reference is not important, all you need to include is the year. For MLA no date is required.

CSE, APA   Foulon and Rousseau (2018) identified the uncertainty of the hydrological parameter.

MLA   Foulon and Rousseau identified the uncertainty of the hydrological parameter.

If, however, the citation is to something specific within the source and not just to the work in general, then you must be specific in your citation. When referring to a particular page, figure, or table, include the page number (note that in the CSE style there is no comma between the author's name and the year, and no period after p). Note that the APA style uses an ampersand ($\&$) within the citation (but not in the text), whereas the CSE and MLA styles use *and*:

CSE   On pages 2 through 4, . . . (Jelinski 2015)
 According to Table 2.1 . . . (Dearden 2016)
 As Figure 1 shows . . . (Bakker 2012)
 . . . as seen in Chapter 8 . . . (North and Church 2014)

APA   (Jelinski, 2015, pp. 1−6)
 (Dearden, 2016, Table 2.1)

(Bakker, 2018, Fig. 1)
(North & Church, 2014, Chapter 8)

MLA   (Jelinski 3)
(Dearden, table 2.1)
(Bakker, fig 1)
(North and Church, ch. 8)

4. Citing a work by multiple authors can be tricky.[7] For a source with two authors, list both authors' names. When shortening a list of three or more authors, use "et al.":
Two authors:

CSE, APA   Bertazzon and Shahid (2015, 2017) are investigating childhood obesity and neighbourhood walkability.

MLA   Bertazzon and Shahid are investigating childhood obesity and neighbourhood walkability.

Three or more authors:

CSE   Mantyka-Pringle et al. (2015, p 4) identify how to transition toward sustainability that encapsulates Indigenous rights and cultures.

MLA   Mantyka-Pringle et al. identify how to transition toward sustainability that encapsulates Indigenous rights and cultures (4).

In APA, when there are three, four, or five authors, cite all authors the first time a work is identified (example *a*), and in subsequent references only the first author's surname and "et al." are used (example *b*) as well as the year if it is the first citation of a reference within a paragraph (example *c*):

a)   Sponarski, Semeniuk, Glikman, Bath, and Musiani (2013) are correct.

b)   Sponsrski et al. are correct.

c)   Sponarski et al. (2013) are correct.

When there are six or more authors, in APA cite only the surname of the first author followed by "et al.":

Leonard et al. (2015) focus on managing the Columbia River Basin for energy and fish.

In MLA, when there are more than three authors, give only the first author's surname followed by "et al.":

> Stewart et al. considered the implications of Arctic sea ice for cruise tourism.

In CSE, an article with three to ten authors is cited within the text using the first author's surname followed by "et al."

5. When more than one work is cited within a single set of parentheses, the items are separated by semicolons. In the CSE style the works are listed in chronological order (example *a*), but in both the APA (example *b*) and MLA (example *c*) styles they are listed in alphabetical order (note the absence of dates in the MLA example):

    (a) (Timmerman 2016; Victor 2017; Benner and Bradley 2018)

    (b) (Benner & Bradley 2018; Timmerman 2016; Victor 2017)

    (c) (Benner and Bradley; Timmerman; Victor)

6. If there are two authors with the same last name, include their initials. The CSE style does not use periods or spaces between two or more initials:

CSE   (Smith JM 2016; Smith SLJ 2015)

APA   (M.L. Hanson, 2015; S. Hanson, 2015)

MLA   (A. Best; C. Best)

7. When citing two or more works by the same author(s), list the surname(s) once, with the dates following. If there are multiple publications for any one year, use a letter marker after the year to distinguish them:

CSE   (Meadows, Meadows, and Randers 1992, 2004).
          (Le Billon 2014, 2015a, 2015b, 2017a, 2017b).

8. When citing a work that you have not read directly but know through a quotation in someone else's work, you should cite the source of your information about the work. Do not cite the original (unless you have searched for and located it). MLA style uses the abbreviation "qtd. in" to indicate information that has been quoted in another source.

> *CSE*   According to Cameron (1887, cited in Merante 2001, p 25), . . .
>
> *MLA*   According to Cameron (qtd. in Merante 25), . . .

9. Lecture or seminar notes can be cited as "personal communications." Because your notes do not contain recoverable (verifiable) data, personal communications can be cited in your text only, and not in your reference list. You could say, for instance:

> In her lecture Professor Draper outlined . . . (D. Draper, GEOG 421 lecture, April 6, 2018, University of Calgary, Calgary, Alberta).

In the reference section

Although specific details vary depending on the subject (see the sample entries below), all subjects in the alphabetical listing share some features of reference style in common. Here are the general guidelines:

1. References are listed alphabetically by author: surname first, followed by given names or initials; do not number your entries.
2. For a work with two or more authors, list all their names, in the order in which they appear in the original source. In some styles only the first author's name is reversed (Zhang, C., X. Guo); in others all the names are reversed (Zhang, C., Guo, X.). In CSE, if there are more than ten authors, only the first ten are listed, followed by "et al."
3. When citing more than one work by a particular author in the CSE and APA styles, list the entries in chronological order (the date should usually follow the author's name); for works published in the same year, add a letter marker to each date (2018a, 2018b, etc.). In the MLA style, multiple works by the same author are listed alphabetically by title, and after the first entry the author's name is replaced by three hyphens followed by a period.
4. For references to journals, always include the volume and issue numbers and inclusive page numbers.

Sample entries

Several variations exist. Note the differences in punctuation (such as the absence of periods after initials in names in the CSE style), parentheses, italicization, presence or absence of page references, and so on.

Journal

For their works cited (reference) pages, each of the APA, CSE, and MLA styles identifies author, title, volume, and issue numbers for journals. The CSE style abbreviates the names of journals and does not underline or italicize them. Also note the placement of initials, and the treatment of *and* (MLA uses the word, APA an ampersand (&), and CSE omits it). In addition, there can be variations in punctuation (colon or comma), italicization, and spacing. Note, too, the location of the year of publication. The APA style italicizes, as a unit, the journal name and the volume number. An author's full name generally is cited in MLA style.

> *CSE*   Shelton, T. 2017. Spatialities of data: mapping social media 'beyond the geotag'. GeoJ. 82(4): 721–734.
>
> *APA*   Shelton, T. (2017). Spatialities of data: Mapping social media 'beyond the geotag'. *GeoJournal, 82*(4), 721–734.
>
> *MLA*   Shelton, Taylor. "Spatialities of Data: Mapping Social Media 'Beyond the Geotag'." *GeoJournal*, vol. 82, no. 4, 2017, pp. 721–734.

Journal, multiple authors

> *CSE*   Aminipouri M, Knudby A, Ho, HC. 2016. Using multiple disparate data sources to map heat vulnerability. The Canadian Geographer. 60:356–368.
>
> *APA*   Aminipouri, M. Knudby, A., & Ho, H.C. (2016). Using multiple disparate data sources to map heat vulnerability. *The Canadian Geographer*, 60, 356–368.
>
> *MLA*   Aminipouri, Mehdi, Anders Knudby, and Hung Chak Ho. "Using Multiple Disparate Data Sources to Map Heat Vulnerability." *The Canadian Geographer*, vol. 60, no. 3, 2016, pp. 356–368.

Book

Note the placement of p or pp: p 10–20 (CSE) and pp. 10–20 (APA). For a whole chapter in a book, refer to the pertinent pages (e.g., "26–41," not "Chapter 2"). In the CSE style, 80 p is the total length of a book; although this is optional it can provide useful information to the reader. The terms *Publisher* (*Publ.*), *Inc.*, or *Co.* and *Press* are generally omitted from commercial publishers (e.g., Wiley) although the word *Press* is included for university presses (e.g., McGill-Queen's University Press). The names of university presses are written out in the APA style but abbreviated in the CSE and MLA styles. Note that when there are more than three authors the MLA and CSE styles allow you to list the first author only, followed by "et al.":

CSE   Lucia L, et al. 2015. Social infrastructure and vulnerability in the suburbs. Toronto: University of Toronto Press. 208 p.

APA   Lucia, L., Preston, V., Anisef, P., Basu, R., & Wang, S. (2015). *Social infrastructure and vulnerability in the suburbs.* Toronto, ON: University of Toronto Press.

MLA   Lucia, Lo, et al. *Social Infrastructure and Vulnerability in the Suburbs.* U of Toronto P, 2015.

In the CSE style, if the place of publication is not well known, include more information, such as the name of the province or state. Note that the APA style always includes the province/state or country. The MLA style does not require the city, state, province, or country.

CSE   Field K. 2018. Cartography. Redlands, CA: Esri Press. 576 p.

APA   Field, K. (2018). *Cartography*. Redlands, CA: Esri Press.

MLA   Field, Kenneth. *Cartography*. Esri Press, 2018.

Book with edition number

CSE   Bone, RM. 2018. The Regional Geography of Canada. 7th ed. Don Mills, ON: Oxford University Press. 480 p.

APA   Bone, R.M. (2018). *The regional geography of Canada* (7th ed.). Don Mills, ON: Oxford University Press.

MLA   Bone, Robert M. *The Regional Geography of Canada*. 7th ed., Oxford UP, 2018.

Book, two authors

CSE   Lydon M, Garcia A. 2015. Tactical urbanism: short-term action for long-term change. Washington, D.C.: Island Press. 352 p.

APA   Lydon, M., & Garcia, A. (2015). *Tactical urbanism: Short-term action for long-term change*. Washington, D.C.: Island Press.

MLA   Lydon, Mike, and Anthony Garcia. *Tactical Urbanism: Short-term Action for Long-term Change*. Island Press, 2015.

Book, edited

CSE   Maniaque-Benton C, editor. 2016. Whole earth field guide. Cambridge, MA: MIT Press. 288 p.

APA   Maniaque-Benton, C. (Ed.). (2016). *Whole earth field guide*. Cambridge, MA: MIT Press.

MLA   Maniaque-Benton, Caroline, editor. *Whole Earth Field Guide*. MIT P, 2016.

Book published in two locations by two different presses

CSE   Rum D, Barley JV, editors. 2011. The geography of drink across an international border. London, UK: Mugs; New York: Saloon. 356 p.

MLA   Rum, Derek, and Julia V. Barley, editors. *The Geography of Drink Across an International Border*. Mugs/Saloon, 2011.

The APA style does not address co-publication.

Chapter in an edited book

CSE   Hansen-Ketchum P. 2015. Engaging with nature in the promotion of health. In: Hallstrom LK, Guehlstorf NP, Parkes MW, editors. Ecosystems, Society and Health. Montreal: McGill-Queen's University Press. p. 99–129.

APA   Hansen-Ketchum, P. (2015). Engaging with nature in the promotion of health. In L.K. Hallstrom, N.P. Guehlstorf, & M.W. Parkes (Eds.), *Ecosystems, Society and Health* (pp. 99–129). Montreal, QC: McGill-Queen's University Press.

MLA   Hansen-Ketchum, P. "Engaging with Nature in the Promotion of Health." *Ecosystems, Society and Health*, edited by Lars K. Hallstrom et al., McGill-Queen's UP, 2015, pp. 99–129.

Government report

CSE   Parks Canada Agency. A natural priority: a report on Parks Canada's Conservation and Restoration Program. Ottawa, Canada: Queen's Printer; 2018. Catalogue No.: R-62-551/2018E-PDF.

APA   Parks Canada Agency. (2018). *A natural priority: A report on Parks Canada's conservation and restoration program* (Catalogue No. R62-551/2018E-PDF). Ottawa, Canada: Queen's Printer.

MLA   Parks Canada Agency. *A Natural Priority: A Report on Parks Canada's Conservation and Restoration Program*. Ottawa: Queen's Printer, 2018. Print

Article in an encyclopedia

CSE   Mower A. 2018. Cutting grass. In: The encyclopedia of gardening. Volume 1. Des Moines, IA. Roots; pp. 307–8.

APA   Mower, A. (2018). Cutting grass. In *The encyclopedia of gardening* (Vol. 1, pp. 307–308). Des Moines, IA: Roots Press.

MLA   Mower, Alex. "Cutting Grass." *The Encyclopedia of Gardening*. Des Moines: Roots, 2018. Print.

Unpublished dissertation

CSE   Reynolds, RP. 2017. Personalizing Tsunami Risk on Vancouver Island with GIS: A Mixed-Methods Case Study Exploring the Use of GIS in Public Tsunami Risk Assessment and Personal Preparedness in Port Alberni, B.C. [dissertation]. [Calgary (AB)]: University of Calgary. 295 p.

APA   Reynolds, R.P. (2017). *Personalizing tsunami risk on Vancouver Island with GIS: A mixed-methods case study exploring the use of GIS in public tsunami risk assessment and personal preparedness in Port Alberni, B.C.* (Unpublished doctoral dissertation). University of Calgary, Calgary, Canada.

MLA   Reynolds, Ryan P. "Personalizing Tsunami Risk on Vancouver Island with GIS: A Mixed-Methods Case Study Exploring the Use of GIS in Public Tsunami Risk Assessment and Personal Preparedness in Port Alberni, B.C." Diss, U of Calgary, 2017. Print.

Presentation

CSE   Dawson, J, Johnston, M, Stewart, E, Têtu, P-L. 2018. Cruise ship passenger experiences of shore visits along the Northwest Passage, Arctic Canada. Paper presented at: 6th International Polar Tourism Research Network (IPTRN) Conference: Whitehorse, Yukon, Canada.

APA   Dawson, J., Johnston, M., Stewart, E., & Têtu, P-L. (2018, June). *Cruise ship passenger experiences of shore visits along the Northwest Passage, Arctic Canada*. Paper presented at the 6th International Polar Tourism Research Network (IPTRN) Conference, Whitehorse, Yukon, Canada.

MLA   Dawson, Jackie, Margaret Johnston, Emma Stewart, and Pierre-Louis Têtu. "Cruise Ship Passenger Experiences of Shore Visits Along the Northwest Passage, Arctic Canada." 6th International Polar Tourism Research Network (IPTRN) Conference, 24 June 2018, Yukon College, Room A2206.

Article in an online journal

When referencing electronic journals follow the format of their print counterparts.

The APA style includes the DOI wherever possible. If none is available, give the URL. No retrieval date is required. Similarly, the MLA specifies that a DOI is preferable, but a URL must be included if a DOI does not exist. Further, MLA does not require a date of access to be included, but it does recommend it as an "optional" element to include. MLA also removes the http:// and https:// from a URL.

CSE   Rousselin M. 2018. A study in dispossession: the political ecology of phosphate in Tunisia. JPE [Internet]. [cited 2018 Jul 16]; 25: 1–19. Available from: https://journals.uair.arizona.edu/index.php/JPE/issue/view/1483

APA   Rousselin, M. (2018). A study in dispossession: The political ecology of phosphate in Tunisia. *Journal of Political Ecology, 25*, 1–19. Retrieved from https://journals.uair.arizona.edu/index.php/JPE/issue/view/1483

APA   Rousselin, M. (2018). A study in dispossession: the political ecology of phosphate in Tunisia. *Journal of Political Ecology, 25*, 1–19. doi: http://dx.doi.org/10.2458/jpe.v25i1

MLA   Rousselin, Mathieu. "A Study in Dispossession: The Political Ecology of Phosphate in Tunisia." *Journal of Political Ecology*, vol. 25, no. 1, 2018, pp. 1–19, doi: dx.doi.org/10.2458/jpe.v25i1.

Website

CSE   National pollutant release inventory. [Internet]. 2018. Ottawa: Environment Canada; [cited 2018 Sept]. Available from: http://www.ec.gc.ca/inrp-npri/default.asp

APA   Environment Canada. (2018, July). *National Pollutant Release Inventory*. Retrieved from http://www.ec.gc.ca/inrp-npri/default.asp

APA   Environment Canada. (2018, July). *National Pollutant Release Inventory*. Retrieved from www.ec.gc.ca/inrp-npri/default.asp

MLA   Environment Canada. *National Pollutant Release Inventory*. 2 Sept. 2018, www.ec.gc.ca/inrp-npri/default.asp.

Using notes with parenthetical references

Both the APA and MLA styles permit the use of notes to supplement the information contained in parenthetical references.

In APA style, notes have two purposes:

1. Content footnotes expand on the ideas in the main text.
2. Copyright permission footnotes acknowledge the source of copyrighted material that has been reproduced or adapted.

In MLA style, notes have two purposes:

1. Content notes provide additional information or comment.
2. Bibliographic notes can either provide an opportunity for you to comment on the value, quality, or importance of your sources, or supply information to clarify references that contain numerous citations.

When using notes, place a superscript Arabic numeral (a number slightly raised above the lines of words, e.g.,[14]) at the appropriate place in the text and insert the note after a matching numeral at the bottom of the page (footnote) or at the end of the text (endnote).

Notes should be used sparingly, since they divert the reader's attention away from the main text. If you find yourself creating many long, complicated notes, it is probably better to use the notes-and-bibliography method of documentation described in section B.

B. Notes and a Bibliography

This system uses notes (either *footnotes* or *endnotes*) and a *bibliography*. It permits greater freedom than the parenthetical reference style does, since it lets you use *bibliographic* and *content* notes to expand upon the material presented in the main text. When using notes, you must also include a full *bibliography* (see pp. 133–5).

Notes

Notes allow the reader to check sources, verify information, and consider points that may not warrant inclusion in the main text. Never put essential information into a note; if it is important to your argument, you should include it within the main body of the paper. Notes are useful for developing an argument (especially when the word count is limited), presenting commentary on your sources, expanding on a point made in the text, identifying specific sources, and so on. But including too many of them can interrupt your reader's progress. Try to include in the text as much of the necessary information as you can to keep the note itself as short as possible. To avoid clutter, remember that you don't need references to common knowledge or undisputed facts. Just be sure to provide source information in a note if you quote or summarize other people's ideas; such acknowledgement will help you to avoid charges of plagiarism.

Use footnotes/endnotes to:

- identify the sources of particular words or ideas;
- provide additional relevant information, subsidiary discussion, amplification, or qualification of points made in the main text;
- point out cross-references within your own work; and
- acknowledge assistance received from people or agencies who, for instance, provided information, or gave you permission to use their data or their lab facilities or to undertake interviews on their premises, using their staff or clients.

Both footnotes and endnotes are identified with superscript numbers in the text. *Footnotes* appear at the bottom of each page. *Endnotes* appear at the end of the paper, usually under the heading Notes. The format for footnotes and endnotes is identical; only their locations differ.

Format

1. For the reader's convenience, you may place your *footnote* at the bottom of the page on which the citation appears. Be sure to leave enough space for it. You should also leave a quadruple space between the text and the footnote, to make the division clear. A line (either about 10 spaces in length, or right across the page) between the text and footnote will help to make the division clear. The Insert menu in your word-processing software usually will have an

option that allows you to easily insert and format both footnotes and endnotes.

2. Footnotes should be indented the same number of spaces that you use for a new paragraph. In your writing footnotes should be single-spaced, in contrast to the double-spaced text. Leave a double space between entries.

3. If you choose to place all your notes at the end of your paper, they become **endnotes**. Using a separate page, underline or italicize your centred title—**Endnotes** or simply **Notes**—and list the notes by number. Leave a triple space between the title and the first entry, and a double space between entries.

4. Whichever format you choose, remember to number your notes consecutively, using Arabic numerals, and to put the corresponding number at the appropriate place in the text (usually at the end of the sentence in which you make each reference), using superscript. The numbers should follow all end punctuation.

5. Some instructors permit the use of smaller font sizes for notes (e.g., 10-point) than the standard text size (e.g., 12-point). Find out what your instructor prefers before you prepare and submit your paper.

The following examples of documentation are restricted to the most common kinds of notes and bibliographic references. They are based on *The Chicago Manual of Style*.

Notes for first references

Article in a journal

The abbreviation *p.* (or *pp.*, for multiple pages) may be used to indicate page numbers, but increasingly it is omitted from references. Most page numbers may be contracted to avoid unnecessary repetition (for example, *33–7, 465–82, 1277–9*); however, numbers between *10* and *20* should always be written in full (*10–11, 12–15, 214–18, 1342–1480*). If the issue of the journal in which the article appears is one of several bound together to form a single volume with *continuous* page numbers, you may leave out the week or month or issue number of publication—see the two examples—and just give the volume number, year (in parentheses), and page numbers. Here are examples of two styles:

1. Andrew Reeves, "Attack of the Killer Algae," *Alternatives Journal* 43, no. 2 (August 2017): 52–5.

2. Andrea Choi, "Equity, Race, and Whiteness in Canadian Geography," *The Canadian Geographer* 60, no. 3 (Fall 2016): 377. https://doi.org/10.1111/cag.12266.

Book by one author

Capitalize the first letter in the title and subtitle, as well as the first letters of all words except for articles, prepositions, and conjunctions (see Chapter 18 for help with these terms). The author's full name, not just initials, can be cited. Terms such as *editor*, *compiler*, and *translator* are abbreviated. When the publisher's name is long, you should use its familiar short form; thus *Macmillan of Canada Ltd.* becomes simply *Macmillan*.

> 3. Maharaj K. Pandit, *Life in the Himalaya: An Ecosystem at Risk* (Cambridge: Harvard University Press, 2017).

Book by two or three authors (with page references)

Although the title page may list more than one place of publication (say, Toronto and Buffalo), you need only name the first place in your reference:

> 4. Moses Brackish and Marshy Puddle, *Crossing the Dead Sea* (Toronto: Shore, 2019), 65–7.

Book by four or more authors

In a note only, the name of the first author is included, followed by "et al." with no intervening comma; in the bibliography, the first 10 authors are listed, followed by "et al."

> 5. Spencer C.H. Barrett et al., *Invasion Genetics: The Baker and Stebbins Legacy* (Hoboken, NJ: Wiley-Blackwell, 2016).

Book with one editor

> 6. Michael A. Burayidi, ed., *Cities and the Politics of Difference* (Toronto: University of Toronto Press, 2015).

Book with two editors

> 7. Alison L. Bain and Linda Peake, eds., *Urbanization in a Global Context* (Don Mills: Oxford University Press, 2017).

Book authored and edited by different individuals

> 8. Mark C. Serreze and Roger G. Barry, *The Arctic Climate System*, 2nd ed., ed. John T. Houghton, Michael J. Rycroft, and Alexander J. Dressler (Cambridge: Cambridge University Press, 2014).

Book by one author translated by another

You need not list the author's name when it is part of the title:

> 9. *Ptolemy's Geography*, trans. J. Lennart Berggren and Alexander Jones (Princeton: Princeton University Press, 2002).

Notes for subsequent references

1. Subsequent note references should be brief. The preferred style today includes only the author's last name, the title in shortened form, and, if appropriate, the pertinent page number. If you are referring repeatedly to the same source, you can use the abbreviation *ibid.* (which is short for the Latin word *ibidem* and means "in the same place") and the page number (if appropriate), provided that there is no intervening reference to a different source:

   20. Sayer and Maginnis, "Forests in Landscapes," 109.
   21. Marcus Doel, *Geographies of Violence* (Sage, 2017).
   22. Ibid.
   23. Kevin R. Ford et al., "Competition Alters Tree Growth," *Canadian Journal of Forest Research* 47 (2017), 53–62.
   24. Morrissey, *Key Concepts*, 53.
   25. Ibid., 62–71.

2. If a bibliography includes all works cited in the document, even the first citation in the text of a particular work's title can be in shortened form.

3. If you are referring repeatedly to a single primary source, after the first mention (with appropriate identification in a foot- or endnote), you may simply cite the page numbers, enclosed in parentheses, in the text.

Bibliography

A bibliography is an alphabetical list of the works cited in an essay. It is normally an essential part of the note form of documentation. Although a bibliography is not required if you document your references fully in footnotes or endnotes, a full bibliography lists all the sources cited. A separate listing in the bibliography, with a subheading, might include particular relevant works not cited in the essay. The bibliography is always the last item in an essay; any appendices precede it.

Format

The format for bibliographies in Chicago style differs slightly from that for notes:

1. Use a separate page at the end of your essay, with an underlined or italicized heading—*Bibliography*—centred on the page.

2. Single space all entries, leaving a double space between entries and a triple space between the heading and the first entry. Entries should

have hanging indents, which means the first line of the entry is not indented but the subsequent lines of each entry are indented. The examples in this chapter all follow this style.

3. Do not number entries; instead, *list them alphabetically* by the author's or editor's surname. If no author is given, begin with the first significant word in the title.

4. Begin each bibliographic entry at the left margin and indent any subsequent line five spaces.

5. Include all cited works in a single list: books, chapters in books, journal articles, etc.

6. For more on annotated bibliographies, see page 78.

Article in a journal

Note that when referencing a work with two or more authors, only the first author's name is inverted:

Buras, Allan, Barbara Spy, Karolina Janecka, and Ryszard Kaczkab. "Divergent Growth of Norway Spruce on Babia Góra Mountain in the Western Carpathians." *Dendrochronologia* 50 (August 2018): 33–43.

If a work has 10 authors or fewer, all should be listed; for references of 11 authors or more, the first seven should be listed, followed by "et al."

Book

If you include more than one work by a particular author, list the entries alphabetically by title. Give the name in the first entry only. For subsequent entries, replace the author's name with three dashes followed by a period:

Spieles, Douglas. *Environmentalism: An Evolutionary Approach*. Routledge, 2018.

———. *Protected Land: Disturbance, Stress, and American Ecosystem Management*. New York: Springer-Verlag, 2010.

Article in an edited book

Alexander, Shelley. "Carnivore Management and the role of conservation GIS." In *Resource and Environmental Management in Canada*, 5 edn, edited by Bruce Mitchell, 293–317. Don Mills: Oxford, 2015.

Government document
> Canada. British Columbia. Legislative Assembly. Speech from the Throne, 41st Parliament, 3rd session, February 13, 2018.

Unsigned newspaper article

If a newspaper article is unsigned, the name of the newspaper stands in place of the author:

> *The Telegram.* "City of St. John's says water safe to drink despite unpleasant taste and odour." July 18, 2018.

Article in an online journal
> Wood, Patricia Burke, and David A. Rossiter. "The Politics of Refusal: Aboriginal Sovereignty and the Northern Gateway Pipeline." *The Canadian Geographer* 61, no. 2 (Summer 2017): 165–77. https://doi.org/10.1111/cag.12325.

Website
> Dowsett, Paul. "Why Simple Is the New Smart." Rethink Sustainability. May 4, 2018. http://rethinksustainability.ca/2018/05/04/why-simple-is-the-new-smart/.

If an access date is required, it is included parenthetically at the end of the entry.

C. Citation-name

The following examples follow the CSE style. In addition to the parenthetical reference style outlined in section A, the CSE advocates two alternative documentation systems: citation-name and citation-sequence. (See section D for examples of the citation-sequence system of documentation for cartographic, archival, and architectural records.) In the *citation-name style*, each new book or article mentioned in the text is assigned a number. Then the same number is used for every subsequent reference to the same work. The numbers inserted in the text—preferably as superscript or in parentheses—direct the reader to the reference section at the end of the paper:

> These findings are supported by Becker and Pandle.[14]

(or)

> These findings are supported by Becker and Pandle (14).

The first citation of each reference is assigned a number; then at the end of the paper the references are listed in the sequence in which they were cited initially.

In the text

Two authors maintain this stance.[14,15] Lindeman,[16] however, takes particular issue with the suggestion[15] that . . .

As shown in the above example, if more than one citation needs to be made at a time, you should insert a comma between the numbers but you should not insert a space.

In the reference list

1. Boyd D.R. 2015. The optimistic environmentalist. Toronto: ECW. 219 p.
2. Louv R. 2011. The nature principle. Chapel Hill: Algonquin Books. 317 p.
3. Jamal S. 2018. Out, damn spot! Alternatives Journal. 43(3–4): 93–95.

The citation-name style has the advantage of interrupting the reading of the text in a minimal way. The obvious disadvantage is that the reader will have to turn to the reference list to find out which work is being cited.

D. Citation-sequence

Maps, architectural records, and various archival sources will include information from which you can select what you need for your citations and bibliography. This information may include the following:[8]

- author
- title
- edition
- scale
- place of publication
- name of publisher
- date of publication or drawing
- specific material designation and extent (e.g., a map, relief model, or architectural drawing)

- other physical details, such as the material used (e.g., vellum, engraved on copper plate, digital)
- dimensions
- series
- location (if unique, name the specific library or archives, CD-ROM, website)
- insets (if any)
- nature (machine-readable, painting, drawing, etc.)

The following examples are formatted according to the CSE citation-sequence style:

Map

Zania. 2017. Population over 50 [demographic map]. Zunila: Census Office. Scale 1:1,500,000. 2 sheets.

Map in atlas

Northern Newfoundland. 2004. [physical features and thematic sections]. In: The Canadian atlas: Our nation, environment and people. Montreal: The Reader's Digest Association; Ottawa, Canadian Geographic. pp. 124–5. Colour, scale 1:1,000,000.

A useful source

Once you know which style you are to use for a particular project, you will save yourself time if you memorize the ins and outs of that style. However, in addition to using this book or a specific style manual (e.g., APA), you also may wish to check out Citationmachine.net, a website that "translates" whatever basic information you provide into one of several styles, including MLA, APA, Turabian, Chicago, Web page, and online non-print. In addition, you can look up DOIs using Crossref, a free website that searches for DOIs using information such as article title, author(s), and publisher information.

Chapter Summary

All universities and colleges expect that you will approach your course work and research projects honestly and with integrity. This means, whether you are working on a project, a paper, or a lab report, you will acknowledge, respect, and act in accordance with the academic principles and values in effect at your institution. One way you can demonstrate your personal academic integrity is through developing your understanding of vital research, writing and documentation skills. Then, you will avoid engaging in plagiarism (see Chapter 1), for example, because you will know how to give credit to other people's work and be able to use appropriate citation methods when you quote or paraphrase various sources. In this chapter we have identified some of the basic styles available for citing sources in your written work.

Notes

1. International Center for Academic Integrity, T. Fishman, ed., *The Fundamental Values of Academic Integrity*, 2nd ed. (Clemson, SC: Clemson University Press, 2014). For more detailed information on the fundamental values of academic integrity you may wish to consult the Fundamental Values section (under Resources) of the International Center for Academic Integrity's website, found at: https://academicintegrity.org/fundamental-values/.
2. Brian Graham, "Ireland and Irishness: Place, Culture and Identity," in *In Search of Ireland: A Cultural Geography*, ed. Brian Graham (London: Routledge, 1997), 7.
3. Patrick J. Duffy, "Writing Ireland: Literature and Art in the Representation of Irish Place," in Graham, 78.
4. Ellen Churchill Semple, *Influences of Geographic Environment* (New York: Henry Holt, 1911), 1.
5. Tony Russell et al., "MLA Formatting and Style Guide," *The Purdue OWL,* Purdue U Writing Lab, June 18, 2018, https://owl.english.purdue.edu/owl/resource/747/1/.
6. Council of Science Editors, *Scientific Style and Format: The CSE Manual for Authors, Editors and Publishers*, 8th ed. (New York: Cambridge University Press, 2014), used mostly by scholars in the natural and physical sciences; American Psychological Association, *Publication Manual of the APA*, 6th ed. (Washington, DC: American Psychological Association, 2010), which is the standard reference for the social, behavioural, and health sciences; and Modern Language Association, *MLA Handbook for Writers of Research Papers*, 8th ed. (New York: The Modern Languages Association of America, 2016), generally used with academic writing in the humanities. Other specialist style manuals include A.M. Coghill and L.R. Garson, eds., *ACS Style Guide: Effective Communication of Scientific Information*, 3rd ed. (New York: Oxford University Press, 2006); Wallace R. Hansen, ed., *Suggestions to Authors of the Reports of the United States Geological Survey*, 7th ed. (Washington, DC: GPO, 1991), and the American Institute of Physics, *AIP Style Manual*, 4th ed. (New York: American Institute of Physics, 1990). Two standard works are Kate L. Turabian, *A Manual for Writers*, 8th ed. (Chicago: University of Chicago Press, 2013), and *The Chicago Manual of Style*, 17th ed. (Chicago: University of Chicago Press, 2017). The latter is available online.
7. The order of names in a work with several authors may be alphabetical, but in science citations the order generally reflects the authors' relative contributions or their relative standing (e.g., the senior researcher—generally called the principal investigator—first, and his or her assistants thereafter, usually in order of their contributions).
8. Based on Terry Cook, ed., *Archival Citations: Suggestions for the Citation of Documents at the Public Archives of Canada*, in collaboration with Victorin Chabot and with contributions from Patricia Kennedy (Ottawa: Public Archives of Canada, 1983), 5–7.

8

Participation, Group Assignments, and Presentations

In this chapter, we examine

- basic points to consider when you are giving a presentation;
- fundamentals you need to know when working in a group;
- visual aids and how best to use them; and
- essentials to keep in mind when creating a poster.

Introduction

This chapter is intended to help you take an active part in seminars, discussion groups, tutorials, and—for upper-level students—conferences. The chapter also offers tips on managing group work and giving formal presentations, and you will also find suggestions about visual aids, including posters, that you can use in those situations.

Participation

The goals of all discussion groups, seminars, and tutorials are insight and understanding, and the key to achieving them is participation. In turn, the key to successful participation is preparation. The following pointers will help you to become a good participant.

Preparing

1. **Know what the assignment is!** In most cases, your assignment (say, to read and comment on a chapter) will be announced in the previous week's meeting. If you miss a session, check with a classmate to find out the topic for the next week; remember that your instructor will determine quickly who is prepared and who is not.

2. **Be prepared to be the first speaker.** Even if you are not scheduled to be first, be ready just in case.

3. **Be prepared to discuss the author's work from a critical standpoint.** Know what you agree or disagree with or are puzzled by. Admit that you don't understand something; others may be in the same situation. Insight and understanding will develop through discussion.

4. **Be aware of time limitations.** If you are assigned to be the main spokesperson, your preparation will be critical. If the meeting is 50 minutes long, you may be expected to speak for five to ten minutes—to present the main ideas derived from the assigned reading and to identify some of the questions that came about after considering what the author(s) had to say. Don't plan to say too much or go into too much detail. As the one assigned to get the discussion started, you should identify the high points, raise some questions, and hope that others will jump in with their thoughts and questions. On the other hand, you may have only two or three minutes to summarize your initial reaction to the reading. Know in advance how much time is allotted for you to speak. Practise speaking for that long, either to yourself or—better—to someone else who can be both a timekeeper and a critic. Whether you have a little or a lot of time to speak, it will never be enough to present everything the author discusses; that isn't the purpose of discussion groups. Following are some ways you can prepare to summarize your interpretation of the author's work.

The topic

Most assignments for discussion groups, seminars, and tutorials relate to a reading assignment, idea, or quotation that you are asked to think about and be ready to discuss. Help the thinking process along by systematically writing down your thoughts and then reorganizing them into a coherent whole. In itself, the act of writing will help you to think.

A reading

First, scan the assigned material quickly to get a feel for the general points made, the types of research data and methods of analysis used, and the conclusions drawn. If the material is from a journal, there may be an abstract. If so, read it, but be aware that the author's abstract may not convey the information you need to summarize the work.

Next, read the whole assigned reading with care, making notes of the major points as you go. It's essential to grasp the main lines of the argument before you begin reflecting on what you have read. Not all questions may be answered by the author, so be prepared to pose those questions in the group meeting.

You'll find that you can participate much more freely if you have prepared some short notes to jog your memory. But keep them brief: lengthy notes will tempt you simply to read out what you have written. Sometimes it's useful to write down a short quotation too, if you think it may be appropriate to cite in the discussion.

An idea

If you are asked to discuss an idea rather than a specific piece of writing, it will probably be presented in the form of a quotation or a brief statement. Such assignments can be more difficult to prepare, but there are some steps you can take that should help:

1. **Think about the context.** In the case of a quotation, try to find out more about the source from which it was taken. If the source is a book or journal in the library's collection, examine it quickly to determine the context of the quotation. Even if you decide that the quotation can be considered without reference to its source, you will certainly have to consider the context of the course in question (see point 3 below).

2. **Think about the contents.** Is there one sentence or several? Is there one idea, or two, or more? If there are several sentences and ideas, identify the main point first; then look at the remaining points in relation to it. What is the author saying? Is the point clear, or is there a subtheme that is not obvious at first glance? Does the author seem to be working from an assumption that you find questionable? Write out your understanding of the author's main point.

3. **Think about the author's statement in relation to the course.** Is there an obvious connection to the readings assigned to support that week's lecture(s), earlier lecture material, or class discussion? There may be a link to material examined several weeks earlier. Think about the sweep of material covered in the course to date. Is there a summarizing quality to the quotation? Does it grasp some essential point that the instructor may be aiming at?

4. **Try writing a one-page summation of your understanding of the quotation and your responses to it.** In contrast to an abstract, which demands objectivity, this exercise includes a subjective element: not only your understanding of the quotation itself, but your exploration of your response. Your summary is a combination of statement of fact and personal reflection. From this exercise will come more questions, which in turn will trigger further thought(s).

In class

Participants likely will sit in a circle, perhaps around a table. On paper, jot down the points made by others in the group—their conclusions and their questions. Try not to become totally immersed in note-taking, though: keep your head raised as much as possible, for two reasons. First, it will help you to see people's faces and/or hear their inflections, both of which can be crucial in conveying meaning. Second, you'll find it easier to participate if you are focusing on the others in the group rather than your notes. Looking at people as you talk allows you to see if they are listening to you. If you notice that someone is "turned off," you might try asking that person a question. Above all, speak clearly so that the other participants can hear what you have to say— what you say does matter.

Working on Group Assignments

Being able to work effectively in groups to produce a research report or other group assignment is a skill that your instructors (and future employers) value highly. Yes, group work can be stressful; however, when your group works well together, the benefits can include increased productivity and performance, enhanced skills development, and greater self-awareness.[1] Each of these benefits (often referred to as "soft" skills) is important during your academic career, invaluable when you enter the workforce, and generally essential throughout life.

To function successfully in small groups, each student needs to

- communicate effectively (including using or developing their interpersonal skills),
- participate willingly and contribute to a healthy group climate, and
- take responsibility for accomplishing their tasks.

Communicating effectively within a group can be challenging because both intellectual and emotional aspects are involved. You might feel somewhat vulnerable in explaining your own ideas to a group (especially early in a term); how carefully others listen to you (and you, to them) matters. Active, tolerant listening is important (see Chapter 3), and asking questions to clarify others' ideas and avoid misinterpretations is vital. Being able to express your feelings in an open but non-threatening way (which means, among other things, paying attention to your body language and tone of voice), and responding empathetically rather than reactively to other people and what they say, are communication skills that can be learned and practised.

No team or group is dependent on the skills of just one person. How well group members collaborate to complete the group assignment is a reflection of the skills each member brings to the group. For example, if you are able to reflect on how well (or not) your group's activities and interactions are going and, if you sense tensions are building, are able to initiate (rather than avoid) the often difficult conversations about group dynamics or processes, you will make an immense contribution to the success of your group.[2] And, if everything is going well, then your encouragement of the group members will be valuable as well.

Table 8.1 identifies key skills that help members develop a healthy group climate and promote effective group work. Often it takes a deliberate effort to

Table 8.1 Skills That Help Members Develop a Healthy Group Climate

Personal Skills	Skills Relative to Other Group Members
Trust and self-disclosure	Mutual trust (honesty)
Active and tolerant listening	Open; receptive to new ideas, different opinions
Communication skills	Respect for others' contributions
Flexibility	Helping others to master content
Accountability	Giving and receiving constructive feedback, offering alternatives
Participation (individual)	Participation (collective)
Patience	Collaborators, not competitors
Motivation and commitment	Awareness of body language, tone of voice
Keeping deadlines	Reflection on group activities and interactions; managing disagreements

Source: After: University of Waterloo, Centre for Teaching Excellence. Teamwork Skills: Being an Effective Group Member. Retrieved from https://uwaterloo.ca/centre-for-teaching-excellence/teaching-resources/teaching-tips/tips-students/being-part-team/teamwork-skills-being-effective-group-member. See also University of Southern California. (2018, 6 July). Organizing Your Social Sciences Research Paper: How to Manage Group Projects. Retrieved from https://libguides.usc.edu/writingguide.

cultivate these skills, and group cohesiveness (which leads to a healthy group climate) is an ongoing process. If each member strives to build and use these skills, group success should follow. Everyone turning up and staying until the end of meetings helps, too!

Successful group work is achieved through effective organization and management of all the tasks required. One of the planning tools groups can use to help organize and monitor the timing and sequencing of tasks that comprise their project is a Gantt chart (Figure 8.1). Developed by mechanical engineer Henry Gantt in the 1910s, the chart displays a time scale on the horizontal axis and rows of bars on the vertical axis that show the beginning and ending dates of individual tasks in the project, enabling group members to schedule the project tasks and monitor the group's progress. Today the Gantt chart and others like it may be prepared manually or by using computer software.[3]

To plan a group project using a Gantt chart, you can follow these steps:

1. **Identify and list all the significant project activities that need to be completed** (e.g., identifying the field site, searching the literature). For each task, show the earliest start date, how long you estimate it will take to complete, the team member(s) who will be responsible for each task, and any resources required. Note that the timing of some of your tasks may depend on other activities being completed first (sequential tasks), while other (parallel) tasks may be done at any time. Initially, it can be difficult to estimate accurately the durations of various tasks; often, doubling your estimate works best! Table 8.2 shows what a work breakdown could look like.

2. **Plot each of the tasks onto the graph (paper).** Starting at the earliest possible date, draw each task as a bar, where the length of the bar represents the estimated duration of each task. The left end of the bar represents the expected start date of your project and the right end marks the expected completion date. Above the bars, identify the time taken to complete each task (e.g., specify the number of days and place in parentheses). Specify a reasonable number of tasks (15 to 20 maximum) so you can fit your chart onto a single page. If you have a more complex project, you can split it into main and subtasks, and complete an overall Gantt chart for the main tasks and separate charts for the subtasks. Don't worry about scheduling each task yet, and don't be surprised if the first draft of your diagram looks untidy.

Specify project title here

Task	September 3 6 9 12 15 18 21 24 27 30	October 3 6 9 12 15 18 21 24 27 30	November 2 5 8 11 14 17 20 23 26 29 …
1. discuss project and its objectives			
2. site selection; field verification			
3. identify and obtain equipment			
4. conduct literature review			
5. collect data			
6. progress report			
7. analyze data			
8. prepare and present final report			

Figure 8.1 A simple example of a Gantt chart

Note: Each inverted triangle represents a milestone in the project.

Table 8.2 Work breakdown (selected elements only)

Task description	Possible start	Time estimate[1]	Who is responsible	Type/ dependent on[2]	Resources
1. discuss project and its objectives	week 1	2 days	MN, DK, EJ, AS	Sequential	
2. site selection; field verification	week 1	2 weeks	DK, EJ	Sequential/ task 1	
3. identify equipment needs; obtain equipment	week 2	1 week	DK, EJ	Parallel/tasks 1, 2	stream gauges, GPS . . .
4. conduct literature review	week 2	7 weeks	MN, DK, EJ, AS	Parallel/tasks 1, 2, 3, 6	
5. collect data	week 4	2 weeks	DK, EJ	Sequential/ tasks 1, 2, 3	
6. progress report due	week 5	1 week	MN, AS	Parallel/tasks 2–5	DVD projector
7. analyze data	week 6	3 weeks	MN, AS	Sequential/ task 5	statistical software package
8. write final report	week 8	4 weeks	MN, DK, EJ, AS	Parallel/1–7	

Notes:

1. Time estimates are illustrative only and are not recommended timeframes.

2. Whether tasks are sequential or parallel largely depends on context.

3. **Schedule the project activities.** On the Gantt chart, schedule the project tasks so that the sequential activities are carried out in the required sequence, ensuring that the parallel tasks do not start until the activities on which they depend have been completed. The timeframes for some tasks may overlap. Try to make the best use of the time each group member has available; remember that, ideally, each person should contribute an equal amount of time to the project, although not necessarily to each task. Ensure that you identify important milestones within the chart, such as when a progress report or presentation is due, and the final due date of the group project. Milestones

or checkpoints may be marked by a special symbol, often an up-side-down triangle.

It's advisable to include a little "slack time" in the schedule to allow for delays, including equipment and computer problems or even the failure of one or more group members to complete their tasks precisely on time. If a group member appears not to be putting an appropriate level of effort into the project, and if your efforts to contact or speak with the person are unsuccessful, consider talking with your instructor as soon as possible; he or she may take additional steps to help ensure that member's participation in the project. If the problem is not resolved, and if your instructor provides a peer-evaluation opportunity at the end of the project, having spoken about your concern previously will help the instructor to assess more accurately every member's contribution to the project.

4. **Monitor your progress.** As the project progresses, regularly update your chart by filling in the bars to a length proportional to how much work has been accomplished on each of the tasks. You can get a "quick read" of overall progress on your project if you draw a vertical line through the chart at the current date. The filled-in portion of the bar representing tasks that have been completed will lie to the left of the vertical line, as will the filled-in portion of the bar for tasks that are behind schedule. Current tasks will cross the line, and ahead-of-schedule tasks will have the filled-in portion of the bar to the right of the vertical line. Future tasks are positioned completely to the right of the line.

Grade determination for group work

Know how grades are to be determined. Is there to be a group grade (determined by an overall evaluation of the submitted work) or an individual grade (based on the specific section or sections you worked on by yourself)? If a group grade is to be assigned, all participants—from the dedicated ones to the "let others do the work for me" variety—will end up with the same mark. You will want to ensure that all members do their best and participate fully. Your group members may choose to sign a contract as a way of holding each person accountable to the group. Be sure to hold and attend regular meetings so each person can provide status updates.

Presentations

Many courses require that each student give a formal presentation on research they conducted during the term. Often, such presentations are initial explorations that you can rework prior to the final write-up and submission of your research project. You may even find that presenting your material in public triggers thoughts quite different from those generated by writing alone. Remember: there is the formal presentation you plan to give, the one you actually give, and the one your audience hears! Try to ensure that what you actually present conveys what you really want your audience to know. Careful preparation and good delivery are the keys.

Oral presentations can be daunting if you have no previous speaking experience. Keep in mind, first, that you are among friends, all of whom will have to make their own presentations; second, that experience in giving presentations can be invaluable in later life. Here are several pointers that will help you to structure your talk.

Preparing

1. **Know your topic.** An effective talk is always based on solid research. For your presentation to be believable, you must become the expert. So, within the time constraints, learn as much about your subject as possible. Having a good grasp of the topic will boost your self-confidence.

2. **Be aware of what your audience needs to know in order to understand what you are going to say.** If your audience does not already know the definitions, concepts, and processes that you will be referring to, identify them clearly. Start by giving the title for the talk; then pose a question, or at least define your aim. If appropriate, remind your audience that your topic relates to some issue, concept, or broader area of discussion that has previously been examined in class. If you are reporting on field work, be sure to identify the location and character of the area where the research was done.

3. **If you are to make an oral presentation, and are asked *not* to read your presentation, then do not write out everything you plan to say.** The following tips may help you speak more effectively:
   - Use numbered index cards or sheets of paper for your speaking notes.

- List the main points, using headings to group your material, along with supporting details or evidence, quotations, and any questions you wish to pose. Include all the main points you wish to make.
- Use visuals when possible to convey any detailed information rather than trying to read it out (see 6 and 7 below and p. 154).
- Number your points as a memory aid. This will help you avoid anxiety over what comes next. Even if you don't identify the numbers to your audience, the numbered points on your outline will make it easier for you to find your place when you glance at your notes after looking at your audience or a visual.
- Underline key words or points that you want to emphasize.
- Jot down any side-comments or jokes (*if* appropriate), in case your memory blanks at the key moment.
- Keep your notes simple. Don't have long run-on sentences. Use point form.
- Use a large font size.
- Don't put too much on one page or card. Leave a large space at the bottom. This will help you avoid looking down as you approach the foot of the page or card. Eye contact with your audience is important.
- Try not to be glued to your written material. Use it as a guide as you speak. Just reading will tend to produce a monotone presentation, which will hamper communication with your audience.

4. **If you are permitted to read your presentation, be sure to know how long you will take to read it.** Fine tune the material so you will be within the time limit. Print your text in larger than usual font size (for ease of reading) and leave a large margin at the foot of the page (so you won't need to look down as you approach the bottom of the page).

5. **You may be asked to provide a handout for each student.** The handout may include a bibliography or an outline of your presentation. If the latter, keep it brief, like a table of contents. Include your name, the course number or title, and the title of your presentation. As you speak, you may choose to use this outline to keep your place in your presentation, even as you refer to your more detailed notes. Even if you aren't asked to do so, it's a good idea to give other students a list of some important references that pertain to your topic; not only will it give them some useful information, but it will help to remind them of your contribution to the class.

6. **Practise giving your talk.** Know the time limit, time yourself, and test your notes. Are they adequate? Is there too much information, or not enough? Practise using your visuals as you speak so that you know when and how to use them and how long you can spend on each. Keep the specific purpose of each item in mind and be aware of the next point you wish to make. Whatever aids you use, remember that if you take longer than planned on one item, you will have to rush later ones. Be aware, too, that you will probably cover your material (and show visuals) faster in a "dry run" than during your actual presentation. If possible, practise with a friend who can give you feedback. Above all, the keys to preparing for any presentation are good thinking, good writing, and good preparation.

7. **Use visual aids when possible.** Visual aids can enliven and inform a class, but because they also can be distracting you should use them with care. For discussion on *posters*, see pages 156–9 for *computer-generated images*, see below; for *photographs*, see pages 152–3 and for *maps*, *tables*, *equations*, *diagrams*, and *graphs*, see Chapter 12. Before proceeding, here are four general points:

   • When possible, use a horizontal image. If you must use vertical visuals, make sure the screen is high enough for people at the back of the room. If the screen is too low, they won't be able to see the bottom of your image.

   • Keep all visuals simple, clear, and focused on a point; multi-purpose visuals may only confuse your audience.

   • Make sure the text you use in any visual (including maps and graphs) is large enough to be seen from the back of the room and be sure that the image is in focus.

   • If you have a lot of numbers to show, consider plotting them on a graph that will be easy for your audience to grasp.

Types of visual aids

You can employ several different types of visual aids to enhance your presentation. Here are a few comments about each of them.

Computer-generated images

Many lecture and seminar rooms are equipped for effective use of PowerPoint or similar software: you just insert your memory card or hook up your laptop to project your material onto a screen.

Computer-generated images can be combinations of slides of places, text, graphs, and maps. Because they can be stored easily on your laptop or other memory devices, they are readily transportable. If you are not experienced with the relevant program or equipment, you might end up wasting some of your presentation time while you figure out the technology. If a course is available on presentation software or hardware, take it, and apply what you learn. With practice, you will find it is possible to generate useful images and use them effectively. As you prepare your material, consider the following guidelines.

- Be consistent in the styles you use for lettering, formatting, and colours.
- Use a plain background for all of the images. Don't overuse colours (e.g., different colours for each slide). White lettering on blue can be effective. Avoid using yellow and orange for words because they are hard to read, but they may be used to show a distributional pattern on a map.
- Don't use several colours on an image unless there is a clear and under-standable reason to do so.
- Choose a simple, clean font that can be read easily from the back of the room. Sans serif fonts work best for onscreen presentation material such as overheads and PowerPoint slides.
- Use a type size that can be read with ease from the back of the room. You may need to try several sizes before identifying the best choice for your purpose.
- Don't overload any one slide with too many words. Use point form for succinct statements. Avoid embellishments. Don't include anything that isn't essential. Normally, each slide should make one point, or two or three (bulleted) related points.
- If you show a quotation, be sure to include quotation marks and iden-tify the source. Given space limitations, you may list only the author's name, but be prepared to give the full citation after your presentation, if called upon to do so.
- Keep graphs, tables, and maps as simple as possible. Don't overload them with too much data.
- Finally, don't be seduced into using only the ready-made templates on PowerPoint. Think differently. Know what *you* want to show, why, and how you want it to appear. Format your own slides—then you can be sure that you will have what you want.

Blackboards and whiteboards

This most basic of tools can be used effectively when you are giving an in-class presentation. When you use a black—or white—board, if possible, put some of the material on it before the class meeting: you don't want to spend too much time with your back to the audience. When eliciting suggestions from others in the class, write their comments in point form on the board. Doing so may assist later discussions, but you may want to have a designated assistant do the actual writing for you. (Make sure you use dry-erase markers on whiteboards!)

Overhead projection

When PowerPoint is not available, an overhead projector is an alternative. Your illustrative material can be copied onto transparency film using either a computer and printer or a photocopier. Overheads are clearer than work done on a blackboard, especially in large rooms; they can be prepared in advance; they can be written on (using special pens) during your talk; they can be partially covered (to hide something in order to highlight one piece of information) and moved on the screen as need be; and, because they are ready to use, the images on the screen can be changed very quickly. Before the presentation, stack your images in the order you plan to show them and know which side to place on the machine. You can write (with non-permanent markers) on the plastic used for overheads, which may be useful for summarizing points made by you or others. (This is especially good if you are allergic to chalk dust!)

Images and photographs

Images and photographs of scenes, people, or equipment may be useful too—but only if they clearly show what you need them to show! All too often, people who take photos see something in them that others do not. If you are unsure about the effectiveness of your images and photos, show them to classmates before the presentation and have them tell you what they see; their answers may not be what you expect. In that case, consider using different images or photos. If you store them on memory stick, check to see that they are in the order you wish to project them (using the projection equipment available to you in the classroom). *Before* class, check your files so that during your talk you are not caught off guard by an image that is oriented incorrectly or is out of order.

Videos

You may be permitted to show a pertinent video or YouTube clip to a discussion group or class. A short section of a video may be all you need show in order to make your point. Check with the appropriate library staff about any copyright limitations that might preclude you from using a video in a classroom setting. If you want to show a YouTube clip, be sure that your classroom is equipped with WiFi and have the clip prepped and fully loaded before you begin your presentation.

Presenting

1. **Dress comfortably (but not sloppily).** Be wary of trying something new for the occasion: the day you give a presentation may not be the best time to wear a tie if you aren't accustomed to one, or to try out new shoes that don't quite fit.
2. **Be on time.** If you arrive at the last minute, you may find that another student is absent and the schedule has been changed to slot you first. If you plan to use equipment, set it up and make sure it is functioning properly before the session begins.
3. **Start by identifying what you are going to do.** Tell your audience what your topic is, and briefly outline how you plan to present it. If your time limit is very short, don't give an outline—just present the essential information.
4. **Keep track of time.** Note the time on your watch (place it on the table where you can see it easily) or cellphone (with the sound turned off) when you start your presentation. Periodically check to see how much longer you have.
5. **Speak loudly, clearly, and with enthusiasm.** Everyone in the room needs to hear you. Pronounce your words distinctly. Try to speak with enthusiasm; a monotone can be deadly. Pace yourself. Don't speak too quickly.
6. **Never apologize.** Comments such as "I'm not really ready to give this talk," "I don't feel well today," or "I'm not very good with this machine"

will irritate any audience. They are there to learn about your topic, not the state of your health or preparations.

7. **Look at your audience.** Eye contact will help you see whether your audience understands what you're saying. Puzzled looks may be a sign that you need to repeat or rephrase a point to make it intelligible.

8. **Use your visual materials.** Having thought carefully in advance about how you intend to use your visuals, proceed in a way that will keep your audience focused on your essential message, not just on the supporting material. Consider the following tips:

   - Don't lose precious time during your presentation by turning on the laptop or projector. Have everything switched on and ready to go before you start.
   - Start with a PowerPoint slide that contains the title of the presentation, your name, and, if you think it is appropriate, the name of the course and the date.
   - Your second slide should give a short outline of your talk so the audience knows what to expect.
   - Don't overwhelm your audience with too many slides. A good rule of thumb is one slide per 40–60 seconds of your talk.
   - Avoid the temptation to speak too long about any one slide.
   - Don't obscure anyone's view by standing in front of the screen, and try not to turn your back on the audience. Presenting from either side of the screen usually works best.
   - A slide with several small images, or many numbers, must remain on the screen long enough for the viewers to grasp the details; otherwise you will lose people's attention, or at least leave them frustrated.
   - End with a slide containing a point-form summary or your conclusions.
   - Avoid fancy transitions between slides. The process of changing the images may become more interesting for the viewer than the content of the images or, for others, the process may simply be irritating. Either way, you could lose the attention of your audience. Keep it simple.

9. **Use humour.** A joke can help to reinforce a point, if it is relevant. Just don't turn your presentation into a stand-up routine—and never, ever tell a joke that includes racial or other slurs, or that may be offensive to others.

10. **Pose questions for your listeners as you speak.** Questions will help to keep them alert.

11. **Summarize your main points and then draw the presentation to a conclusion.** Your conclusion should bring the audience back to the main issue or question(s) raised during your talk. Try to end with a question (or a controversial observation) that will stimulate your audience to respond.

12. **Finish on time.** You don't want to be told by your instructor that your time is up when you still have information to share. Keep within the specified limits and don't expect to be granted additional time to finish.

13. **Be prepared for questions.** It's a good idea to repeat any question so that everyone can hear it before you respond. Keep your answer short and to the point. If you didn't hear or didn't understand a question, don't be afraid to request that the person repeat or clarify it. If you can't answer a question, you can always say you don't know and ask whether others in the group have any ideas; or you can refer the question to your instructor.

Tutorials

Although most of the above points also apply in tutorials, there is one fundamental difference between these small groups and large seminar or discussion groups. Whereas the latter usually have anywhere from 12 to 20 participants, a tutorial normally will involve only the instructor, you, and perhaps one or two other students. The intimacy of such a small group means you cannot escape behind someone else—you simply must be prepared. The structure of tutorials varies from instructor to instructor, but you always will have to read carefully and be prepared to discuss your reading. Make sure you keep your reading notes throughout the term, since you may have to write a summary paper, usually in the form of a literary review, as part of the tutorial requirement.

Giving a Paper at a Conference

Upper-level undergraduates and, more often, graduate students may be invited to give papers at conferences, sometimes with a professor as co-author. Many of the comments in this chapter apply to conference presentations as well as class work. Rehearse thoroughly, speak in a structured but freestyle manner (if possible, don't read your paper word for word), enunciate clearly, speak directly to the audience, keep within the allotted time—and be ready for questions!

Posters

A poster is a self-contained visual display that generally uses a mix of narrative and visuals (e.g., maps, tables, graphs, and pictures) to convey information. In some courses posters may be required to display findings from a field project or as part of a senior undergraduate project, but they can be useful in other situations too, including labs, seminars, and departmental open houses. In addition, posters are used frequently at professional meetings, where instead of giving papers, participants may stand beside their posters and answer questions from other conference participants.

The dimensions of the poster may be determined for you, either by your instructor or by the size of available display boards. Some instructors will have you use the dimensions required by learned societies, e.g., for the Association of American Geographers (AAG), 1.2 metres by 2.4 metres (about 4 feet by 8 feet). Creating an effective poster—one that is unified and coherent—requires careful planning. Here are some pointers.

Basic elements to include
- Subject title
- Author(s) and, if needed, affiliation
- Textual material: statement of problem, research methods and data used, evidence and results, conclusion
- Visual material: maps, graphs, tables, photos, as required
- Short list of pertinent references
- Acknowledgements, if appropriate

"Viewability" and "catchability"
- The title of your poster should be in print large enough to catch someone's eye from at least 4 metres (about 13 feet) away.
- Other material should be legible from a distance of about 1.2 to 1.5 metres (4 to 5 feet); 18-point type is the absolute minimum size (used for captions under graphics, for instance). Also, remember that text printed all in upper-case letters is hard to read.
- Related to "viewability" is "catchability": your poster needs to *catch* the attention of potential readers. Good overall design is essential. Vibrant

colours can be effective in attracting attention, but to keep the reader's attention they should be used selectively.

Textual material

- Be concise. Editing—and re-editing—are required to make a point with brevity and clarity.
- If possible, use point form rather than paragraphs of text. Constantly ask yourself whether the textual material you want to present is essential; if the answer is no, delete it. Your final word count should be between 250 and 450, with the lower limit likely if there are several visuals.
- If you have information that you believe is essential to your case but is too detailed to include on the poster, prepare a handout for people who want to know more. Bear in mind, though, that if the assignment was to prepare a poster, with no addenda, your instructor may not consider this "extra" material when grading your work.
- Experience has shown that most readers will start with the title, glance at your statement of problem, and then read your conclusions. Only if you have captured their interest will they consider the rest of your material. Keep this tendency in mind as you decide on the poster's title and write your conclusion.

Visual material

- Include only those visuals that directly inform readers about your project. Don't include tangential illustrations just because they are "nice."
- Keep your visuals as clean and simple as possible, so that readers grasp them quickly.
- If you must use multi-purpose visuals, ensure that your graphic selections are clear and distinct, so that readers can understand the essential information easily.
- Consider presenting your data on a graph or map rather than in a table.
- Ask yourself whether the visuals convey essential information. Have you chosen the best type of graph? Are the patterns on maps and graphs clear and readily understood? Presenting different sorts of information in different forms will make it clear that they are discrete. If in doubt, make separate visuals.

Layout

- If you have sufficient room, mark off a space on the floor or on a table top that is the same size as your poster. Having printed off your text (minimum size of 24 point for text in the body of your poster), identified the size of your poster title, and using mock-ups of your image files, lay your text and images in place on the floor or table—how does it look? What changes do you need to make to present your message clearly? Ask a friend to look at it—do they "get it"? If you don't have a large enough space, you can use a computer to do the layout or sketch a small poster to scale or use graph paper—cut proportionally to the dimensions of the poster board—and small pieces of paper (representing your text and visuals) to plan the layout of your poster.
- Identify everything that you wish to include (text and visuals). Regardless of your medium, place the elements of your poster in various arrangements to see what works best. Keep the figures, tables, and text blocks balanced (see Figure 8.2).
- Place your explanatory text blocks close to the pertinent visuals.
- To help your readers move easily from one section to the next in a logical manner, use columns and rows, with sequential numbers or letters as guides. You also could use arrows or pointing hands.
- Don't overload your poster—aim to leave about 30 to 40 per cent of the poster area without text and images. If you have too much material, edit again. Aim to make your presentation increasingly more precise, especially the textual material. Edit and rewrite until the message of your text is absolutely clear, using as few words and, consequently, as little space as possible. Accept that posters cannot convey as much information as written essays or oral presentations.
- Leave additional blank space as a frame around sections you want to highlight.
- Lastly, before you finalize the poster, check to see that your visual materials are legible from at least 1.2 metres (4 feet) away.
- If all your materials (text, photos, graphs, and maps) are in digital form, or can be converted to it, you may be able to assemble your poster on a desktop computer using an illustration program such as Adobe Illustrator, CorelDRAW, or a free, open-source program such as OpenOffice Draw. Access to a large-format printer (either in your department or at a printshop) will permit you to print your work on a single large sheet.

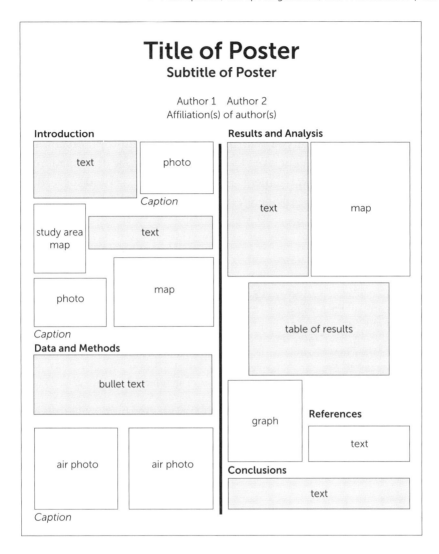

Figure 8.2   Sample layout

Caring for your poster

- Posters can be awkward to carry, especially if you have to walk any distance through rain or snow. Consider laminating your poster. Check with your department's technician to see whether you can have this done "in house" (undoubtedly for a fee); if not, you can get it done commercially. If all else fails, a cardboard tube will help protect your poster.
- Go to the session prepared: take your own pins and tape!

Chapter Summary

Course instructors enjoy seeing each of you gain the insight and understanding that comes from active participation in class discussions, seminars, and the like. As you take part in and learn to contribute in meaningful ways to group assignments and presentations, you will develop a variety of important skills that will serve you well in the future. Teamwork, organizational strengths, task management, even leadership skills can be developed through participation in group work. There are many tools to learn and suggestions to apply; your classrooms provide great opportunities to practise and become more proficient in their use.

Notes

1. "Organizing Your Social Sciences Research Paper: How to Manage Group Projects," University of Southern California, July 6, 2018, https://libguides.usc.edu/writingguide.
2. "Teamwork Skills: Being an Effective Group Member," University of Waterloo, Centre for Teaching Excellence, https://uwaterloo.ca/centre-for-teaching-excellence/teaching-resources/teaching-tips/tips-students/being-part-team/teamwork-skills-being-effective-group-member. See also "Organizing Your Social Sciences Research Paper: How to Manage Group Projects," University of Southern California, July 6, 2018, https://libguides.usc.edu/writingguide.
3. There are many software programs for project management available online today; many of them have free versions that would be suitable for use with group projects in geography, sustainability studies, and environmental sciences.

9 Writing a Lab Report

In this chapter, we examine
- the essentials when you write a lab report; and
- style issues when preparing lab reports.

Introduction

Laboratory exercises have several purposes, but the most important is the "hands-on" working through of a problem, often using equipment or materials that cannot be used readily in the lecture room or at home. Whatever the specific content and purpose of the exercise, the overall goal is to clarify, amplify, and apply basic concepts, principles, theories, processes, and research methods in the particular field under consideration. Because labs generally work as building blocks, providing detailed insights into the subjects discussed in lectures and assigned readings, it's important that you complete the exercises systematically, in the order indicated by your instructor. See Appendix I for a list of pertinent weights, measures, and notation (pp. 330–1). For advice on taking lab exams, see page 181.

Lab Books and Lab Assignment Sheets

While some instructors give individual assignments for each lab, one by one, others will require you to buy a lab book. If you have a book, look through it to see what is coming later in the course; knowing what lies ahead can sometimes help you handle earlier assignments. In either case, before you begin any lab assignment, be sure you have read the required course material for that day and have thought about the relevant lectures. Whether or not you have a lab book, the following information will help you to complete your lab reports.

Purpose and reader

Because your lab report will be read either by your course instructor or a teaching assistant (TA), you can assume that he or she is familiar with scientific terms; you may not have to define or explain them—unless you are specifically told to do so as part of the assignment. You can assume also that your reader will be on the lookout for any weaknesses in methodology or analysis and any omissions of important data. Usually you will be expected to give details of your calculations, but even when asked to provide just the results of your calculations, you should include any experimental uncertainty that might affect them.

Objectivity

Objectivity is critical in lab work. You must never allow your preconceived opinions or biases, or even expectations, to get in the way of the facts; otherwise you may, perhaps unwittingly, distort the findings. You must follow through with the experiment or exercise as objectively as possible and present the results in such a way that anyone who reads your report or attempts to duplicate your procedure would be likely to reach the same conclusions that you did.

Recording findings

All lab assignments involve making and recording observations (perhaps during an experiment) or measurements (reading a contour map, considering the application of an equation, determining grain size, measuring rates of erosion in a wave tank, etc.). Some assignments may require a numerical response. Others will call for words—perhaps nothing more than a simple "yes" or "no," "true" or "false." In other cases there may be fill-in questions, with space for only one or two words. Although you may be asked to write a little more, in general a precise, succinct summary statement or a point-form response will be all that you have time (or space) for. If a space is provided for your answer, make sure your writing is neither so small nor so large as to either "undersell" or "overkill"! In summary, read the question or direction and then consider your observation or response with care, answering in as few words as possible.

Format

Because the information in scientific reports must be easy for the reader to find and assess, it should be grouped into separate sections, each with a heading. One of the differences between writing lab reports and writing essays is that in a report you should use headings and subheadings whenever possible, as well as graphs, tables, and diagrams. Most lab reports follow a standard order:

1. Title Page
2. Abstract (*or* Summary)
3. Introduction (*or* Statement of Purpose *or* Objective)
4. Experimental Design (*or* Methodology)
    (a) Materials
    (b) Method
5. Results
6. Discussion (*or* Analysis)
7. Conclusion
8. Attachments (*or* Appendices)
9. References

Some instructors will prefer that you identify *Materials* within the *Method* section, not separately. The guidelines presented below assume that the lab work to be reported is based on an experiment.

Title page

The title page is the first page of your report. It should include the title of the experiment, the date it was performed, your name, and the date of submission; for practical purposes it also should include the name and number of the course, the lab section number, and the name of your instructor and, if applicable, your TA. The title should be brief but informative, clearly indicating the subject and scope of your experiment. Avoid meaningless phrases, such as "A study of . . ." or "Observations on . . ."; simply state *what* it is that you are studying.

Abstract

Also known as a *Summary*, the *Abstract* appears on a separate page following the title page. It is a brief summary of the purpose of the experiment, as well as the method, results, and conclusion. For a simple experiment, your abstract may only be a few lines (75–100 words); even for a complex one, you should keep it to about 200 words. (Note: some instructors may not require you to write an abstract.)

Introduction

Sometimes called the *Statement of Purpose* or, simply, *Objective*, this introductory section should include a succinct yet complete statement of your purpose. If, as is often the case, the purpose is to test a hypothesis arising from a specific problem, you should state, clearly and explicitly, the nature of both the problem and the hypothesis. Your introduction should include the theory underlying the experiment and, in general terms, any pertinent background data or equations. Although you may refer to papers relevant to the experiment, it's best to avoid quoting extensively.

Experimental design (or methodology)

This section often is divided into two parts: *Materials* and *Method.* However, some departments prefer that students, especially in first- and second-year courses, omit the subheadings. Certainly a single section is adequate when the description of materials used is short. The following pointers apply in either case.

Materials

First, list the materials and equipment used and explain how the experiment is set up. If different arrangements of equipment are required, give a full list of the equipment in this section, and then in the *Method* subsection describe each separate arrangement before you describe the respective tests. A simple diagram will help the reader visualize the arrangement of equipment. If the diagram is too large for a regular page, you can draw it on an appropriately numbered and labelled attachment at the back of the report, as an attachment (or appendix), and refer to it within the body of the report. Some departments require that you specify the source or supplier of any reagents you have used. Such information should be included in this section: for example, "Hydrochloric acid was obtained from BDH Chemicals."

Method

Describe the procedures step-by-step, in the order in which you actually performed them. You should include enough detail that others will have no difficulty in repeating the experiment—and, you hope, in achieving the same results. (Of course, if you are following instructions in a lab manual, you may not need to copy them out word for word; simply refer to the instructions and give details of any deviation.) When a certain procedure is long, complicated, or not necessary to a full understanding of the experiment, you may describe it in a labelled appendix.

Although your description of the experimental method should be concise, it must include all the essential details, so that readers will know exactly what materials to use, when to use them, and what controls to apply if they try to perform the experiment themselves. If you heated a test tube, for example, report at what temperature it was heated and for how long; if you performed a chromatography or other process at a faster or slower rate than usual, state the rate; or, if you used a piece of equipment that had to be set to particular specifications, identify the calibration. You should be consistent also in the way you identify your material (degree of detail, units of measurement, and so on). Identify what statistical tests you have used to analyze your data.

If you have undertaken a number of tests, statistical or otherwise, begin with a short summary statement listing and numbering the tests so that the reader will be prepared for the series. To avoid confusion, describe the tests in the same order in which you have listed them, giving them the same numbers and subheadings.

Experiments always are described in the past tense. When you want to give instructions rather than a description of your method, use the imperative: e.g., "Cut off the top 20 cm of the soil sample."

Scientists writing for scientific journals are divided on whether you should use the active or passive voice. Most prefer the passive voice ("The water flow was started," rather than "I started the water flow") because they believe that its impersonal quality helps to maintain the detached, clinical tone appropriate to a scientific report. Nevertheless, some scientists use—and accept in students' work—the active voice ("I started the water flow") because it is clearer and less likely to lead to awkward, convoluted sentences. Ask your instructor about the department's preferences. Whichever voice you use, remember to strive for *clarity*, *objectivity*, and *consistency*.

Results

This is where you report your observations, data, and calculations. Find out from your instructor whether you are expected to give the details of your calculations or only the results they produced (calculations are sometimes placed in an appendix). In either case, you should pay special attention to the units of any quantities: to omit or misuse them is a serious scientific mistake. Taking care to include all units will also reveal mistakes in your calculations that might otherwise go undetected. If your units don't cancel properly to yield the result you expected, you will know that you have made an error.

Where possible, you should also make sure that the calculated values you report include the "uncertainty" in each of them. For example, you might report that the calculated volume of a hollow sphere is 23.45 ± 0.05 cc (where ± 0.05 is the uncertainty in the volume measurement). Whenever you report any calculations or measurements, check to see whether you need to include the standard deviation, the standard error of the mean, or the coefficient of variation.

The format of the *Results* section depends on the type of experiment performed. Whenever possible, use a computer-based spreadsheet with a quick and efficient graphing capability to summarize your findings. A graph (or chart) usually is preferable to a table because it will have more visual impact, but if you have made several measurements it probably is best to report them in a table. When devising a graph without the aid of a computer, be sure to remember the following steps:

- Use properly ruled graph paper.
- Use a scale that will allow you to distribute your data points as widely as possible on the page.
- Put the independent variable (the one you have manipulated) on the horizontal axis, and the dependent variable (the one you measured) on the vertical axis.
- Make the vertical axis about three-quarters the length of the horizontal axis.

And, whether or not you use a computer, remember these three important rules:

- Put error bars (±) on data points, where possible.
- Label the axes, including the units used, so that the reader knows exactly what you have plotted on the graph.
- Title the graph and label it (for example, "Figure 1"), so that you can refer to it by number in your report.

Discussion (or analysis)

This is the part of the lab report that allows you the greatest freedom because your purpose is to analyze and interpret the test results and to comment on their significance. You want to show how the test produced its outcome, whether expected or unexpected, and to discuss those elements that influenced the results. In determining what details to include, you might try to answer the following questions:

- Do the results reflect the objective of the experiment?
- Did the experimental method help you to accomplish that objective?
- Do the results you obtained agree with previous results as reported in the literature on the subject? If not, how can you account for the discrepancy between accepted values and those you have found experimentally? What (if anything) went wrong during your experiment, and why? What was the source of any error?
- Could the results have another explanation?

For a good discussion, remember to think critically not only about your own work but about how it relates to previous work.

Conclusion

This is a simple statement of the experiment's conclusion. You don't necessarily need a separate section; the conclusion can also appear as a short summary at the end of the *Discussion* section. Although you may include a summary table or other graphic illustration if it will clarify the conclusion, you should not introduce new information into your conclusion—i.e., do not include data that are not identified within the body of the report.

Attachments (or appendices)

Numbered and titled attachments should include only detailed material that is too extensive to place within the body of the report, such as the diagram and detailed material noted above in the *Experimental Design* section, or extensive statistical analyses.

References

For most reports on work done in the lab, in one day's session, you may not have to include any references. Your instructor will be impressed, though, if you take the time to find and note one or two relevant references (including, perhaps, appropriate sections of the textbook). If the lab test takes several days to run, then you will have time to do a little extra research. You should list the sources of any information used in your report. If you use endnotes to cite some references or present a brief explanatory discussion, you will need to have a separate endnote section, preceding the list of references. If you need to acknowledge a number of sources, you may list them in separate categories, such as *Books* and *Journals*. Be sure to use the referencing style pertinent to your course of study (see Chapter 7). If in doubt, ask your instructor.

Report-Writing Style

Scientific reports, like essays, must be written with the reader in mind. Because your reader will be your instructor or TA, you don't need to define elementary terms or explain a method that would be taken for granted by anyone with scientific training. At the same time, you should avoid filling your report with technical jargon when non-technical language will suit just as well. The watchwords are *clarity* (because your thoughts need to be expressed clearly) and *precision* (because what you write needs to be accurate); you want to make it easy for the reader to understand exactly what you mean.

Although the basic rules are the same as for any other kind of writing, scientific reports do pose special problems. Here are a few words of advice.

Avoid using too many nouns as adjectives

Clusters of nouns used as adjectives can create cumbersome phrases:

| *orig.* | high acid mine drainage sulfate concentrations |
| *rev.* | high concentrations of sulfate in acid mine drainage |

| *orig.* | apparatus construction |
| *rev.* | construction of apparatus |

Of course, some nouns are frequently—and acceptably—used as adjectives: *rock* glacier, *reaction* time, *block* stream, *sheet* wash, *stream* channel, *ice* sheet, *loess* plain. Your ear is probably the best judge of what is awkward and what is not.

Avoid using too many abstract nouns

Whenever possible, choose a verb rather than an abstract noun:

orig.	The <u>addition</u> of acid and subsequent <u>agitation</u> of the solution resulted in the <u>formation</u> of crystals.
rev.	When acid <u>was added</u> and the solution <u>shaken</u>, crystals <u>formed</u>.
rev.	When I <u>added</u> acid to the solution and <u>shook</u> it, crystals <u>formed</u>.

Avoid vague qualifiers

As a scientist you must be exact. In particular, you should avoid words such as *quite*, *very*, *fairly*, *some*, or *many* when you can use a more exact term. *Relatively* is especially dangerous unless you are actually relating two or more things.

Avoid unnecessary passive constructions

Although you may prefer to use passive verbs for describing methods and results, you should try to use active verbs in your *Introduction*, *Discussion*, and *Conclusion* sections. Your sentences will be clearer and more direct:

| *orig.* | pH4 <u>is needed</u> for the enzyme. |
| *rev.* | The enzyme <u>needs</u> pH4. |

| *orig.* | It <u>was reported</u> by K.Q. Truong . . . |
| *rev.* | K.Q. Truong <u>reported</u> . . . |

Avoid ambiguous pronouns

The pronoun *it* will cause confusion if the reader can't tell which noun it refers to:

> To germinate, the seed requires water. It must be warm.

Is it the seed or the water that must be warm? If there is any chance of ambiguity, you should repeat the pertinent noun:

> The <u>water</u> must be warm. (or) The <u>seed</u> must be warm.

Be especially careful that the pronoun *this* clearly refers to a specific noun:

> *orig.*   When removed from the water, the stalk lost its leaves. <u>This</u> occurred over eight hours.
>
> *rev.*   When removed from the water, the stalk lost its leaves. <u>This</u> <u>loss</u> occurred over eight hours.

Chapter Summary

An effective lab report will present more than the data you have derived through your lab work: through the clarity of your thinking and organized manner of writing, your lab report will demonstrate how well you understand the concepts and principles that the instructor intended you to examine through the experiment. Documenting your findings (both the expected and the observed results) and discussing their significance (why and how differences occurred) allows you to demonstrate your comprehension of the purpose of the experiment, to explain it, analyze it, interpret it, and come to a meaningful conclusion.

10 Writing Examinations

In this chapter, we examine

- points to consider while you prepare for an examination;
- things to help you during the examination; and
- different types of examinations.

Introduction

You may feel nervous before tests and exams. Knowing what to expect can help. This chapter offers advice on how to handle different types of written exams, including open-book and take-home exams, objective exams (notably multiple-choice), and lab exams.

Special Needs

If you learn you are to take a type of exam that is new to you, find out what it will entail and set aside time to practise. This suggestion is not far-fetched: some students have never written an essay exam before they get to college or university, while other students may never have taken an objective test. If you need help, seek it out—from your instructor or from the student support services—*well before* the exam.

If you have a documented medical reason to contact your college or university's student accessibility services centre (often named "disability" resource centres or services), then do so when you begin your studies or as soon as your condition is identified medically. When you follow its protocols, that centre serves as an intermediary between you and your instructor. Some centres provide forms for you to take to your instructor that identify the accommodations you require. If that is not the case at your college or university, always inform your instructor at the start of the term or semester. Don't wait until just before a scheduled exam because your request for special consideration may be refused.

Before the Exam

Review regularly

There are three equally important types of post-lecture reviews:

- the *immediate post-lecture review*, to get things organized in your mind;
- *periodic reviews,* to get the material and concepts embedded in your memory; and
- the *full-course review* to sharpen your memory just before the exam.

As you review, especially during the periodic and full-course reviews, don't remember just the important material, lecture by lecture (and all the readings and any other assignments), but relate all of that material to new information and insights subsequently gained. If you don't review regularly, at the end of the term or semester you'll be faced with relearning rather than remembering.

What should you do about material you have not yet mastered? While studying, try to pay attention to trouble spots: areas you don't feel you understand or know enough about. You can then concentrate on bothersome issues: if you have trouble with certain facts or concepts, draw upon course material you know well and seek to place the difficult material into a broader context. If your trouble is methodological (i.e., how an experiment was done or a result derived), work at the problem systematically, with reference to your lecture and lab notes. If you are stuck, seek help from the instructor or TA prior to the exam time. Make good use of any student meeting times your TA has available. Joining (or starting) a study group can also be an effective way to understand and review material.

Set memory triggers

As you review, write down in the margin key words or phrases that will trigger details in your mind (if you are reviewing typed notes, either print out a copy or use the "new comment" function to add comments into the file). The trigger might be a concept word that names or points to an important theory or definition, or a quantitative phrase such as "five reasons for soil degradation." Try creating an acronym or a nonsense sentence that will trigger an otherwise hard-to-remember set of facts (e.g., use the acronym HOMES for the Great Lakes—Huron, Ontario, Michigan, Erie, and Superior). Any method you use that will help you memorize numerous items will increase the effectiveness of your study habits.

Ask questions

Think of questions that will get to the heart of the material and cause you to examine the relations between various subjects or issues; then figure out how you would answer them. The Three-C approach (pp. 81–3) may be helpful. For example, reviewing the *components* of the subject could mean focusing on the main parts of an issue or on the definitions of major terms or theories. When reviewing *change* in the subject, you might ask yourself what elements caused that change directly or indirectly. To review *context* you might consider how certain aspects of the subject—issues, theories, actions, results—compare with others in the course. The Three-C approach forces you to look at the material from various perspectives.

The most useful review questions you can pose are not those that require you to recall facts, but those that force you to analyze, integrate, or evaluate information. Ask your instructor if old examinations are available to you, perhaps through the course website or in the library. If they are, take advantage of them: check the types of questions you might be asked and the kind of material that is typically covered. Be aware that new instructors may ask different types of questions than appear on previous exams.

Allow extra time

Where is the exam to be held? Give yourself plenty of time to get there. If travelling by car or public transit, allow for traffic problems. Always anticipate difficulties and allow yourself a good time margin.

Important items

Take extra pens and pencils, an eraser, some tissues, and, if permitted, a ruler, coloured pencils, and a calculator. Be sure to have your student ID card: it may be needed for admission to the exam room or to receive the exam paper.

If the exam is to take place in a computer lab, arrive early so you can ensure your computer is working. Reboot it and log in with your student ID to clear it of others' work or school profiles.

Writing an Essay Exam

Long-essay and short-answer exams

Listen to your instructor so you know in advance whether you are to write short-answer questions, one or more long essays, or a combination of the two. Both types of writing test your ability to demonstrate your knowledge and understanding of the course material, conceptual and theoretical issues, and methods. Short-answer questions demand less writing and more focused thinking because there is little space (or time) for giving illustrative examples. Longer essays will be more discursive, likely requiring a basic question or thesis statement and supporting evidence.

Read the exam

Don't start to write immediately. Take time to read the instructions and all the questions, and then devise a plan of action. A few minutes spent on thinking and organizing will produce better results than the same amount of time spent on writing a few more lines.

Apportion your time

Identify how many questions you must answer and whether you have any choice among questions. Subtract five minutes or so for the initial planning, and then divide the remaining time by the number of questions you must answer. Include in your apportionment the approximate time you will need to draw pertinent maps, diagrams, or graphs—but don't spend too much time on such illustrations unless they are critically important. If possible, allow for a little extra time at the end to reread and edit your work. If the exam instructions indicate that not all questions are of equal value, apportion your time accordingly (work on the most important ones first).

Choose your questions

Decide which questions you will answer, and in what order. Your answers don't have to be in the same order the questions appear on the exam—*but always be sure to write each question's number (from the question sheet) at the start of every answer*. Decide which question you can answer best. Even if the exam seems disastrous at first, you probably can find one question that looks manageable: that's the one to begin with. It will get you rolling and increase your confidence. Some think it's a good idea to place your best answer first, your worst answers in the middle, and your second-best answer at the end, in order to leave the reader on a high note, but if you think you will be rushed you should work from best to worst. That way you will be sure to get all the marks you can on your good answers, and you won't have to cut a good answer short at the end.

Keep calm

Keep calm; take 10 slow, deep breaths as a deliberate relaxation exercise. Try not to rush. Plan how you will proceed and then tackle things bit by bit. Computer and smart phone apps can help you—before the exam—learn how to battle stress and anxiety and help you improve your ability to focus.

Read each question carefully

As you turn to each question, read it again carefully and underline all the key words. The wording probably will suggest the number of parts your answer should have; be sure you don't overlook anything (a common mistake when people are nervous). Because the verb used in the question is usually a guide for the approach to take in your answer, it's especially important that you interpret the following terms correctly:

- **explain:** show the *hows* or *whys*;
- **describe:** identify the qualities that best explain or illustrate the issue;
- **evaluate:** measure or assess the relative worth, or merit, of something;
- **compare:** give both similarities and differences—even if the question doesn't say "compare and contrast";
- **outline:** state simply, without much development of each point (unless specifically asked);

- **discuss:** develop your points in an orderly way, considering contrary evidence or ideas;
- **define and discuss:** give the pertinent definition and then explore it by giving illustrative examples;
- **demonstrate:** state the issue and then provide evidence that supports the case or provides an understanding of a process. If pertinent, include formulae, diagrams, or other pertinent material.

Make notes

To start an exam question, jot down key ideas and information related to the topic in your answer book (perhaps at the back of the exam book, where your notes will be separate from your exam answers). These notes will spare you the worry of forgetting something by the time you begin writing. Next, arrange the points you want to use into a brief plan, using numbers to indicate their order (that way, if you change your mind, it will be easy to reorder them). At the close of the exam be sure to cross out these notes so that the evaluator won't think they are your actual answers.

Be direct

Get to the points quickly and illustrate them frequently. Use a direct approach. Don't worry about composing a graceful introduction: simply state the main points that you are going to discuss, and then get on with developing them. Be as clear as possible in your answers. For each main point give the kind of specific details that will prove you really know the material. General statements will show you are able to assimilate information, but they need examples to back them up.

Write legibly

Bad handwriting makes readers grumpy. When the marker has to struggle to decipher your ideas, you may get poorer results than you deserve. If for some special reason (such as a physical handicap) your writing is hard to read, ask whether you can make special arrangements to use a computer or, in special cases, a tape recorder (the accessibility services centre should facilitate such arrangements). If your writing is just plain bad, it's probably better to print. Some instructors will allow pencils; others will demand you use a pen.

Write on alternate lines

Writing on every other line may make your writing easier to read and will leave you space for changes and additions.

Keep to your time plan

Keep to your plan and don't skip any questions. Try to write something for each question rather than focusing just on the question that is best for you. If you find yourself running out of time on an answer, summarize the remaining points and go on to the next question. Leave a large space between questions so that you can go back and add more if you have time. If you write a new ending, remember to cross out the old one—neatly.

Reread your answers

No matter how tired or fed up you are, reread your answers at the end if there is time. Check especially for clarity of expression; try to get rid of confusing sentences and increase the logical connections between your ideas. Revisions that make answers easier to read are always worth the effort.

Check question numbers

Before handing in your exam, re-check that each of your answers starts with the number that correctly links it to the question you have addressed. An un-numbered answer may not be graded.

Writing an Open-Book Exam

If you are permitted to take your books into the exam room, be forewarned: don't fall into the trap of relying too heavily on them. Rifling through pages and looking things up may result in you not having time to write good answers. Use the books only to check information or for specific, hard-to-remember details. For instance, if the exam is on fluvial processes, you could check on detailed formulae; if in a political geography exam the issue is electoral studies, you may want to look up voting statistics. In other words, use the books to make sure your answers are precise and well illustrated. Never use them to replace studying and careful exam preparation.

Writing a Take-Home Exam

The allotted time for a take-home exam will be limited; perhaps one afternoon, or overnight. Plan accordingly and carefully: time for reviewing the questions; time for culling from your notes and pertinent source material; time for organizing your thoughts; time for writing; time for reviewing, rewriting, and making any needed corrections; and time for submitting your work before the deadline. If the time is short, charge ahead but leave time for rereading what you have written, so you can catch any errors. If the timeframe you are given is overnight, or even longer, build in time for eating, sleeping, and other breaks. Try to avoid working yourself into a frenzy. Plan, and proceed according to the plan, always with an eye on the clock.

As with other exams, you will be expected to demonstrate your command of the material. Don't look for fresh sources if time is very limited. Because you will have been doing your periodic reviews on a regular basis, use that knowledge to get the best result. Keep in mind that a take-home exam is intended to test your overall command of the course's concepts, methods, and subject matter. Your reader is less likely to be concerned with your specialized research than with evidence that you have understood and assimilated what you have learned.

The guidelines for a take-home exam are similar to those for a regular exam; the only difference is that you don't need to keep *such* a close eye on the clock. Be sure to follow this advice:

- Keep your introduction to each answer short and get to the point quickly.
- Organize your answer in a straightforward and obvious way, so that the reader easily sees your main ideas.
- Frequently use concrete examples to back up your points.
- Where possible, show the range of your knowledge of the course material by referring to a variety of sources, rather than constantly using the same ones.
- Demonstrate that you can analyze and evaluate material and not simply repeat information.
- If you are asked to acknowledge the sources of any quotations you use, be sure to jot them down as you go; you may not have time to do so at the end of the exam.
- You may be asked to provide a list of all the works you consulted while writing the exam. If so, attach a list of them to your exam.

Writing an Objective Test

Objective tests—whether true or false, or multiple-choice—are common in the sciences and social sciences. Be wary: some questions are designed to confuse students who aren't certain of the correct answers. Preparation for objective tests is the same as for other kinds. Here, though, it's especially important to pay attention to definitions and unexpected or confusing pieces of information, because they can so readily be adapted to make objective-test questions. Although there is no sure recipe for doing well on an objective test—other than knowing the course material completely and confidently—these suggestions may help you to do better:

What is the marking system?

If marks are based solely on the number of correct answers, pick an answer for every question even if you aren't sure it's the right one. For a true-false question you have a 50 per cent chance that it will be correct; and even for a multiple-choice question with four possible answers, you would get an average of 25 per cent right if you picked the answers blindfolded. On the other hand, if there is a penalty for wrong answers—if marks are deducted for errors—guess only when you are fairly sure you are right, or when you are able to rule out most of the possibilities. Don't make wild guesses.

Do the easy questions first

Go through the test at least twice. On the first round, skip over troublesome questions. Because the questions usually are of equal value, it's best to get all the marks you can on the ones you find easy. Tackle the more difficult questions on the next round.

Make your guesses educated ones

If you decide to guess, at least increase your chance of getting the answers right. Forget about intuition, hunches, lucky numbers, and so-called patterns of correct answers—the idea that if there have been two "A" answers in a row, the next one can't possibly be "A," or that if there hasn't been a "true" for a while, "true" must be a good guess. Many test-setters either don't worry about patterns at all or else deliberately mislead pattern-hunters by giving the right answer the same letter or number several times in a row.

Constructing good objective tests is a special skill that not all instructors have mastered. Often the questions they pose, though sound enough as questions, do not produce enough realistic alternatives for answers. In such cases the test-setter may resort to some less-realistic options, and if you keep your eyes open you can spot them. James F. Shepherd has suggested a number of tips that will increase your chances of making the right guess—that is, if you are quite sure you don't know the correct answer.[1] Drawing from his work, with some additions, consider the following:

- Weed out the answers you know are wrong, rather than looking for the right one. Placing a stroke through the first word or two of an obviously incorrect statement or question may help you eliminate options.
- If no obviously correct statement leaps out at you, rephrasing the possible statements as "true" or "false" may help you identify the correct answer.
- If two of the several statements seem to be correct, ask which one is less likely than the other.
- Avoid any terms you don't recognize. Don't be fooled by sophisticated terminology. An unfamiliar term may be a red herring, especially if it is close in sound to the correct one.
- Avoid extremes. Most often—but not always—the right answer lies in between. For example, suppose that the options are the numbers 800,000; 350,000; 275,000; and 15: the highest and lowest numbers are likely to be wrong.
- Avoid absolutes, especially on questions dealing with people. Few aspects of human life are as certain as is implied by such words as *everyone*, *all*, or *no one*; *always* or *invariably*; and *none* or *never*. Statements containing these words usually are false.
- Avoid distracters, i.e., look for essential information, not extraneous material.
- Avoid jokes or humorous statements and those that appear to be demeaning or insulting.
- Choose the best available answer, even if it is not indisputably true.
- Choose the long answer over the short (it's more likely to contain the detail needed to make it right) and the particular statement over the general (generalizations are usually too sweeping to be true).
- Don't automatically dismiss "all of the above" over individual answers. Test-setters know that students with a patchy knowledge of the course

material will often fasten on the one fact they know. Only those with a thorough knowledge will recognize that all the answers listed *may* be correct.

- Don't be afraid to skip a question and return to it later. The gap in time, and the successful handling of other questions, may trigger your memory.

Lab Exams

Lab exams usually focus on material directly related to lab work, although you may also need to draw upon material from lectures and assigned readings. This type of exam poses a particular issue for you to examine, for example the identification of a rock type, the composition of a particular soil sample, or a set-up for testing deposits in a water sample. Some lab exams are timed, notably those that are set up with several stations for you to visit. The signal for you to move from one station to the next may be a verbal command or, possibly, a bell. Whether you are at one station for the whole exam or at several, be aware of the time so you can keep on top of what you must do within the set time constraints.

When preparing for lab exams, pay special attention in your notes to diagrams and charts. You may be asked to respond to identification questions or to questions about how something functions. In some lab exams you will be expected to compare and contrast two or more items or processes. Do not rush! Take your time to read carefully the question(s) you are to answer or the problem(s) you are to solve. Then, knowing what is expected of you, tackle the matter with confidence. If your mind goes blank, try to refresh your memory by systematically working your way through the posed question or, if that does not work, pose your own questions related to the issue at hand.

Some Final Tips

Whatever the type of exam, always keep your eye on the clock so you know how much time remains. If you have time at the end of the exam, go back and reread the questions. One or two wrong answers caused by misreading can make a significant difference to your score. On the other hand, don't start second-guessing yourself and changing a lot of answers at the last minute. Studies have shown that when students make changes they are often wrong (your first answer often is the correct one). Stick to your initial decisions unless you know for certain you have made a mistake.

If you find that your anxiety about examinations is extreme and is impeding your ability to perform, it might be wise to seek help. Many campuses have improved their physical and mental health support facilities, including services such as counselling and student wellness centres, fitness opportunities, nutrition assistance, pet therapy days, and more. These types of services may be possible sources of assistance. Remember, though, that exams are intended to measure your learning in a course; they do not demonstrate anything about your worth as a person.

Chapter Summary

While you can target your studying to what seems most likely to be on an exam (e.g., by studying old exams and assessing what the professor emphasizes in class), and while you can practise answering the kinds of questions that you expect to appear on an exam, keeping up with your regular review of the course material throughout the term is the strategy that is most likely to ensure your success in writing exams. There are methods you can use to prepare and study for different types of exams and plans of action to employ while writing an exam, but the key to success involves taking good lecture notes, doing your assigned readings and deliberately taking time to review and study your course materials.

Note

1. James F. Shepherd, *College Study Skills*, 6th ed. (Boston: Houghton Mifflin, 1998) and *RSVP: The College Reading, Study, and Vocabulary Program*, 5th ed. (Boston: Houghton Mifflin, 1995).

11 Doing Field Work and Writing about It

In this chapter, we examine

- things to consider as you prepare to do field work;
- fundamentals for writing and using field notes;
- essential points about questionnaires; and
- basics for reporting your findings.

Introduction

In all environmental disciplines, the environment itself is a source of information. Doing field work is fundamentally important. Your focus will depend on your discipline and the nature of the course you are taking. For example, attention may be directed to the physical or biological properties and processes in a particular place or region; to the spatial patterns of human-made features or processes; to the interplay between human and natural processes; or to human understanding of a particular place and its people and the way they interact. These broad statements don't encompass all that you will do as you seek to make "sense of that vast panorama of fact and fiction, pattern and event, on the surface of the earth,"[1] but they are a general guide. The topics for investigation are diverse, and huge in number, but the information obtained by field work will provide you with primary data. It takes time to learn how to "read" and "understand" what you "see," thus the need for field courses in which you will learn a variety of techniques.

Two types of writing (with illustrations) are associated with field work: field notes (which may or may not be evaluated by the instructor) and assignments (which are submitted for evaluation). Following some pointers on preparing for field work, this chapter focuses on keeping a field notebook; making sketch maps, sketches, and photographs; keeping a field diary; constructing a questionnaire; and writing a formal field report based on analysis of your data.

Preparation

Statement of purpose

You will want to know what you are going to do, and so—likely with guidance from the instructor—you need to identify the purpose of the field trip and what is to happen. Reading and some initial map work may be required, and perhaps also some initial data collection and analysis, before you can develop a clear statement of purpose (unless one is provided for you) and what exactly you plan to do. Whether you are to study soil types or the crops farmers grow on different soil types, you will want to identify the parameters of your research design and the methodology to be used. Depending on what you learn as you prepare, you will know what you will have to take along on the trip, including extra clothes, food, and equipment.

Equipment

The basic items needed for most types of field work are a bound notebook (with both lined and graph paper), a clipboard (with a plastic cover in case of rain), several pens and pencils, paper clips, and a small, durable backpack or shoulder bag. Other items to take with you depend on the weather, the season, and the location where the field work is to be carried out: you might need a whistle, water bottle, boots or sturdy waterproof shoes, sunscreen and sunglasses (UV protected), first-aid kit, insect repellent, hat, raincoat or winter jacket, and so on.

A smart phone or tablet can be useful for recording data in the field, and a laptop is invaluable for recording and analyzing data immediately, either in the field or at home afterward. You also may need maps (e.g., topographical, soils, land-use), air photos if available, a multi-metre tape measure (usually one per group is enough), a calculator, and, if you don't have a computer with you, a ruler and a compass for constructing graphs. A handheld Global Positioning System (GPS) or directional compass (in certain types of terrain) is essential for certain types of field assignments. Depending on the instructor's directions, other special instruments (such as soil augers, wind gauges, thermometers, tree corers, trail counters, etc.) may be needed as well.

If you use a GPS, you will need an accurate sketch map to verify any digital analysis of your data that you may do at a later time. To use a GPS effectively when recording field data, you will need to know the location of set benchmarks, their coordinates and elevation. A topographical map can be used for ground truthing.

Safety

When doing any kind of field work it's wise to establish a "buddy" system; each set of buddies should have at least one loud whistle, in case of emergencies. If you expect to be away from a settlement for an extended period, you should give someone in authority a detailed plan of your anticipated route and check-in places and times. Additional measures are essential if you are going to conduct research in a remote or isolated location. If you are undertaking upper-level field studies—independently or in a group—your department may require that you first complete a risk assessment. You might also consider formal first-aid training.

Permissions

To do certain types of field work it is necessary to obtain permission prior to any data collection efforts. If your research requires you to administer a questionnaire, conduct a survey, or otherwise engage in direct contact with people, it is highly likely that an ethics committee must approve the types of questions and research methods (e.g., sampling method) you intend to use. Check with your professor so you understand what is required. If you will be doing work that involves other people—for instance, if you have to walk through someone's property—it may be necessary to get prior permission, perhaps by a phone call but preferably by letter. In any event, be sure you have a letter of introduction from your professor to show if the occasion arises.

Finally, remember that while you are in the field you are a representative of your institution: always be polite to people and respectful of property. It would be a pity if some sarcastic comment or questionable behaviour on your part turned anyone against later generations of students. In a rural area it's wise to let the local police know what you are doing. Your instructor may do this, and may also arrange to have an article appear in the local newspaper to inform local residents that they can expect to see strangers undertaking research in their area.

Field Notes

Field notes are not for your eyes only: they must be legible and understandable to others—including your instructor. This is critical if your field research is part of a larger project concerned with change over time at a particular location because future researchers may require your data. Record your observations in an orderly fashion, whatever the length of the field exercise—two hours, a day, or several weeks. Specific *systematic observations*, recorded on the spot, make up the first part of field notes; the second part consists of later reflections on those observations (*summary statements*). Systematic observations can be recorded in point form, whereas summary statements usually are more formal and written in complete sentences. If you are to make observations at several sites, they need to be standardized, so it's important to prepare your format in advance. That way you can see easily whether you have obtained all the required information before you move on. Similarly, if you are using classifications, you should work them out (as far as is practical) in advance; if using abbreviations or symbols, place summary lists or tables in your field notebook for ready reference.

The data you gather in the field may later be mapped using a computer-assisted cartography program, perhaps as part of a geographic information system (GIS) study, or used in some other fashion, but first they must be recorded in the systematic observations section of your field notebook (or in a hand-held computer notebook).

Systematic observations

First things first

Your instructor may give you a handout outlining the purpose of the field assignment; if so, keep it with your field notes (perhaps taped or glued into your notebook). At a minimum, record at the top of the first page:

- the basic premise of the study,
- a statement of purpose,
- any basic questions or hypotheses, and
- an outline of the methods to be used.

These set the stage for everything that follows. What should you do if your instructor doesn't provide a question, but just tells you to "investigate" a particular problem? First, always seek to explain an observed pattern; don't simply describe it. Never be satisfied with merely writing down whatever data you gather, unless the instructor has explicitly stated that nothing more is expected. Second, to help you "investigate," take the problem statement provided by the instructor and either reformulate it into a central question or advance a hypothesis; this will serve as a guide to the types of information you must gather. Third, with those requirements in mind, consider the types of research methods you will need to use. Together, your basic question or hypothesis and research methods will help you determine both what to include and what to exclude from your field observations and data collection.

Format, time, locations, and headings

At the start of each day, write down the date and time at the top of a new page. Record the name of anyone who assists you in gathering data. You may find that each instructor has a particular format for recording field notes, but the following schema is typical. Divide the paper into two sections: a narrow column on the left—perhaps 6 to 8 centimetres (2.5 to 3 inches) wide—for locational and time references and headings for different types of observations (e.g., "soils," "slope," "land use," and—if these might influence the data and therefore be needed later to explain any possible discrepancies—"weather conditions" such as precipitation, wind direction, and cloud cover); and a wider column, taking up the rest of the page, for recording your observations.

Whenever you note an observation, also record the time and location. The latter will be particularly important when you are analyzing the day's findings far away from the site because data may have been gathered from numerous locations. Map referencing to the coordinates of the topographical sheet is best. References to "near the maple tree" (how near?) or "20 metres west of the farm house" are of no use, unless the locations of the maple tree and the farm house are recorded, too. Using a GPS makes precision easy.

Headings, as noted above, can be useful for keeping your observations discretely organized on the page, especially when you are recording several types of data at each site. At first it may be advisable to take more summary, point-form notes than you think are really necessary. In time, as you gain experience in determining what is important and what is not, your field notes will become increasingly useful.

Selectivity

You need to be selective in deciding what observations to record in your notebook. Either the instructions you receive from the course instructor or the purpose that you and your colleagues have established will help you determine what is important. For example, if you are to read the landscape for evidence of particular forms of architecture, you may not need to record observations about soil types—unless, for instance, (a) you have hypothesized that there is a relationship between soil type and crops being grown and thus the architectural style on site, or (b) you know that a record of such data could be useful in the future, for another purpose. If, on the other hand, you are to observe existing recreational land uses in order to determine the potential for further recreational development, you will need to seek and record a wide variety of data, including soils; slope; existing land uses; population density, distribution, and pattern; recreational activities; settlement types and spread, and economic base; governmental institutions; and so on. In short, the nature of the problem will help you define what you need to observe, measure, and record. Before beginning to collect your data, you also should have an idea of the types of analysis and presentation that will be required at a later time. These requirements may dictate your sampling methodology and will help you identify any additional information that you may need to record, such as the distance from a benchmark.

Consistent and accurate recording

It is important that you record *all* your raw field observations in a consistent manner first, before grouping them into categories, adding interpretations, or drawing conclusions. If you record the data one way at one site and another way at the next, they may be useless. At the outset, then, consider the exact nature of the data to be collected, and then record them consistently, accurately, clearly, and completely. If you use equipment to record data, make sure the instrument is calibrated accurately, that the settings and units on the instrument(s) are appropriate to the task, and that the settings are taken from the pertinent instructional manuals.

Analysis, tables, and graphs

In some cases it may be appropriate to present your findings in tables for each site for which you have data; in others it may not be possible to put the information into tabular form until all the field work has been done. The data tables you develop then will be available for further analysis and display using various methods. For instance, if you are gathering data on truck travel flows at a particular intersection, you might summarize the findings by time periods on tables before graphing and mapping them. All three methods can be useful, and much of the work can be done in your field notebook, although entering your data into a computer spreadsheet will save a lot of time and effort.

Not all the information you record will be numerical; subjective data can be essential for certain types of field work (especially in some cultural and social geography courses). Such data can be more challenging to work with than simple, objective numbers, but they can be rewarding. What you want to do is find patterns or linkages among observations that at first glance may seem completely unrelated. To do that, you need to experiment. Sort the data into different categories—and don't get stuck on the first ones that come to mind. You may need to manipulate the data in some way before you can draw any inferences from them. Thus the data carefully recorded in your field notebook from each observation, at each site, and (depending on the nature of the study) perhaps between sites, may become useful to you only later, once you have analyzed the total data set using any of a wide range of statistical and quantitative techniques. If such analysis is necessary, be sure to include the results in your field notebook.

Sketch maps

The old saying that "a picture is worth a thousand words" applies to field work. Two types of "pictures" are important for field notes: sketch maps and drawings of the scene under consideration. If the scale is not critical—if all you need is the approximate pattern of distribution—then a sketch in map form may be adequate. Such sketch maps are easy to do because they are only approximate recordings of what you see. If more accurate information is needed, you will want to use graph paper and a tape measure. In cases where you don't have time to take accurate measurements, there is an alternative: simply count the paces it takes you to walk the distance you want to measure. For practice, lay out an exact course of 15 metres (approximately 49 feet) or more, pace it forward and backward (to make sure you've counted correctly), and divide the length by the number of paces. Walk in a relaxed but steady manner; don't take unnaturally long strides. This will give your average pace (from instep to instep or, if you prefer, from heel mark to heel mark). Thereafter, all you need to do is pace out the line to be measured (e.g., the perimeter of a property, or a building's dimensions) and multiply the number of paces with the known length of your pace. On any sketch map you make, remember to include a scale, an informational key, and a directional indicator (north arrow).

Sketches

Even if you think you can't draw, with practice your sketches will become quite adequate to record information that relates directly to the field project.

In fact, sketches often are more useful than photographs because you can omit what is not essential to the problem at hand. The scale of the observations will help you determine how much detail to include. Imagine, for instance, that you are to sketch a soil profile of the area 1 metre by 4 metres (approximately 3 feet by 13 feet): a proportional scale (say, 10 centimetres to 1 metre, or perhaps 3 inches to 1 yard) will have to be determined so that your sketch will reflect accurately what you see and measure. The components of the profile should be labelled. Or, perhaps you have to draw a particular form of joint in a log building; here again, exact measurement may be important. In a sketch of a large area, by contrast, it would be impossible to record everything you see. An artist sketching the scene would need to be selective; so do you. How selective should you be? Ask yourself why a drawing would be useful. The answer will depend on the purpose of the field work:

- Are you studying specific rural or urban land uses, drainage, valley slope, vegetation patterns, architectural forms, river bank erosion, upland ecosystems, plant colonization and succession, glacial land forms, garbage dumps, or wildlife habitat patterns?
- What particular things are you examining? Would a drawing show its outline, distribution, or pattern to advantage?
- What should you include? What should you emphasize? What can you omit?
  - When sketching a valley from a nearby hilltop, for example, you may want to record the vegetation (such as wind breaks) or field patterns in some detail, to the exclusion or downplaying of buildings.
  - If you are to draw a river meander, the location of above-water gravel in the river will be more important than trees that are well away from the bank.

Just as you think about what to record in words, think about what might be useful to record in a drawing or a sketch map.

Whereas some of your sketches may suggest only approximate scale and measurements, others will need to be accurate. For instance, a sketch or block diagram (essentially a relief model) of a woodlot edged by an old rock wall can be approximate (within reason), but a cross-section derived from topographical maps must accurately reflect the scale and contour intervals shown in those printed sources. Sketches of equipment you use in the field must also be accurate in detail, especially if proportional relationships are important, or if a dial or other means of measurement is recorded. Finally, accuracy obviously is important if you are asked to produce a detailed sketch of, for instance, the precise placement of equipment in a field-study site.

Photographs

Photographs can be invaluable for certain types of field work. You will need to ensure that you are close enough to isolate the subject—unless you intend to show it in relation to other features in the landscape—and that the details you want are clearly visible. If the scale is not evident, place an item (such as a lens cover or a marked measuring stick) in the scene or beside the subject of the photo. A digital camera permits you to edit the image at a later time and transfer it to a program such as PowerPoint, or, if you are set up for it, to print photographs on-site. Set up your digital camera to record the date and time on each photograph. Remember to include in your field notebook a reference to each photograph taken. Never digitally manipulate a photograph with the intent to deceive; to do so would be unethical. As David Griffen notes, "To change a photo—beyond minor tweaks to correct color balance or remove red-eye, for example—is to undermine the truth."[2]

If you aren't set up to print digital photos on-site, consider bringing along a digital instant print camera and tiny printer because they make a colour image available almost immediately for insertion in your field notebook. Be sure to write down your comments about the contents of the photograph.

Summary statements

Periodically you will want to summarize your observations. Summarizing sessions during the course of the day may be possible, but at a minimum a late-afternoon or evening session is needed. Here are three suggestions:

- After gathering data at one site and recording them in your notebook, you may be able to take a few minutes to reflect on what you have been doing. If you have questions that can't be answered readily, jot them down for later reference. Also, take the time to note any overarching observations you may have made about what you have been doing. These insights may be useful later.

- A lunch break can be a good time for interim summarizing, collating data, or, more importantly, reflecting on what you have written in your notebook that morning. Are there questions that come to mind once you step back from the actual data-gathering?

- The most important time for summarizing is late afternoon or evening; don't put this task off until the next day. Reflect on what you have done during the day and jot down your major observations while they're still fresh in your mind. You will be pleasantly surprised later, when these observations help you in writing your field report. Your summary observations may include anything from specific insights to general feelings about what you have seen and recorded. The evening is a good time to compile summary tables of the data gathered; then you will have a summary of the day's data ready either for immediate analysis or for later compilation and analysis with data from other days.

General comments

Keep your field notes tidy because they may be examined and graded by your instructor. Field notes can serve other purposes too. Clearly written systematic observations, with the pertinent data, sketch maps and drawings, and sound summarizing statements, will be invaluable, whether for class assignments—such as lab work using your data, or research papers based on your field work—or in studying for an examination. Without care, accuracy, and consistency, however, your field notes will be of questionable value. Be sure to think in advance about what you plan to record, why, and how you will do it; check all your field notes the same day you take them, to make sure no important data are missing; and, finally, make sure that everything you write is legible.

Field diary

In addition to field notes, some researchers find it useful to keep a separate *field diary* or *journal* for general thoughts and reflections. In contrast to a field notebook, with its step-by-step, detailed record of observations, a diary is more reflective, recording your musings, ideas, insights, questions, tentative conclusions, and possible hypotheses that may be worth further consideration.

One way to start is with a succinct summary—no more than a sentence or two—of your activities and general observations from that day's work. Then stand back from those observations and allow yourself to think more broadly and abstractly than you can when you're preoccupied with the nitty-gritty of field work. For some types of field work in human geography and in sustainability studies, recording your emotional responses to the day's activities can also be useful. Leave space at the end of each day's entry so that you can return to it and add further reflections, perhaps days or even weeks later.

Preparing a Questionnaire

Designing a questionnaire is not something that can be hurried. Knowing your purpose for using a questionnaire, and the population to be sampled, will help you design a document that is unambiguous and, thus, easily understood by all. A well-designed questionnaire should provide you with useful primary data. There are many types of questionnaires, as you will learn in a qualitative research methods course. Here are several fundamental points to help you as you proceed (assuming you have received any necessary approval from your departmental or university ethics committee to administer your questionnaire, and have fulfilled the expectations of your department or university).[3]

- You may be required to obtain an informed consent form, signed by the people you intend to speak with, prior to proceeding with your questionnaire. You may also need to leave each of your respondents with a copy of that consent form. (Ethics committees often have templates for developing an informed consent form.)
- At the top of your questionnaire, list the project's title, your name, and the names of your department and institution. You might also include a contact phone number or e-mail address, especially if the questionnaire is to be left for respondents to complete on their own.
- By way of introduction, as briefly and clearly as possible, identify the project's purpose and state precisely what your respondents will be asked to do.
- Keep the questionnaire focused. Don't include superfluous material or unnecessary questions that will distract the respondents.
- Avoid ambiguity and jargon. Be precise and clear when you pose a question.

- Avoid bias. Select your words (and sentence structure) with care to avoid influencing the respondents' reactions to the questions you pose.
- Think about the order of your questions. A logical flow should be evident, which will help your respondents. You may use headings or brief explanatory comments to indicate any change in the line of inquiry.
- Get the attention of your respondents by putting factual questions first. More complex material can be placed later.
- Be tidy. If your questionnaire is messy (e.g., with spelling errors, mixed fonts, inadequate spacing) or is poorly organized, you may lose the attention of your respondents.
- Conclude with a "thank you."

Reporting Field Assignments

When field notes are to form the basis of a more formal report, your instructor may give you the headings required to organize your paper. Note that requirements regarding format, quality of sketches and mapping, terminology, and so on in geography differ from those in biology; physical geography generally calls for a different style than human geography. Whatever the style, organize your thoughts according to the instructions given in class; ignoring them may seriously affect your grade. If, on the other hand, your instructor simply tells you to "write a report on the field assignment," with no elaboration, you shouldn't take this as permission to write a rambling, unstructured report. Always present your observations and findings in a clear, succinct, systematic, logical manner. What should go into your report? Consider the following suggestions.

1. **Title.** A clear, descriptive title will leave no question about what you are reporting. For instance, "Contemporary Commercial Land Uses in Red Deer, Alberta" is preferable to "A Pretty Neat Place for Today's Shopping: Variations in the Commercial Patterns of a Small City"; a simple "Leda Clays in the Ottawa Valley" is better than "Clays that Subside and Flow When They Get Wet in the Ottawa Valley Region." If a scientific name is applicable—say, for a plant study—use it so that your reader knows at once what the report is about. Also, be sure to identify yourself, the course, the date, and your instructor on the title page.

2. **Introduction.** Your introduction should identify, in general terms, the purpose of the field study, its basic premise, and the essential question you sought to answer or the hypothesis you sought to test (all these will have been determined *before* the field work was done). The introduction is also the place to situate your study within a broader context. The latter may be given to you by your instructor, but if you have to establish the context yourself, you may need to refer to the course readings, or perhaps a lecture. As has been observed elsewhere in this book, all research has a context, so you must indicate what it is. In addition, you should indicate where and when the field research was carried out; it may also be important to state why that particular place was chosen for study, or if seasonal effects were evident.

3. **Research methods.** Identify what research methods you used and why. If, in the course of the research, you encountered problems and had to make modifications, note these too.

4. **Data gathered.** Present your findings in a straightforward manner, without interpretation. It may be appropriate to present some data in tables, graphs, or maps as well as in your text. Some lengthy supporting material can be located in an appendix so as to not interrupt the flow of ideas in the main text.

5. **Data analysis.** Identify the methods you used to analyze the data, whether qualitative, quantitative, general cartographic, or GIS. State what statistical tests you applied and note the results. Again, data may be presented in tables, graphs, and maps. You need not include all the data or workings of the analysis, although an appendix of that material may be attached. In any event, be sure to keep your detailed analysis of the data—if only so that, later on, you can see where you might have gone wrong.

6. **Discussion.** Identify the observations you have drawn from the data you have gathered and analyzed. Are there any patterns and processes that became obvious only after you worked with the raw data? What are they? How do they relate to the basic purpose of your study? Do they provide a reasonable answer to your essential question? Do they support your hypothesis? If not, explain why. What unanswered questions remain? Were there any problems with the data, or perhaps with your analysis? Spell these out in your report.

7. **Conclusion.** State your conclusion. Succinctly declare whether or not your original purpose has been fulfilled. Finally, *don't* include any new material here.

8. **Appendices.** Pertinent maps (whether by you or published topographical or other maps), air photos, or other material may be included in one or more appendices. Remember to refer in your text to any appended material, with appropriate numbers.

Chapter Summary

Field work is a "trademark" of geography, sustainability studies, and environmental studies. It is a key to understanding how and why both natural environments and human societies vary from place to place. Field work certainly can be challenging as we study complex environments and issues, but the pointers we have provided—about preparing for field work, keeping a field notebook, making sketches and sketch maps, using photographs, keeping a field diary, and writing a formal field report based on analysis of your data—should help guide you through the process.

Notes

1. Anne Buttimer, *The Practice of Geography* (London: Longman, 1983), 12.
2. David Griffen, "A Question of Trust," in Chris Johns, ed., *National Geographic Guide to Digital Photography* (Washington, DC: National Geographic Society, 2006), 16.
3. For additional suggestions, see G. Bridge, "Questionnaire Surveys," in A. Rogers and H.A. Viles, eds, *The Student's Companion to Geography*, 2nd ed. (Oxford: Blackwell, 2003), 230–41. See also P.M. McGuirk and P. O'Neill, "Using Questionnaires in Qualitative Human Geography" in I. Hay, ed., *Qualitative Research Methods in Human Geography*, 4th ed. (Don Mills, ON: Oxford University Press, 2016), 246–73.

12 Illustrating Your Work

In this chapter, we examine

- basic considerations for creating and submitting illustrations;
- points to keep in mind when designing an effective map;
- essential aspects of geographical information systems; and
- different types of maps, tables, equations, diagrams, and graphs.

Introduction

Not all your course work will require writing. Some kinds of data are communicated most effectively using tables, equations, diagrams, graphs, and maps, and some types of analysis cannot be done without such illustrations. *Graphicacy* (dealing with graphic images) and *numeracy* (dealing with quantifiable data) are as important as *literacy* (dealing with written language) for students in the environmental sciences, sustainability studies, and in geography specifically. Visualization and experimentation are important parts of the creative process. Like writing, creating an illustration is a complex process that takes time and reflection. A successful illustration will convey something about your data that might not be captured as quickly or effectively by words—if words could convey it at all.[1] Care must be taken, however, to ensure that your illustrations represent the data accurately.

This chapter briefly identifies some basic considerations to keep in mind as you create illustrations. Helpful suggestions are provided on *maps* and *computer-generated images* (see also pp. 150–1), *tables, equations, diagrams,* and *graphs*. For *photos*, see page 191; for *sketch maps* and *sketches*, see pages 189–91; and for *posters*, see pages 156–9.

The Basics

Currently, both the fields of cartography and of graphics technology are changing a great deal. No longer are maps simply flat images with numerous symbols on them. Now they are part of the much wider field of *geovisualization*, which uses perspective (3D) drawings from different viewpoints or moving images "flying" through a landscape. Other illustrations called *drapes* show your data on a natural topographical surface (see more on *draping* below), while still other illustrative media use *haptics* (touch-sensitive symbols) and sounds.

The "surfaces" used in such media commonly are thought of as natural topography, but they can also represent a statistic other than elevation. These techniques currently require specialized training to use, but because things change so quickly in the digital world it may not be long before some of them are readily available for anyone to use; for example, consider how common interactive maps such as Google Maps are (you can zoom in and out, change orientation, choose different routes, or fly your cursor over an area to see more information about that area), and then think about how rare they were not that long ago.

Geographic information systems (GIS) also have evolved quickly as technology has developed. These computer hardware and software systems let us visualize, organize, manage, and display spatial data and information about our world, enabling us to analyze, interpret, and understand spatial relationships and to model spatial processes. GIS maps and charts allow us to see existing patterns and relationships as well as to anticipate future conditions. Applying the geographic knowledge gained through use of GIS, for example about flooding patterns on Canadian rivers, may help us identify and take preventive or corrective actions to reduce flood damage in both urban and rural settings. The use of UAVs (unmanned aerial vehicles, or drones), equipped with video cameras, infrared heat sensors, and other equipment that instantly deliver high resolution images for use in GIS, has enhanced our capacity to fight wildfires, count wildlife, monitor reservoirs and dams, and support many other environmental management efforts.

With practice, you will be able to refine the expression and execution of your ideas in your own maps and diagrams. Careful compilation of data and consideration of what you want to show, along with thoughtful composition and clean, uncluttered final copy, are the keys to success. Two basic approaches are possible:

- For some work, including field studies, you may be encouraged to use traditional techniques—for instance, to sketch a landscape element or an urban streetscape (on plain or graph paper) using pencils, pens, and rulers. You may be able to incorporate information collected in the field using data loggers and other hand-held devices.

- For most work—especially at advanced levels of study and for theses—you may be expected to use computer programs to analyze data and create visual displays of the results. As the shift to digital data collection and visualization continues, you should take advantage of opportunities to enroll in software courses at your institution or online. Additionally, by learning one major new technique for each paper you prepare—such as indexing, footnoting, or inserting a figure—you will quickly become proficient with a range of necessary tools.

For all visual materials, the following points are fundamental:

- Know clearly what topic you want to illustrate and keep to it.
- Identify who you expect to view your visual material and what its purpose is; both these points help guide you toward creating maps and illustrations that communicate effectively.
- Know why you want to include the illustration. What will it contribute to your paper or poster?
- Because poor data will not make useful illustrations, be sure that your sources are reliable. For GIS data, check the lineage and metadata: find out who made the illustration, what processing occurred, what reference system was used, what date the data was acquired, and what errors (if present) there are in the position and attributes of items (such as community names, tree types, population numbers, etc.).
- Think carefully about how best to show the data: with a graph (which type?), a map (what kind?), a diagram (which style?), a table, or an equation? Can the data be shown on a line graph? Or can they be aggregated into discrete groups to be plotted on a bar graph or listed in a table? Or do they have a spatial aspect that will be shown most clearly on a map?
- Don't try to cram too much information into an illustration, otherwise the illustration may be difficult to follow.
- Make sure your illustration contains all the information necessary to be intelligible on its own and yet also to relate to the text, by expanding upon or clarifying a point.
- Refer to each illustration by citing its number in the text: maps, graphs, and diagrams are all figures (e.g., "Figure 1"), whereas tables are listed as such (e.g., "Table 1").

- Identify your source(s). If you have taken material from someone else's work, state that it is "from . . ." or "excerpted from. . . ." If you have taken material from one or more sources and manipulated it in some way, state that it is "based on . . ." or "adapted from. . . ." If you are presenting your own original data, gathered from interviews, field work, or laboratory observations, be sure to give yourself credit in a manner acceptable to your instructor or supervisor: for instance, "author's field work" or "original data gathered by the author."

When sourcing and adapting online graphics, the following points are fundamental:

- As you search the vast amount of graphic material available on the Internet, you may wish to copy or save images for use in your work. As you do so, ensure that you record the source URL, along with any permission or use restrictions that are found on the page, for every image you save.
- If the image shows exactly what you need, note any restrictions on its use (that you copied with the image). Many government agencies give permission to download and use their maps, graphics, images, and text for educational purposes, provided the materials are cited. See, for instance, Parks Canada's notice regarding use of illustrative material and graphics found on their website (www.pc.gc.ca/avis-notice_e.asp). Such statements can be hard to find, so copy them and keep them with your image notes. Note that a request you make for permission to use materials from other sources may be ignored or, if a response is provided and permission is granted, it may take a very long time to obtain.
- If you use an image in a PowerPoint presentation, always provide the source URL with the image.
- If you use an image from an image retrieval service (e.g., Google Images), be certain to cite the image in its original context (use the URL of the page where the image originally was shown, not the URL of the enlarged image). Here is an example of the correct way to cite an online image:

> Parks Canada/Wayne Roach. "National Marine Conservation Areas, Arctic Marine Regions." Map. Parks Canada: Feasibility Assessment for the Proposed Lancaster Sound National Marine Conservation Area. 17 August 2010. 9 September 2010. http://www.pc.gc.ca/eng/progs/amnc-nmca/lancaster/intro.aspx.[2]

The following sections offer suggestions on several types of illustrations.

Maps

Maps show spatial patterns and relationships. They can display either data required for the purpose of analysis or information derived from the analysis. Geographic information about the (actual and perceived) contents of the earth's surface is recorded in three basic forms. *Points* represent things that have discrete locations: depending on the scale, examples range from monuments to houses or from schools to towns to cities. *Lines* represent things that have length, such as roads, railways, rivers, and political boundaries. *Areas* represent features such as parks or lakes, or distributions (for instance, of soil types).

In the digital world, there are several types of maps you should know about and, provided you have the data, you can use basic desktop GIS to create these types of visuals:

- *Continuous data surfaces* represent phenomena such as elevation (where each location is measured from a fixed registration point, e.g., sea level), and other phenomena such as air movement (where air flows vary across a surface from a source, e.g., smoke plumes from a forest fire).
- *3D graphics* represent three-dimensional, real-world objects (such as buildings or trees) in a map or scene, along with their elevation values.
- *Digital elevation models* (DEMs) are created from terrain elevation data (commonly obtained using remote sensing techniques) and represent terrain relief (see Figure 12.1a).
- *Hillshading* adds a lighting effect to a map based on elevation variations within a landscape; this technique mimics the sun's effects (e.g., shading and shadows), to help provide a clearer picture of the topography in an area (see Figure 12.1b).
- *Draping* superimposes a two-dimensional image onto a three-dimensional surface, such as when an aerial photograph is draped over a DEM, resulting in a realistic visualization of terrain (see Figure 12.1c).

All maps are selective. They include only the data that the compiler wants them to show; in other words, they present an abstraction of reality. Because the compiler may (knowingly or unknowingly) misrepresent data through the use of inappropriate projections or scales, poor classification of

Figure 12.1 Selected examples of types of digital maps

A – A digital elevation model (in raster format): each grey shade represents a different elevation

B – A hillshade, derived from the digital elevation model, viewed from above

C – The hillshade draped over the digital elevation model to provide a realistic, oblique view of the topography

data, inaccurately manipulated data, inappropriate symbols, poor selection of colour or shading, incorrect plotting of locations, or omission, maps also can lie.[3] Thus, care must be taken to ensure accuracy. As with written work, you need to think about the most effective way to express your data visually, what data to include, and how best to display them.

Location maps generally are quite simple: they show the absolute and relative locations (i.e., sites and situations) of one or more features within a particular locale or region. Other types of maps have other uses. For example, Figure 12.2 shows patterns of land use, identifying the distribution of buildings in an older area of a large city by selected categories (using point

Business Categories:

- ● Contemporary – entertainment sector
  (mainly eating/drinking establishments)
- ○ Contemporary – other
  (unequivocal, relevant, partial)
- ⊕ Conventional with contemporary market appeal
- + Conventional – other
- △ Low Grade

( ) Vacant

A Automotive

Inset from street indicates
centre block or upper storey

Heritage Designations, Ottawa City Planning Department

- Notable Heritage
- Heritage
- Heritage Compatible

(Other buildings
not shown)

Merchants' Perceptions

- ■ Prime Heritage Motivation
- ◻ Secondary Heritage Motivation

Figure 12.2 Heritage properties in Lower Town, Ottawa

Source: J.E. Tunbridge, *Of Heritage and Many Other Things* (Ottawa: Carleton University, Geography Discussion Papers, No. 5, 1987), pp. 4, 19. Reprinted with permission of author.

symbols) and by heritage value, actual and perceived (using a combination of area shading and point symbols). Figure 12.2 offers good examples of large-scale maps: they cover a small area.

In contrast, Figure 12.3 covers a much larger area, the entire continental United States. Clearly, the degree of generalization is very different, yet each map shows a distribution. The two maps together reveal time-space changes. Specifically, for the years 1995 and 2004, the maps identify the locations, and

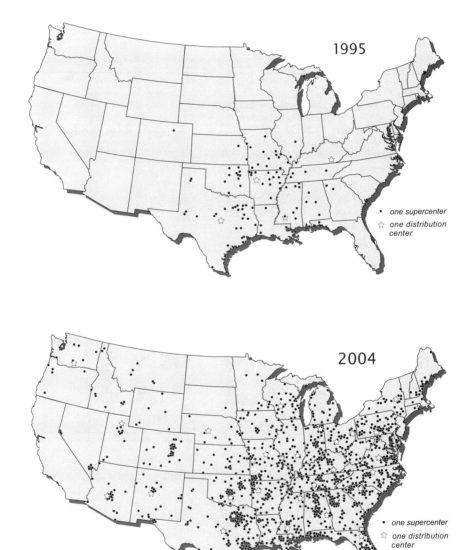

Figure 12.3 The distribution in the United States of Walmart superstores and regional distribution centres in 1995 (top) and 2004 (bottom)

Source: "Unequal Competition among Chains of Supercenters," Thomas O. Graff, *The Professional Geographer*, Vol. 58, Blackwell Publishing 2006, reprinted by permission of the publisher.

thus the distribution, of Walmart superstores (averaging 181,692 sq. ft.) and of the regional distribution centres that fed them. The maps not only reveal the changed distribution but, implicitly, they raise questions about how and why the areal spread occurred as it did between 1995 and 2004. Even a quick glance is enough for us to identify the basic patterns on these static maps. Using dynamic maps to show the spread of phenomena over time—including the distribution of Walmart stores, or the spread of an infectious disease, or the movement of invasive zebra mussels into the Great Lakes—is another way to gain insight into geographical phenomena.

Mental maps are unique to every individual. Whether we are a deep-sea fisherman, a tourist in a foreign land, or someone out for a walk in our own city, our brains are navigating, helping us find our way from point A to point B. Along the way, our brains also store and organize spatial information for future reference, enabling us to visualize that information in our own minds. The "mental maps" (or, cognitive maps) we create combine factual information (e.g., about landmarks) with our subjective interpretations of spatial information (e.g., where those landmarks are relative to other elements of the environment), resulting in each person's unique characterization of space. These mental maps, created from our memories, are useful to geographers and planners involved in designing urban spaces as they can reveal people's preference for different environmental characteristics in various places. Geographers also use mental maps to gain insight into how people's perceptions of their environment influence various decisions they make; for example, to understand why immigrant ethnic groups move into specific urban areas, or why women and elderly people avoid certain parts of town because they are perceived to be unsafe.[4]

Why maps matter

Maps can be part of the process of analysis: they can identify potential solutions to problems by revealing insights that otherwise might not be evident immediately. One example of the power of maps (and the GIS data and analytical tools that underlie and accompany them) to assist in "making a difference" in the real world is seen in a simple map of food availability in Vancouver. By identifying the locations of chain grocery stores, grocery stores selling local produce, community gardens, and farmers' markets, a clear pattern emerges. The map reveals that, in 2011, more than half of Vancouver's grocery stores were located in the affluent northwest neighbourhoods, while residents of the southeast lacked access to affordable food. The southeast portion of the city was a "food desert" (see Figure 12.4). If you had investigated this situation in more detail, adding map layers such as income and age data, you would have found that within the apparently wealthy and well-serviced northwest area, a large pocket of low-income seniors has access to only one (expensive) grocery store. Lack of food security for seniors and other vulnerable populations in the area is a reality, in Vancouver and many other Canadian centres. Layered information helps to identify the dimensions of these kinds of issues, and this dimensionality, in turn, contributes to improved understanding of the issue being investigated.

Beyond identification, maps can also be used to help analyze these issues. For example, past and present city councils in Vancouver have tried to address security of and equitable access to food by creating the Vancouver Food Policy Council and the Greenest City 2020 Action Plan. However, the challenges remain difficult to resolve. This is why, and where, mapping and Web 2.0 technologies can unite to bring together the perspectives of citizens and their communities, governments, industry, and others. Web 2.0 technology includes cloud computing, social media, and GIS data and analysis capabilities, which can enhance traditional data. Because it can be geo-referenced,

Figure 12.4 A food desert in Vancouver, BC

Source: Courtesy of Robin Poitras. After Aleksandra Sagan. "Ritzy South Granville: a food desert," http://vancouver. openfile.ca/vancouver/file/2011/05/ritzy-south-granville-food-desert. Accessed 30 June 2011.

information from social networks such as Twitter, Facebook, YouTube, and blogs may be mapped. Maps created from this information may help citizens discuss and find solutions to issues in their neighbourhoods. In turn, citizens may use their enhanced geospatial knowledge to convey the ideas that they are passionate about to their local government, for example to help develop more sustainable food and agricultural systems within a food-policy context. Maps and other illustrative materials may help citizens and governments to collaborate in generating effective, place-based governance policies.

Maps also have been invaluable in natural disasters and humanitarian crises, including Haiti's 2010 earthquake (e.g., to show estimated numbers of persons exposed to varying intensities of shaking and subsequent severity of structural damage), and in identifying numbers and locations of displaced people in Rwandan refugee camps. In the Zaatari refugee camp in Jordan, ten Syrian refugees were trained to use GIS and produced camp reference maps showing locations of schools, mosques, and shops. Learning GIS map-making skills provided refugees with a livelihood in the camp and a marketable skill if they returned home or adopted a new country.[5]

Presently it is unclear exactly what Web 3.0 will become. Some suggest it will be a combination of the semantic web (which searches and analyzes content based on the ability to understand the meaning of words) and artificial intelligence (where computers understand information as humans do).[6] The extensive use of 3D graphics combined with greater connectivity of all information, and the 24/7/365 availability of computers and mobile devices, suggests there is enormous potential for Web 3.0 to present highly accurate geographical and environmental information to individual users. The cognitive technology used in Web 3.0 may help people interpret maps more accurately and gain new insights into their surroundings, wherever they are!

Maps also may show distributional patterns and quantities: for example, a network of settlements showing their sizes and the routes between them, or the varying types and yields of agricultural production in a given region. Figure 12.5 (which includes an inset map showing the relative location of the research study area) identifies n'Daki Menan, the ancestral homeland and geopolitical territory of the Teme-Augama Anishnabai. The named traditional family territories—which would be hard to describe in words alone—are delimited by the broken lines. By contrast, the area and bounds of the Wendaban Stewardship Authority follow the straight-line, government-imposed township boundaries. Major bodies of water, highways, and towns are also identified. Note the inclusion of scales and directional indicators.

Figure 12.5 The traditional lands of the Teme-Augama Anishnabai and the areal extent of the Wendaban Stewardship Authority

Source: Recompiled from Jeremy Shute and David B. Knight, "Obtaining and Understanding Environmental Knowledge," *Canadian Geographer*, Vol. 39 (1995), pp. 101–11.

Making maps (by hand, and using GIS)

While most maps today are made using GIS software (and databases) of various types, there may be occasions when you will need to create maps and graphic material by hand. For instance, if you are undertaking course work in the field, being able to create your own illustrative material may be crucial. (Note that hand-constructed illustrations may use Mylar, drafting, or graph paper, and require sharp pencils, a ruler, and squares; to draw pie graphs you may also need a compass). Regardless of whether you draw by hand or use a computer, you need to consider several points in order to design a meaningful map, and you need to make sure you include all six required elements (see pp. 210–11).

- **Delimitation of scope.** For effective map design, define the map's purpose and intended audience. These points will help you determine what to show or omit, and which key features to highlight, so that you help focus the user's attention on your concept.
- **Scale, projection, and orientation.** Before you make your map, you will need to decide on its final size and scale, and the projection, symbols, and colours (see pp. 212–13) you will use. For your particular topic and data, at what scale can you include all the pertinent detail? Think about the best orientation for your map. While north usually is at the top of a map you may find that another orientation better suits your purpose. Be sure to indicate the orientation you select (see Fig. 12.5 and p. 210).

    Many outline maps of Canadian provinces, counties, and census tracts, and of various other regions and nations, are available online for your use (for instance, GeoGratis [http://geogratis.ca] provides information on where to find free geospatial data in Canada.

- **Construction.** Don't assume you will get it right the first time! Just like writing, preparing effective maps and illustrations takes time, reflection, and, usually, revision. Examine as many examples as you can of maps similar to what you have in mind and remember not to "re-invent the wheel"—use the current symbols and colour standards and specifications employed by leading map-making agencies. (ESRI's Map Book Gallery [www.esri.com/mapmuseum/index.html] is a go-to website.) Carefully select patterns, line widths, symbols, and fonts to ensure that the distinctions between different items are clear—neither too sharp nor too subtle. Ensure that all the information can be read with ease, and that type sizes are appropriate both to the scale of the map and to the categories of information they identify. Include only the necessary level of detail and leave out distracting embellishments. Does the final product show the data as clearly as possible? Are there any changes you could make to clarify an especially important point? Make sure that important things *look* important and are evident even with a quick glance.

- **Following and double-checking instructions.** Before submitting work, you must ensure that you have followed your instructor's policies and technical requirements regarding acceptable file sizes and formats, compression, and submission method (e-mail, learning-management system such as D2L or Blackboard, or hard copy, for example). Then, carefully review your work for completeness, accuracy, and readability—and be sure to proofread before you push the submit (or print) button! Proofreading means checking that locations, routes, boundaries, and other lines are placed accurately, that all the spellings are correct, and that every number is accurate and complete. Make sure that all the patterns are correctly placed and are readable. Did you include a short, informative title? Is a written explanation necessary, in the text or under the illustration? Have you included scale and directional indicators? Have you credited your sources?

Each time you create or adapt a map, make sure to include these six required elements, as follows:

- The **data frame** displays the data layers; the data frame is the map of the phenomena you are interested in, such as the distribution of specific tree species in a forest, or the numbers of graffiti incidents in community neighbourhoods.
- A **legend** (or **key**) contains the symbols (both their shapes and their colours) used to represent real-world objects. For instance, a small circle or square may represent a point of interest, while a large green area may represent forested land.
- A succinct **title** quickly tells the viewer the subject and location of the mapped data.
- A **north arrow** orients the viewer to the direction of the map (relative to due north). Note that most (but not all) maps tend to be oriented so that due north faces the top of the page (you will need to justify any changes from this pattern). Some maps show latitude and longitude instead of a north arrow.
- Maps usually are made to **scale**; the scale represents the ratio of a distance on the map to the actual distance on the ground (e.g., if measured in centimetres, 1:10,000 would mean 1 centimetre on the map equals 10,000 centimetres on the ground).

- Information on the **source(s)** of a map, the data used to compile the map, information about the projection used, and any caveats are also placed on the maps.
- Two optional elements you may include are a **border** and an **inset map**.

Basic issues concerning geographic information systems

Geographic information systems use two main types of geographic data models to represent real-world data. GIS programs based on *vector data models* employ points, lines, and polygons to represent the world. Each vector feature has an attribute value and locational coordinates associated with it. Vector GIS systems use overlays (superimposed map layers) containing digitized data on different features that occupy the same geographic space, to create maps showing the relationships among the map layers. Examples include field patterns, ground water availability, well sites, drainage systems, crops grown, seasonal livestock densities, and land values; or elevation, streams and rivers, soils, population distribution, political boundaries, roads, telephone and electricity lines, water and sewage pipes, and present and planned buildings. Individual overlays can be combined, erased, or modified as necessary to reveal different types of interrelationships. Vector data models have numerous practical applications in the work world; hence, vector system GIS is an important part of the training of geographers and other environmental scientists. To begin familiarizing you with GIS, some instructors may have you create a personal website on which you can display your GIS course assignments.

GIS programs based on the *raster system* portray geographic space as rows and columns of equal-sized cells arranged in a grid matrix. Each cell has both an attribute value and locational coordinates. Although the mapped results may look coarse because of the grid structure into which data are placed,[7] the results are invaluable for analyzing geographic phenomena.

Like any map, GIS shows points, lines, and areas—although in GIS jargon *areas* are generally referred to as *polygons*. Two kinds of data are gathered: *attribute* data, which pertain to specific areas such as census tracts (and which often come packaged with map data), and *image* data, which can be scanned and digitized from satellite images, aerial photographs, or various other printed sources. If you are creating maps using a GIS program, be careful not to combine too much overlapping information. Clarity should be your goal.

Here are some basic questions to ask if you are considering using a computer mapping program:

- Is your software package capable of doing what you wish? For instance, MS Office will let you make minor modifications such as cutting the file size or snipping out a section of an image. But, to turn an image into a water colour, or a negative, requires software such as Adobe Illustrator. Knowledge of these types of programs is to your advantage.
- Are you familiar with the digital techniques? Do you have enough experience with them to complete the project within a reasonable time?
- Is your data set in a form that the software can read?
- Is the essential locational (geo-referenced) information (map boundaries, rivers, contours, etc.) available in a digital form that the software can read? Your library or department may have a collection of standard base maps and thematic maps in digital form. If not, is a suitable up-to-date base map available for digitizing?
- Have you been careful to differentiate between point, line, and polygon (area) data?
- Have the data in your database been given the coordinates required for use in an automated program? If not, is conversion software available to transform the existing digital data into the required format?

You should also keep the following points in mind:

- If you are digitizing or extracting information from a map with a scale or projection different from your base, the fit will not be precise enough for accurate comparisons. However, there are ways of coping with this problem, so don't hesitate to ask your instructor for help.
- Whatever program you use, be careful to select patterns and densities that fully reveal what *you* want to display and reveal in the illustration. If they are not right for your illustration, don't use pre-set displays just because they are there.
- Check to see that all your data (points, lines, patterns) are where they should be.
- Check the spelling on the map, as you would the text of a paper.

- Check to be sure that you have provided all the required map elements (noted above).
- Make sure that the hard copy will be of suitable quality for your intended purpose.
- If you can use colour, be aware that your mapped results will direct the viewer to think in certain ways. Assume, for example, that you are to map the majority of percentage *yes* and *no* responses to a questionnaire as they pertain to a question posed for the people of region X and that you are able to plot the data by census tracts. If you chose a dark colour (e.g., red) for *yes* and a light colour (e.g., yellow) for *no*, your viewer will be attracted to the *yes* pattern, whether or not it is in the majority of tracts. In other words, think carefully about what and how you want to convey the information, using colours. The same holds true for black-and-white patterns because more densely packed patterns may attract the eye quicker than lightly packed patterns.
- Be careful how you mix colours on the page. For example, if you use blue and purple, or purple and red, you might mask the order of your data, and your viewer may find it difficult to identify quickly what is important. Use of pure colours might be better, such as blue and red. Be aware that some colours connote different things in different cultures. For instance, pink is feminine for most people in Canada, the United States, and Britain, but not in Japan; green is a sacred colour for Muslims; and purple means prostitution in some Southwest Asian countries.[8] In short, know your intended audience because the use of some colours may be inappropriate in certain circumstances.

Be aware that the colours that are printed may not be identical to those that appear on your computer screen. Before you decide on a final colour, print some test pages on the printer you will be using; this is especially important if the colour appears on a legend or a graph label.

Although a working acquaintance with computers is now an essential part of anyone's education, it is possible to become too caught up in the technology. You don't want to get so bogged down in technical issues that you lose sight of your primary goal: to portray spatial data accurately and effectively. GIS training resources, many offered in cooperation with the Environmental Systems Research Institute (ESRI), are available through variously named university geospatial centres.

Tables

Tables present data in a systematic manner, using rows and columns under appropriate headings. How do you decide whether a table is the best way to present your data? Ask yourself these questions:

- What is the purpose of the table? Could the data simply be listed in the text? Is time a variable? If so, perhaps a graph is in order, possibly in addition to a table. Is area or location significant in the distribution of the data? If so, perhaps a map would be more useful than a table.
- Do the data in the table complement—not duplicate—what is in the text? While you need to avoid repetition as much as possible, be aware that a table is not intended to be read straight through as a necessary part of the text. When you place a table in your paper, ensure there is sufficient space between your words and the table so that it clearly stands alone (because it is intended to be read separately from the text).
- What categories should the table show? Are there different ways you might group the data in the table? Which ways will most effectively convey the information and make the point you intend?
- Tables must be easily readable, so do not use extra-small fonts in an effort to cram more data in (consider creating an additional table instead if you have too much information to convey in one table). Also, tables that run over several pages may be better placed in an appendix rather than in your text (try to limit tables to no more than one full page each).

The following elements are essential for any table:

- **Table number and title:** The assigned number should appear at the top of the table and in the text at an appropriate place. The title should be brief and informative. Avoid abbreviations in titles (see Table 12.1).
- **Headings:** The headings for each row (reading across) and column or group of columns (reading down) must be clear; make sure that any abbreviations are explained either in the text or in a footnote. In Table 12.1, years, totals, and percentages appear along the top; employment categories at the left identify the data in each row.

Table 12.1 Non-governmental labour force in Zania by industry, 2007 and 2017

Activity	2007 Total	2007 Percentage	2017 Total	2017 Percentage
Agriculture	101,649	16.5	104,343	15.7
Forestry and Fishing	20,000[a]	3.2	27,000[a]	4.1
Mining	16,940	2.8	19,648	2.9
Manufacturing	156,353	25.4	162,773	24.4
Construction	98,282	16.0	99,345	14.9
Commercial Services	196,643	32.0	226,783	34.0
Professional Services	24,980	4.1	26,862	4.0
TOTAL	615,847	100.0	666,754	100.0

[a] Estimated.

Source: Government of Zania, *Annual Labour Force Statistics* (Zunila: Bureau for Statistics, 2018), p. 10. [All data are fictitious]

- **Footnotes:** If you need to define or otherwise explain something, use a footnote, as in Table 12.1.
- **Source(s):** List the sources of your data.
- **Cross-reference:** Double-check to make sure you have referred to the table in the text (e.g., "See Table 4").

Table 12.1 presents fictional data for which percentages have been determined. Data from two time periods, and their proportional importance, are shown in an orderly manner. The table thus shows both absolute and relative data.

Equations

Place short and simple equations (such as "$E = mc^2$") in the line of text, and long or complicated equations apart from the text, as in the two examples on page 216. If you are presenting two or more equations, you can identify them with numbers (in parentheses) in the right margin, as in these examples. Unless an equation is standard—and thus is generally well known—you should explain any abbreviations in one of three places: immediately below the equation (example 1), in the equation itself (example 2), or in the text (example 2, for reference to "RF").

Example 1

The equation for deriving standard deviation is:

$$(\sigma) = \frac{\Sigma(x_i - \bar{x})^2}{n} \tag{1}$$

where σ (the Greek letter *sigma*) = standard deviation;
Σ = sum of;
x_i = score of measurement, with $_i$ the value of observation;
$\bar{x}$ = mean of a group of scores or measurements; and
n = number.

Example 2

The equation for determining the vertical exaggeration on a topographic map is:

$$\text{vertical exaggeration (VE)} = \frac{\text{vertical scale (VS)}}{\text{horizontal scale (HS)}} \tag{2}$$

Once this is noted, you can use abbreviations. The vertical and horizontal scales are expressed as representational fractions (RF).

Suppose that the HS is 1:50,000 and the VS is 1 inch to 400 feet. The VS expressed as a RF is 1:4,800.

Thus:

$$VE = \frac{1}{4,800} \div \frac{1}{50,000}$$

Be aware that "composing" and "typesetting" an equation can be quite daunting. While mathematical symbols, as well as the ability to make font subscript or superscript, generally are available in word processors, equations with more complex structures may require use of an equation composer (and these are often difficult to use). If you are in a discipline where you frequently need to write equations, you should learn to use composer software. If you use equations only infrequently, you might seek assistance from an experienced user. Alternatively, you could write the equation by hand, scan it, save it as a separate image file (such as a JPG), and then insert it like a figure into your text (scaling it as necessary).

Diagrams

Diagrams can help readers to visualize relationships and processes. Cross-referencing with the text is essential, using the appropriate figure numbers, to ensure that the relationship between any diagram and the ongoing text is clear. Any abbreviations should be explained either in the text or in a legend. To construct some simple diagrams, you may be able to use the templates found in common software (PowerPoint, for example), but more complex diagrams may require use of graphics programs to build the diagrams piece by piece. Three examples of diagrams follow.

Figure 12.6 shows, in outline form, a student's strategy for undertaking research on the environmental worldview of Buryats in Siberia. This imaginative, visually appealing diagram makes it easy for readers to grasp the step-by-step process.

Figure 12.7 shows how the same student captured diagrammatically the relationships between constructs and themes explored in her work—relationships that would be difficult to explain in words alone. Note the use of different type sizes, symbols, and lines.

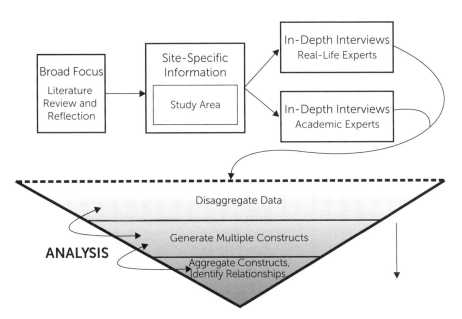

Figure 12.6 A graphic illustration of a research strategy

Source: Kamilla Bahbahani. Used with permission.

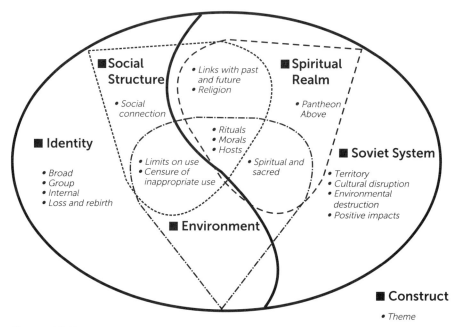

Figure 12.7 Model of the integration of the five constructs

Source: Kamilla Bahbahani. Used with permission.

Figure 12.8 reveals linkages between various present-day factors that act in and on farms and relates individual farms to others within a regional system. The end result is both attractive and instructive: the diagram communicates essential information about various "forces" that impinge on an individual farm, identifies key factors within the farm, and indicates that effects and responses occur at various levels within the system. The use of different boxes, types, shading, and arrows creates an informative illustration that says, in effect, "read me." The descriptive title places the information in a broad context (agricultural adaptation to climate variation) and indicates that the diagram represents a conceptual model.

Graphs

A graph is useful for providing a visual image of the numerical relationships among several observations. Take your time when compiling a graph; think about the style as well as the content. Figure 12.9 shows two ways of presenting the same data: one "bad" and one "good." On the left, the "bad" example uses the kind of 3D effect that is common in advertising and is often

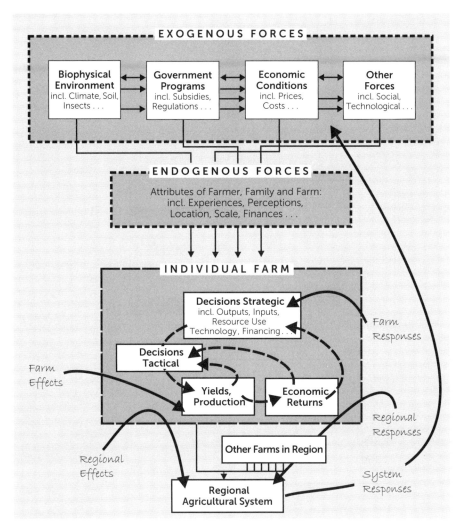

Figure 12.8 A conceptual model of agricultural adaptation to climate variation

Source: Barry Smit. Used with permission.

available in elementary computer-graphing programs. Such illustrations may be appealing, but they are not suitable for academic work. The direct style and clear patterns of the "good" example make it easy to read and also facilitate comparison of data.

There are several kinds of graphs:

- **Line graphs** reveal continuous change by using an actual or implied linking of data between observations (e.g., yearly measures of farmland

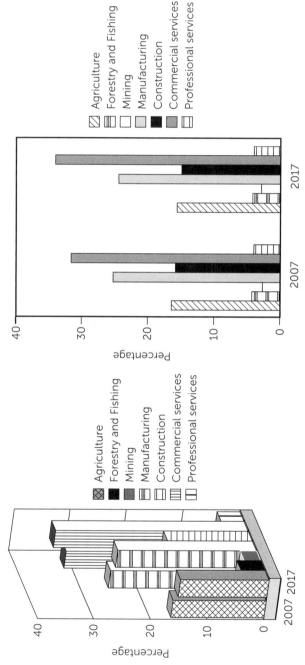

Figure 12.9 Two examples of bar graphs (a "bad" style on the left and a "good" one on the right), showing the non-government labour force in Zania by industry

Source: Table 12.1 on p. 215.

devoted to grapes). As an example, Figure 12.10 shows the numbers of students employed within a jurisdiction (on the vertical or *y*-axis [ordinate]) over a period of 24 years (on the horizontal or *x*-axis [abscissa]). A variant of a line graph is a logarithmic graph, used when data values are too high to show on an arithmetic axis.

- **Bar graphs** consist of either vertical or horizontal columns; the length of each column is proportionally equal to the value being displayed. Two vertical types are used in Figure 12.9, each with 2007 and 2017 data, to demonstrate their usefulness for comparative purposes. Figure 12.9 uses separate columns for each category; the height of each column indicates the proportional value of the category it represents. Figure 12.11, in contrast, uses one column, the total of which is 100 per cent, so the relative importance of each category is shown within the column. A **histogram** is a type of bar graph often used to show frequency of observations over time. Figure 12.12 is an example

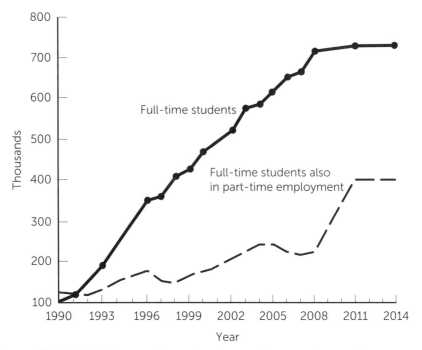

Figure 12.10 Full-time students also in part-time employment

Source: Fictitious.

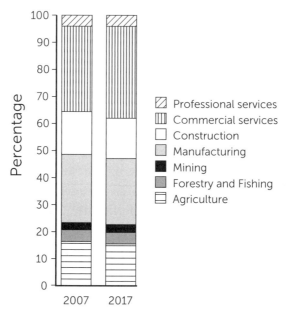

Figure 12.11 A subdivided 100 per cent bar graph, showing the non-government labour force in Zania by industry

Source: Table 12.1 on p. 215.

of a **climagraph**, which uses a histogram in the lower half to show rainfall totals for each month in "Mothvale," and a line graph to show average monthly temperatures.

- **Pie graphs** or **proportional circles** are divided into wedges indicating proportions (Figure 12.13). They are used to emphasize the proportions of individual items making up a whole (e.g., amounts of land by usage, the ethnic components of a population, or the various fauna within a particular region). These graphs show at a glance the relative importance of each category.

- **Scattergrams** show graphically the amount of correlation between two sets of statistical data. The vertical or y-axis generally depicts the dependent variable while the horizontal or x-axis depicts the independent variable. Figure 12.14 includes three scattergrams, each of which shows a different set of data, plotted according to the x and y-axes. The graphs show that differences between the sets of data exist in terms of the strength and direction of relationships. The latter are shown by a line that identifies the goodness of fit to the regression equation, with r obtained by measuring deviations from the line computed by

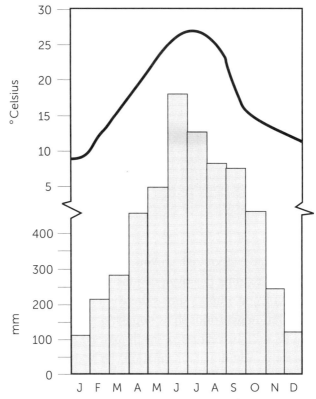

Figure 12.12   Climagraph for the Mothvale weather station

Source: Fictitious.

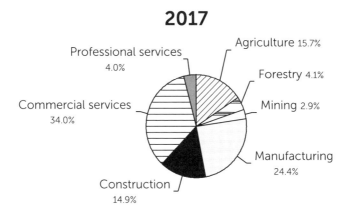

Figure 12.13   Pie graph showing the non-government labour force in Zania by industry, in 2017

Source: Table 12.1 on p. 215.

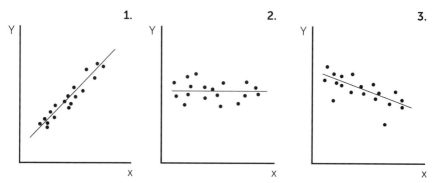

Figure 12.14 Three scattergrams

Source: Fictitious.

least squares (about which you will learn in methods courses). Graph 1 shows a strong positive relationship; graph 2 shows there is no relationship; and graph 3 shows there is a weak negative relationship.

- **Population pyramids** show population distribution by age categories— say, in 5- or 10-year steps—with males on the left half and females on the right. Additional information can be added, as in Figure 12.15.

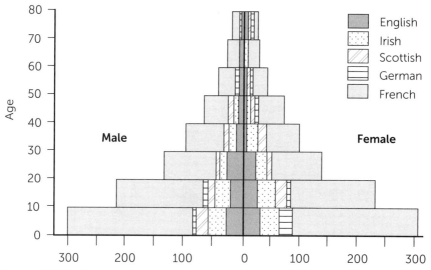

Figure 12.15 Population characteristics of L'Orignal, Ontario, by gender, age, and ethnic origins, 1871

Source: Compiled by David B. Knight from data obtained from the manuscript copy of the 1871 Census of Canada.

A basic consideration when you are deciding what kind of graph to use is the nature of the data to be shown. *Discrete data* (collected at a single time) normally are presented on bar or pie graphs, whereas *continuous data* (showing a sequence through time) generally are displayed as line graphs or histograms.

Many computer programs now permit you to develop all sorts of graphs; often it is possible to change the form of your graph simply by changing a setting. Be attentive if you are going to print your work in black and white; the finished product you see on your coloured screen may look quite different once printed on paper. Don't be lured into using some gimmicky elements of a computer program. They may look good on the screen, but they may not convey the data clearly or accurately. Indeed, the program may even *distort* your data on a graph—just as can happen on a map. Your resulting illustration would therefore be a lie.

If you don't have access to a computer, you still can make acceptable graphs if you follow these guidelines:

- Use a ruler and black ink. Draw a rough version on graph paper and then trace it onto plain paper.
- Place your dependent variable (the one you measure) on the *y*-axis and your independent variable (the one you have manipulated) on the *x*-axis. The ordinate is normally about three-quarters the length of the abscissa, although there are exceptions to this rule.
- Label the axes clearly.
- Use large and distinctive symbols, with different line thicknesses and styles.
- Include only essential details (a cluttered graph is difficult to read).
- Include a legend to show what various symbols represent.
- Identify the source(s) of the data.
- Give the graph a title and number and refer to it by that number in your text (e.g., "See Figure 7").
- Ensure that your work is neat, clean, and clear, and that all your spelling is correct.

Even if you construct your graphs by hand, you could scan them at high resolution, then add labels for the axes, the legend, and any other required text that you have created using a graphics program. This will give a more attractive result than an entirely hand-drawn graph.

Submitting Your Illustrative Work

You may be expected to submit your illustrations as part of an essay or report. Print the illustrations on high-quality paper, and number each page appropriately. Or, you may be asked to submit a map or diagram (and perhaps your whole paper or report) as a PDF (portable document format), possibly on a memory stick or as an e-mail attachment. As mentioned before, you might be assigned to place your illustrative material, likely as part of the full report, on a designated website.

No matter what method you use, always include the title of your work, your name, the course name and number, and the date of submission (be it a report, a paper, or just an illustration). Finally, remember to number each figure or table, cross-referenced to your text.

Chapter Summary

Whether you use hand-drawn pencil sketches or multi-layered GIS maps, illustrations can be a very important way to express the results of your research. Often, graphics—maps, tables, diagrams of various sorts, graphs, equations, and posters—provide the best way to present your findings clearly and accurately. As technology continues to develop, enabling each of us to improve our knowledge and understanding of the nature, patterns, relationships, and processes operative in the world that surrounds us, knowing the basics (and more) of how to design and express spatial information is an important skill. The more you practise illustrating your work, the better you will become!

Notes

1. See, for instance, J. Krygier and D. Wood, *Making Maps: A Visual Guide to Map Design for GIS*, 3rd ed. (New York: Guilford, 2016); T.A. Slocum et al., *Thematic Cartography and Geovisualization*, 3rd ed. (Englewood Cliffs, NJ: Prentice Hall, 2008); B.D. Dent et al., *Cartography: Thematic Map Design*, 6th ed. (New York: McGraw-Hill, 2008); E. Tufte, *Visual Displays of Quantitative Information*, 2nd ed. (Cheshire, CT: Graphics Press, 2001); M.-J. Kraak and F. Ormeling, *Cartography: Visualization of Spatial Data*, 3rd ed. (New York: Guilford, 2010); and M.W. Pearce and O.J. Dwyer, *Exploring Human Geography with Maps*, 2nd ed. (New York: Freeman, 2010).

2. To cite an online image correctly, follow these steps carefully:
    a) image creator's surname, first name (if available), or page author's name if available, followed by a period and a space
    b) title of image followed by a period, in quotation marks. If there is no title provided, describe briefly within quotation marks
    c) descriptive word (map, photo, drawing, etc.) followed by a period and a space
    d) website title in italics, followed by a space
    e) website publication date (in this format: DD MM YYYY) followed by a period and a space
    f) date image was viewed (in DD MM YYYY format) followed by a space
    g) Web address in angle brackets, followed by a period
3. M. Monmonier, *How to Lie with Maps*, 3rd ed. (Chicago: University of Chicago Press, 2018). Monmonier's book *No Dig, No Fly, No Go: How Maps Restrict and Control* (Chicago: University of Chicago Press, 2010) builds on *How to Lie with Maps*. See also his *Bushmanders & Bullwinkles: How Politicians Manipulate Electronic Maps and Census Data to Win Elections* (Chicago: University of Chicago Press, 2001), and J. Black, *Maps and Politics* (Chicago: University of Chicago Press, 2003). For the impact of technologies and their consequences for society, see M. Monmonier, *Spying with Maps: Surveillance Technologies and the Future of Privacy* (Chicago: University of Chicago Press, 2002).
4. Studies in this area of behavioural geography date from the 1960s; in 2018 the *Journal of Cultural Geography* published a collection of essays regarding current and historical research in mental maps. See: N. Gotz and J. Holmen. Introduction to the Theme Issue: 'Mental Maps: Geographical and Historical Perspectives,' *Journal of Cultural Geography*, 25, no. 2 (2018): 157–61, doi: 10.1080/08873631.2018.1426953.
5. Brian Tomaszewski, "I teach refugees to map their world," *The Conversation*, 18 May 2018. https://theconversation.com/i-teach-refugees-to-map-their-world-94160
6. Daniel Nations, "Is Web 3.0 Really a Thing? A Brief Intro to Web 3.0 and What to Expect," *Lifewire*, 24 March 2018. https://www.lifewire.com/what-is-web-3-0-3486623; "5 main features of Web 3.0." *Expert System* (blog), 31 January 2017. https://www.expertsystem.com/web-3-0/
7. See, for example, P.A. Longley et al., eds., *Geographic Information Science and Systems*, 4th ed. (Chichester: Wiley, 2015); C.P. Lo and A.K.W. Yeung, *Concepts and Techniques of Geographic Information Systems*, 2nd ed. (Toronto: Pearson, 2007); C.A. Brewer, *Designing Better Maps: A Guide for GIS Users*, 2nd ed. (Redlands, CA: ESRI Press, 2016); K-T. Chang, *Introduction to Geographic Information Systems*, 9th ed. (New York: McGraw-Hill, 2019); I. Heywood et al., *An Introduction to Geographical Information Systems*, 4th ed. (Englewood Cliffs, NJ: Prentice-Hall, 2012).
8. J. Krygier and D. Wood, *Making Maps: A Visual Guide to Map Design for GIS* (New York: Guilford, 2005), 267.

13 Words: Gender, Race, and Other Sensitivities

In this chapter, we examine

- why it is important to understand the meaning of words;
- ways that meanings may change; and
- how to deal with words that may have negative connotations.

Introduction

Words convey meaning. The words you use give shape to the world in which you live. But are you sure that the words you use convey the meanings you intend, with due consideration for the way they will be read and interpreted by others? Certain words may mean one thing to one reader and quite a different thing to another. To *rap*, for example, to someone of your grandparents' generation, may mean to make a quick, sharp blow with the hand on a hard surface; to someone who grew up in the 1960s, it may mean to talk, while to someone younger it likely means to sing a rapid rhyming song. The meanings of some words change slowly, others quickly, and new words are forever coming into popular use, so dictionaries have to be updated periodically. Glance through the *Oxford English Dictionary*, the *Shorter Oxford English Dictionary on Historical Principles*, or any other sound dictionary that gives etymological information and you will see the roots of words, when they were first used, what they meant then, and how they may have changed in meaning through time. We live in an age of heightened sensitivity to people's rights, and in which people readily take offence when they feel slighted. Be aware of how the words you use may be interpreted. This chapter focuses on some issues related to words and the importance of choosing them carefully.

Cultural Conventions

Cultural conventions guide us in the ways and the situations in which we may use certain words. Slang, swearing, and other expressions used in casual conversation are usually unacceptable in other settings, such as the classroom or a formal essay. A minute's reflection will bring to mind many words that may offend other people, especially in formal situations. Be aware, too, that using certain words may lead to misunderstanding, at a minimum, and at worst, some words may convey bigotry and intolerance.

Language is powerful. It can reinforce and pass on attitudes, good or bad; derogatory language, for instance, can reinforce discriminatory attitudes, actions, and institutions. Paying attention to the words we use can help us to examine our own prejudices, attitudes, and values, and even our actions toward others. As a researcher, you must acknowledge and understand your own biases and thought patterns. Knowing the importance of words as conveyers of meaning will help you achieve clarity of expression in a manner that is not offensive to others. In so doing, you may find that it is necessary to challenge conventional usage. In short, don't assume that "cultural conventions" are always "correct."

Man and . . .

Until the 1970s there were many courses and books with titles such "Man and the Land," or "Man and Environment." *Man* was taken to mean *Homo sapiens* in general, all of humankind. Yet in much of the older literature it is clear that women were indeed neglected, in research and in public life generally. While in some cases the absence of reference to women may be an accurate reflection of the author's intent, in others the use of *man* is totally misleading. For instance, to say that "ancient man developed agriculture" is to ignore the fact that in hunting and gathering societies the females largely were responsible for the domestication of plants. That's why, in this instance, it would be more accurate to use the term *ancient people*. Another example comes from an early twentieth-century geography book: ". . . man carries on his devastating activity particularly in forested regions."[1] What does *man* mean in this sentence? Men? Humans? All human societies, or only some? The same book, in a discussion of materials used for houses, states that "man finds them equally suitable for his work and for his needs."[2] Here again, you must use your imagination to realize that the author was using *man* in the generic sense, to mean human beings in general.

Today, however, it is acknowledged that the use of *man* is inappropriate when the reference is to people of both sexes: use *humankind*, or *people*, or *women and men* instead. Try to avoid the use of compound words starting or ending with *man*. For instance, you can use *police officer* for *policeman*, *fishers* for *fishermen*, *synthetic* or *artificial* for *man-made*, *English people* for *Englishmen*, and so on, if the term is intended to be inclusive. If gender is pertinent, on the other hand, specific terms such as *policewomen* and *policemen* are appropriate: don't hide gender identity when it is important for your reader to know it. (Be aware, too, that some words that may appear to be based on *man*, such as *manage, manipulate, manufacture, manner*, and *manual*, are in fact derived from the Latin *manus, hand*, so there is no need to avoid them.)

Gender-inclusive terms are easy to find, as with *the average person* for *the average man*, and *workforce* or *personnel* for *manpower* or *workmen*. Where pronouns are concerned, simply changing a singular to a plural often takes care of the problem (see pronoun agreement and gender, p. 262). Excessive dedication to gender-inclusive language can lead to awkward terms such as *horsepersonship*. Occasionally you may be able to use humour to your advantage but, in most cases, you can express the same idea in different words (in this case, *equestrian skill*).

Sometimes avoidance of a certain word can cause a loss in meaning; for instance, a *manhole cover* is generally found in a street, whereas a *maintenance cover* could be anywhere. In such cases you may have to add extra information in order to make your meaning clear. And, of course, sometimes it is necessary to use gender qualifiers, as in "The number of female geographers is increasing."

In addition to avoiding use of sexist language, you must be careful not to demean others through your choice of words. For example, don't trivialize women by making foolish or stereotypical generalizations (e.g., "Women are caring, men are not"). Pay attention to what you are writing and saying and be aware of the assumptions underlying your choice of words.

Some students confuse the terms *sex* and *gender*. *Sex*, as a noun, refers to either of the two main divisions (male and female) into which living things are placed on the basis of their reproductive functions; as an adjective, *sex* refers to sexual characteristics or instincts (such as sexual activity, sex appeal, and so on). *Gender*, as a noun, refers either to the grammatical classification of words (masculine, feminine, or neuter, as in *it*) or, notably, to psychological associations, or other characteristics (for example, role differentiation) that reveal behavioural dimensions of being. Be careful to select the appropriate word.

Race and Culture, and Racist Language

As noted above, the meanings of words may change. Such is the case with the word *race*. Beginning in the seventeenth century, early anatomists, anthropologists, and other scientists sought to categorize humans based on their shared physical traits (e.g., skull and bone measurements, as well as skin colour) or social qualities (e.g., language, national history). By the late eighteenth century, people often were identified as belonging to racial categories (e.g., Caucasian,[3] Mongolian, Negroid), but these categories increasingly have been challenged (and largely abandoned) as new understandings have been reached regarding human genetics.

All human beings alive today belong to the same sub-species, *Homo sapiens sapiens*; the Human Genome Project (1990–2003) determined that 99.9 per cent of the DNA of all living human beings is identical at the genetic level.[4] Currently there is widespread agreement among scientists that, in humans, race is not an inherent quality, neither physically nor biologically; there are no subspecies, no races, within our human species. As in any species, however, variations among individuals exist (e.g., eye colour and shape, skin tone, body size, head shape). The movement of modern humans (likely from Africa) throughout the world and into different physical environments, resulted in the development of both cultural and body feature adaptations. Sometimes because of chance genetic developments, but usually because they were environmentally appropriate, certain characteristics became dominant in particular areas of the world (e.g., darker skin tones in tropical areas, lighter skin tones in temperate areas). Globally, these genetic differences are minor; there is greater (but still small) genetic variation within populations in the same geographic area than there is between populations across the continents.

Many scholars have recognized the false beliefs associated with the term "race" and have sought to address the misconceptions among the public. For instance, in 1998 the American Anthropological Association's *Statement on Race* confirmed that all humankind is a single species, and that ". . . present-day inequalities between so-called 'racial groups' are not consequences of biological inheritance but products of historical and contemporary social, economic, educational, and political circumstances."[5] In other words, "racial" categories are socio-cultural constructs, often created by dominant social and political groups to subjugate other groups deemed to be "racially" inferior. While the causes of discrimination, racism, xenophobia, and other such issues are complex, they must be addressed if policies and practices that allow intolerance are to cease and all human rights declarations and conventions are to be upheld.

Use of language that is racist may imply—or be read by others as implying—that you accept discriminatory attitudes toward others. Don't use descriptors when they aren't required (e.g., "two black men" or "two Asian women" when "two men" or "two women" is adequate) to convey pertinent information in certain situations. Clearly, it is inappropriate to use derogatory words or racial slurs and adjectives to describe people.

Consciously try to use appropriate terminology: while not without their own challenges, words such as *origin*, *ancestry*, *identity*, or *ethnicity*, and *culture* may enable people to reflect what is meaningful about themselves to others. But the choice of words can be problematic; for instance, although Statistics Canada no longer uses the term "race" in its national census measurements, the definition of visible minority in Canada's *Employment Equity Act* uses both "Caucasian" and "race." In 2015, Statistics Canada adopted that Act's definition for use in the census, so both words remain in use despite their known sensitivities.

Culture is a complex term; typically, it includes the ideas, attitudes, behaviours, and traditions that underlie the way of life of the members of a society. The learned attributes that make one group of people culturally distinct from another include features such as language, religion, rituals, customs, celebrations, and ways of doing things. Be aware that the human capacity to identify and name different groups of people according to these cultural differences often leads to an "us" *versus* "them" distinction. This kind of binary thinking can lead beyond a mere acknowledgement of difference to include value judgments about status (superiority) and, ultimately, lead to conflict. The world does not need more conflict; let's choose our words carefully to unite our species.

Ethnicity and Visible Minorities

Associated with a concern for race and culture is the need to be aware of the appropriate words to use when referring to people with attributes that differentiate them from others in society. For example, in Canada many people speak English or French with an accent, observe holidays or traditions that may differ regionally, or are members of visible minorities. The term *South Asian*, for instance, is used to refer in a general way to people from several different countries, including India, Pakistan, Bangladesh, and Sri Lanka. Within each of these countries, significant differences of language, religious beliefs and practices, dress, and customs exist. At minimum, it is important to be aware of a person's country of origin, and to know that a Sri Lankan will not want to be called an Indian, or vice versa.

The same holds true for other parts of the world. Japanese and Chinese people, for instance, are different from one another, and would not appreciate being identified incorrectly. Belgians are not French—not even when they are Walloons (as opposed to Flemings). And while Botswana is in southern Africa, the people of that country are emphatically not South Africans. At times, of course, it may be correct to link peoples—for example, from southern Africa, or northern Europe, or South Asia—if the discussion pertains to a whole region and not simply to part of it. But keep in mind the danger of cultural "blindness": there is a tendency for North Americans to generalize about less developed countries—for instance, to consider a reference specific to Zambia as being representative of all Africa—in a way they would never do where a European country (say, Scotland or Germany) is concerned. Also, beware of generalizing about people's belief systems: not all Arabs are Muslims, and not all Muslims are Arabs; not all Jews are Zionists; not all socialists are communists; and so on.

What about "Indians" in Canada and the United States? Particularly in governmental and bureaucratic situations, the word *Indian* is used to refer to people indigenous to North America (as opposed to those who have come, or whose ancestors came, from India in South Asia). The terms *Native people* or *First Nations* (in Canada), *Native Americans* (in the United States), *Aboriginal people*, and *Indigenous people* also have been and are used, but not all of them are appropriate. The term *people* has international legal meaning; hence Canada's First Nations intentionally use the term *people* to describe themselves. Likewise, whereas Europeans used to refer to the people of the Arctic as *Eskimos*, the people themselves prefer the term *Inuit*, which means simply "the people." And, depending upon the context, it may be more appropriate to use the specific name—Cree, Naskapi, Nisga'a, Anishinaabe, Oneida, Chippewa, Navajo, etc.—rather than a broad term such as *Indigenous people*. In Canada as well as in the United States, some Indigenous people refer to themselves simply as Americans—but do not consider themselves to belong to either country. In short, be aware of what people call themselves, and use the appropriate term. And remember, never use racial slurs or derogatory or insensitive adjectives: they are demeaning and could lead you to be seen as a racist, even if you believe you are not.

Whites and Blacks and . . .

Indigenous people in Canada often use the term *white* to refer to anyone who is not Indigenous—including "non-whites." *White* often is used by "whites" to refer to themselves—to the exclusion of all "non-whites"—although contemporary governments generally do not use or accept either term. Unlike non-Maori New Zealanders, who have adopted the Maori word *pakeha* for people of European origin, non-Indigenous Canadians have not yet found a suitable term to describe themselves. Similar problems arise in designating the people in both Canada and the United States who formerly were referred to as *Negro* or *coloured*. These terms reflected the enslavement of their ancestors but were not self-chosen; instead they were applied to the population by "whites."

As a new, revitalized sense of individual and group self-worth developed in the 1960s, a determined effort was made by the people themselves to find acceptable descriptors. First *Afro-American* and then *African American*—and, similarly, *Afro-Canadian* and *African Canadian*—became popular, but *black* has also come into widespread usage (though you should be aware that not everyone today accepts *black* either; some prefer *people of colour*, and some prefer the use of country-of-origin terms). If we were to replace "white" with country-of-origin terms (e.g., European-Canadian, or Armenian-Canadian), could the term "white" then be discarded?[6] In Britain, however, *black* is used inclusively to refer to people of African, Caribbean, and South Asian origin; as you read reference sources, and as you write, keep this distinction in mind. Above all, once again, use the words that the people in question prefer, and avoid prejudicial, discriminatory terms.

Disabilities

The advocacy movement for *people with disabilities* (not *the disabled*) continues, yet many members of the general public remain unsure of the preferred terms. Here is a guide to some of them:

Do not use	Do use
afflicted	person with a disability, visually impaired, etc.
confined to a wheelchair; wheelchair-bound	person who uses a wheelchair, wheelchair user
cripple	person with a mobility impairment, a spinal-cord injury, arthritis, etc.
differently abled	person with a disability
handicapped; mental handicap	person with a disability (unless referring to an environmental or attitudinal barrier, in which case "handicapped" is appropriate); intellectually disabled
normal	person who is non-disabled ("normal" is acceptable only in reference to statistics, e.g., "the norm")
suffers from . . .	use the appropriate verb: has cerebral palsy, is hard of hearing, etc. (Disability is not synonymous with suffering.)

What is the common denominator in the right-hand column? In each of these examples the emphasis is on the person, not the disability. Remember that disabilities are incidental; they do not define people, nor do they reflect the individuality, equality, or dignity of people with disabilities.

Some terms, such as *deaf*, are in common use; but, it might sometimes be appropriate to use the phrases "person with a hearing impairment" or "person who is hard of hearing," if the disability is not total. The word *blind* is also used, but there are some people who are "visually impaired" as opposed to being totally blind. Know who it is you are referring to, and the nature of the disability they live with.

Some Final Thoughts

You must be attentive to the words you use when describing people. This chapter has identified a number of terms that may be hurtful, offensive, and divisive (and that could cause outright rejection of your work). But the list here is far from complete. How can you avoid other discriminatory terms? Although there is no foolproof method, in practically every case the best advice is simply to find out what term the people you are writing about prefer:

the more you know about any subject—including people—the less likely you are to make mistakes. An even better solution is, when possible, to do research *with* the people in question, rather than *about* or *on* them.

Chapter Summary

Words have enormous power and importance because they have meanings that allow us to communicate our ideas and to pass on knowledge about our cultures and the environment. Even though languages and the meanings of words change over time, it is very important that we carefully choose the words we use, not only to convey our meaning accurately but also to avoid racist words and those with negative connotations. Taking time to look up the meaning of any word you're not sure about, before you use it, is a good practice.

Notes

1. Jean Brunhes, *Human Geography* (Chicago: Rand McNally, 1920), 335.
2. Ibid., p. 98.
3. As much as the term *Caucasian* is an outdated, pseudo-scientific term, it is still used in forensic fields and in policing to mean a "white" person, of European origin. For a useful discussion of racial and ethnic classification schemes in the censuses of three countries that have similar demographic histories, see Gillian Stevens, Hiromi Ishizawa, and Douglas Grbic, "Measuring Race and Ethnicity in the Censuses of Australia, Canada and the United States: Parallels and Paradoxes," *Canadian Studies in Population*, 42, no. 1–2 (2015): 13–34, doi: http://dx.doi.org/10.25336/P6PW39.
4. Smithsonian Museum of Natural History, "What Does It Mean to Be Human?" June 11, 2018, http://humanorigins.si.edu/evidence/genetics/one-species-living-worldwide. For a brief overview of the Human Genome Project see National Human Genome Research Institute, "An Overview of the Human Genome Project: What was the Human Genome Project?" May 11, 2016, https://www.genome.gov/12011238/an-overview-of-the-human-genome-project/. For a brief history of the Project, see National Human Genome Research Institute, "An Overview of the Human Genome Project: A Brief History of the Human Genome Project," November 8, 2012, https://www.genome.gov/12011239/a-brief-history-of-the-human-genome-project/.
5. American Anthropological Association, "AAA Statement on Race," May 17, 1998, http://www.americananthro.org/ConnectWithAAA/Content.aspx?ItemNumber=2583.
6. Yolanda Moses, "Is the Term 'People of Color' Acceptable in This Day and Age?" December 7, 2016, https://www.sapiens.org/column/race/people-of-color/.

14 Writing with Style

In this chapter, we examine

- how to write clearly;
- how to write concisely; and
- how to become a more effective writer.

Introduction

Writing with style does not mean stuffing your prose with fancy words and extravagant images. Any style, from the simplest to the most elaborate, can be effective, depending on the occasion and intent. Writers known for their style are those who have projected something of their own personality into their writing; we can hear a distinctive voice in what they say. Obviously it takes time to develop a unique style. To begin, you have to decide what general effect you want to create. Journalists have led the trend toward short, easy-to-grasp sentences and paragraphs. When writing in an academic context, by contrast, you may expect your audience to be more reflective than the average newspaper reader, but the most effective style is still one that is clear, concise, and forceful.

Be Clear

Because sentence structure is dealt with in Chapter 15, this section focuses on the use of clear words and the creation of clear paragraphs.

Choose clear words

The key to good writing is the use of clear (easy-to-understand, unambiguous) and appropriate words. Think carefully about what you want to say and then write it out in words that convey your meaning accurately and effectively. Remember to refer to specialized disciplinary dictionaries. For hints on using dictionaries and thesauruses built into computer programs, see Chapter 1. On the changing meanings of certain words related to gender, race, and so on, see Chapter 13.

Use plain English

Plain words are often more forceful than fancy ones. If you aren't sure what plain English is, think of everyday speech (apart from profanities): how do you talk to your friends? Many of our most common words—the ones that sound most natural and direct—are short. A number of them are among the oldest words in the English language. By contrast, most of the words that English has derived from other languages are longer and more complicated; even after they've been used for centuries, some can still sound artificial. For this reason you should be aware of words loaded with prefixes (*pre-*, *post-*, *anti-*, *pro-*, *sub-*, *maxi-*, etc.) and suffixes (*-ate*, *-ize*, *-tion*, etc.). These Latinate attachments can make individual words more precise and efficient, but putting a lot of them together will make your writing seem dense and hard to understand. In many cases you can substitute a plain word for a fancy one (see Table 14.1).

Table 14.1 Examples of "fancy" and "plain" English

Fancy	Plain	Fancy	Plain
accomplish	do	oration	speech
cognizant	aware	prioritize	rank
commence	begin, start	proceed	go
conclusion	end	remuneration	pay
determinant	cause	requisite	needed
fabricate	build	sanitize	clean
finalize	finish, complete	subsequently	later
maximization	increase	systematize	order
modification	change	terminate	end
numerous	many	transpire	happen
obviate	prevent	utilize, utilization	use, use

Suggesting that you write in plain English does not mean that you should never pick an unfamiliar, long, or foreign word: sometimes those words are the only ones that will convey precisely what you mean. Inserting an unusual expression into a passage of plain writing may be an effective way to catch the reader's attention—as long as you don't do it too often. And, of course, writing clearly does not mean that you should avoid all words that have specific scientific meanings. In many circumstances, such words are invaluable for conveying precise and appropriate meanings, and using them correctly will indicate your understanding. Just remember that when you use technical language your instructors will not be impressed by the mere presence of such words; appropriate disciplinary terminology must be used correctly (see "Jargon" on p. 241). In other contexts—for example, if you are reworking an essay for submission to a newspaper—it is wise to avoid scientific terms that may not be familiar to the general reader.

Be precise

Always be as precise or exact as you can. Avoid all-purpose adjectives such as *major, significant*, and *important*, and vague verbs such as *involve, entail*, and *exist*, when you can be more specific. The two pairs of sentences, following, illustrate how precision may be improved:

> *orig.* Wagner and Mikesell <u>were involved in producing</u> the influential book *Readings in Cultural Geography*.
> *rev.* Wagner and Mikesell <u>co-edited</u> the influential book *Readings in Cultural Geography*.

> *orig.* Burning petrochemicals has a <u>significant</u> impact on the environment.
> *rev.* Burning petrochemicals has a <u>detrimental</u> impact on the environment.

Avoid unnecessary qualifiers

Qualifiers such as *very, rather*, and *extremely* are overused. Experienced writers know that saying something is *very beautiful* may have less impact than saying simply that it is *beautiful*. For example, compare these sentences:

> They devised an <u>elegant</u> hypothesis to explain the data.
> They devised a <u>very elegant</u> hypothesis to explain the data.

Which has more punch? Here are a few more examples of unnecessary qualifiers:

hard evidence	evidence
mountainous in character	mountainous
positively rejected	rejected
really dangerous	dangerous
truly substantial	substantial

When you think that an adjective needs qualifying—and sometimes it will—first see if it is possible to change either the adjective or the phrasing, and then try to write a precise statement. Instead of writing

Maple syrup production was really great last year,

write a statement such as

Maple syrup production last year was 30 per cent higher than the year before.

In some cases, qualifiers not only weaken your writing but are redundant because the adjectives themselves are absolutes. To say that something is *very unique* makes as much—or as little—sense as to say that someone is *rather pregnant* or *very dead*.

Cut redundant words

Avoid saying the same thing twice (redundant repetition is known as tautology). For example:

Tautology	*Meaning*
each individual person	each person or each individual
enclosed with this essay	enclosed
grouped together	grouped
I personally agree	I agree
my own personal opinion	my opinion
percolated down	percolated
postponed until another time	postponed
the reason for this is because	because
at this present time	now, or currently

Jargon

All academic subjects have their own terminology or jargon: special, technical language. It may be unfamiliar to "outsiders," but it helps specialists explain things to each other. Precise disciplinary jargon is appropriate for informed audiences, such as your professors and the students in your lab or seminar section. Remember, though, that you must be certain of what a specialized term means, and that you shouldn't use jargon unnecessarily, simply to make yourself seem more knowledgeable. Too often the result will be not clarity but complication. The guideline is easy: use specialized terminology only when it's a kind of shorthand that will help you explain something more precisely and efficiently to a knowledgeable audience. If plain prose will do just as well, stick to it, especially when your audience is unlikely to know the disciplinary jargon.

Create clear paragraphs

Paragraphs come in so many sizes and patterns that no single formula could possibly cover them all. There are three basic principles to remember in writing clear paragraphs:

1. A paragraph is a means of developing and framing an idea or impression.
2. The divisions between paragraphs are not random, but indicate a shift in focus.
3. Paragraphs normally include at least two sentences.

With these principles in mind, you should aim to include three elements in each paragraph:

- the topic sentence, to tell the reader the subject of the paragraph;
- a supporting sentence or sentences, to convey evidence or develop the argument; and
- a conclusion, to indicate to the reader that the paragraph is complete. The conclusion may summarize the paragraph, especially if the discussion is long or complex, and may include a reference (direct or indirect) to the topic sentence.

Keep these points in mind as you write. The following sections offer additional advice.

Develop your ideas

You are not likely to sit down and consciously ask yourself, "What pattern shall I use to develop this paragraph?" What comes first is the idea you intend to develop: the pattern the paragraph takes should flow from the idea itself and the way you want to discuss or expand it. (The most common ways of developing an idea are outlined on pp. 87–90.)

You may need one or several paragraphs to develop an idea fully. For a definition alone you could write one paragraph or ten, depending on the complexity of the subject and the nature of the assignment. Just remember that ideas need development and that each new paragraph signals a change in idea or focus in the development of your discussion.

The topic sentence

Skilled skim-readers know that they can get the general idea of a book simply by reading the first sentence of each paragraph. The reason is that most paragraphs begin by stating the central idea to be developed. If you are writing your essay from a formal plan, you probably will find that each section and subsection will generate the topic sentence for a new paragraph.

Like the thesis statement for the essay as a whole, the topic sentence is not obligatory: in some paragraphs the controlling idea is not stated until the middle or even the end, and in others it's not stated at all but merely implied. Nevertheless, it's a good idea to think out a topic sentence for every paragraph. That way you'll be sure that each one has a readily graspable point and is connected clearly to what comes before and after. When revising your initial draft, check to see that each paragraph is held together by a topic sentence, either stated or implied. If you find that you can't formulate one, you probably should rework the whole paragraph.

Focus

A clear paragraph will help to focus attention and to facilitate understanding for yourself and the reader. The lead sentence normally identifies the central idea of the paragraph and, to maintain focus, what follows should contain only details that are linked to the central idea. In addition, each paragraph should be structured so readers can see that the details are related. A good way to maintain focus is to keep the same grammatical subject in most of the sentences that make up the paragraph. When the grammatical subject is shifting all the time, a paragraph loses focus, as in the following example:

orig. In metropolitan centres, <u>main street redevelopment</u> in favour of major shopping-hotel-convention centres or large cultural complexes has become almost obligatory. <u>Rehabilitation</u> of the oldest and often the most distinctive parts of the city centre, typically identifiable with the "zone of discard" of the central business district, often takes place at the same time. <u>Economic, demographic, and cultural factors</u> of international relevance have provided the impetus for such changes. <u>Energy concerns and the return of the urban lifestyle</u> as a fashionable ideal among an influential elite are some of the factors. <u>Substantial dislocation</u> of the physical, functional, and social components of the inner city takes place, mostly at the expense of its poorer residents, as redevelopment occurs.

Most readers would lose their focus on the central message of this paragraph because the grammatical subject (underlined) constantly jumps from one thing to another. Notice how much stronger the focus becomes when all the sentences have the same grammatical subject—either the same term, a synonym, or a related pronoun:

rev. <u>Main street redevelopment</u> in metropolitan centres now favours major shopping-hotel-convention centres or cultural complexes. <u>Such redevelopment</u> usually takes place as the oldest parts of the city centre (typically the "zone of discard" of the central business district) are rehabilitated. The <u>revitalization of inner cities</u> is a response to economic, demographic, and cultural factors of international relevance, and reflects changing energy concerns and the return of the urban lifestyle as a fashionable ideal for the influential elite. Whatever its merits, the <u>revitalization process</u> entails a substantial dislocation of the physical, functional, and social components of the inner city, mostly at the expense of its poorer residents.

Naturally it's not always possible to retain the same grammatical subject (focus) throughout a paragraph. If you were comparing the athletic pursuits of *boys and girls*, for example, you would have to switch back and forth between boys and girls as your grammatical subject. In the same way, your focus would need to shift if you were discussing examples of an idea or exceptions to it.

Avoid monotony

If most or all of the sentences in your paragraph have the same grammatical subject, how do you avoid boring your reader? There are two easy ways:

- **Use stand-in words.** Pronouns, either personal (*I, we, you, he, she, it, they*) or demonstrative (*this, that, those*), can stand in for the subject, as can synonyms (words or phrases that mean the same thing). Stand-in words can be useful, but be aware that pronouns may reduce the clarity of your writing (because pronouns are less precise than the grammatical subject). In particular, avoid starting a sentence with *It* or *This* unless your referent (or, antecendent—the noun or noun phrase that a pronoun refers to) is clear and correct.
- **"Bury" the subject by putting something in front of it.** When the subject is placed in the middle of the sentence rather than at the beginning, it is less obvious to the reader. If you take another look at the revised paragraph above, you'll see that in some sentences there is a word or phrase in front of the subject, giving the paragraph a feeling of variety. Even a single word, such as *first, then, lately*, or *moreover*, will do the trick. (Incidentally, this is a useful technique to remember when you are writing an application letter and want to avoid starting every sentence with *I*.)

Link your ideas

To create coherent paragraphs, you need to link your ideas clearly. Linking words are those connectors—conjunctions and conjunctive adverbs—that show the *relations* between one sentence, or part of a sentence, and another; they also are known as transition words, because they bridge the transition from one thought to another. Make a habit of using linking words when you shift from one grammatical subject or idea to another, whether the shift occurs within a single paragraph or as you move from one paragraph to the next. See Table 14.2 for examples of commonly used connectors and the logical relations they indicate. Note that numerical terms such as *first, second*, and *third* also work well as links.

Table 14.2 Examples of connectors and their logical relations

Connectors (linking words)	Logical relation
again	addition to previous idea
also	
and	
furthermore	
in addition	
likewise	
more	
moreover	
similarly	
although	change from previous idea
but	
by contrast	
despite	
even so	
however	
in spite of	
nevertheless	
on the other hand	
rather	
yet	
accordingly	summary or conclusion
consequently	
for this reason	
hence	
so	
thus	

Vary the length, but avoid extremes

Ideally, academic writing will have a comfortable balance of long and short paragraphs. Avoid the extremes—especially the one-sentence paragraph, which can state only an idea, without explaining or developing it. A series of very short paragraphs is usually a sign that you have not developed your ideas in enough detail, or that you have started new paragraphs unnecessarily.

On the other hand, a succession of long paragraphs can be tiring and difficult to read. In deciding when to start a new paragraph, remember always to consider what is clearest and most helpful for the reader.

Be Concise

At some point, you may be tempted to pad your writing. Whatever the reason—because you need to write 2,000 or 3,000 words and have only enough to say for 1,000, or just because you think length is strength and hope to get a better mark for the extra words—padding is a mistake. You may fool some readers some of the time, but remember that your instructors are not likely to be fooled by this tactic.

Strong writing always is concise. It leaves out anything that does not serve some communicative or stylistic purpose, in order to say as much as possible in as few words as possible. Concise writing will help you do better on both your essays and your exams.

Guidelines for concise writing

Use adverbs and adjectives sparingly

Avoid the shotgun approach to adverbs and adjectives: don't include numerous modifiers unless you are sure that they clarify meaning. One well-chosen word is always better than a series of synonyms:

> *orig.*   As well as being <u>costly</u> and <u>financially</u> <u>extravagant</u>, the venture is <u>reckless</u> and <u>foolhardy</u>.
>
> *rev.*   The venture is <u>foolhardy</u> as well as <u>costly</u>.

Avoid noun clusters

A trend in some writing is to use nouns as adjectives, as in the phrase *noun cluster*. This device occasionally can be effective, but frequent use can produce an awkward pile-up of words. Breaking up noun clusters may not always produce fewer words, but it may make your writing easier to read:

> *orig.*   MP3 player utilization manual
>
> *rev.*   manual for using MP3 players
>
> *orig.*   pollution investigation committee
>
> *rev.*   committee to investigate pollution

Avoid chains of relative clauses

Sentences full of clauses beginning with *which*, *that*, or *who* typically are more wordy than necessary. Try reducing some of those clauses to phrases or single words:

orig.	The solutions <u>which</u> were discussed last night have a practical bene-fit <u>which</u> is easily grasped by people <u>who</u> have no technical training.
rev.	The solutions discussed last night have a practical benefit, easily grasped by non-technical people.

Try reducing clauses to phrases or words

Independent clauses can be reduced by subordination. Here are a few examples:

orig.	The report was written in a clear and concise manner and it was widely read.
rev.	Written in a clear and concise manner, the report was widely read.
rev.	Clear and concise, the report was widely read.
orig.	His plan was of a radical nature and was a source of embarrassment to his employer.
rev.	His radical plan embarrassed his employer.

For more detail on subordination and reduction, see pages 250–1

Strike out hackneyed expressions and circumlocutions

Trite or roundabout phrases may flow from your pen without a thought, but they make for stale prose. Unnecessary words are deadwood; be prepared to hunt and chop ruthlessly to keep your writing vital:

Wordy	Revised
at this point in time	now
consensus of opinion	consensus
due to the fact that	because
examined on a day-to-day basis	examined daily
if at all possible	if possible
in all likelihood	likely
in the eventuality that	if
in the near future	soon
it goes without saying	obviously
there was a large degree of agreement	most people agreed
we were in the process of testing	we were testing
when all is said and done	(omit)

Avoid beginning with "it is" and "there is"

Although it is not possible always, try to avoid beginning your sentences with *it is* or *there is* (*are*). Your sentences will be crisper and more concise if you do:

orig.	There is little time remaining for the industrialized countries of the world to reverse the effects of carbon dioxide on the ozone layer.
rev.	Little time remains for the industrialized countries to reverse the effects of carbon dioxide on the ozone layer.
orig.	It is certain that pollution will increase.
rev.	Pollution certainly will increase.

Be Forceful

To develop a forceful, vigorous style, you need to learn some common tricks of the trade and practise them until they become habit. Here are some suggestions.

Choose active over passive verbs

An active verb creates more energy than a passive one does:

Active: Rivers erode valley soils.

Passive: Soils in valleys are eroded by rivers.

The use of passive constructions tends to produce awkward, convoluted phrasing. Writers of bureaucratic documents are among the worst offenders. The passive verbs in the following mouthful make it hard to tell who is doing what:

It <u>has been decided</u> that the utilization of small rivers in the region for purposes of generating hydro-electric power <u>should be studied</u> by our department and that a report to the Government <u>should be made</u> by our Director as soon as possible.

Passive verbs are appropriate in four instances:

- When the subject is the passive recipient of some action:

   The politician <u>was heckled</u> by the angry crowd.

- When you want to emphasize the object rather than the person acting:

  The anti-pollution devices in all three plants <u>will be improved</u>.

- When you want to avoid an awkward shift of subject in a sentence or paragraph. Using the passive sometimes will help you maintain focus:

  The contractor began to convert the single family homes to apartments, but <u>was stopped</u> by the police because a permit had not been issued.

- When you want to avoid placing responsibility or blame:

  The plans <u>were delayed</u> when the project leader became ill.

When these exceptions don't apply, make an effort to use active verbs for a livelier style.

Use personal subjects

Many of us find it more interesting to learn about people than about things—hence the enduring appeal of gossip columns. Wherever possible, make the subjects of your sentences personal. This trick goes hand in hand with the use of active verbs. Almost any sentence becomes livelier with active verbs and a personal subject:

orig.   The <u>outcome</u> of the municipal referendum <u>was</u> the <u>decision</u> to increase the area to be preserved as green space.

rev.   <u>Residents</u> of the municipality <u>voted</u> to increase the area to be preserved as green space.

Here is another example:

orig.   It can be assumed that <u>an agreement was reached</u> because <u>there were smiles</u> on both city and developer sides when the meeting <u>was finished</u>.

rev.   Apparently, <u>the city and the developer reached an agreement</u> because <u>both bargainers were smiling</u> when <u>they finished</u> the meeting.

Use concrete details

Concrete details are easier to understand—and to remember—than abstract theories. Whenever you are discussing abstract concepts, always provide specific examples and illustrations; if you have a choice between a concrete word and an abstract one, choose the concrete word. Consider this sentence:

> The French explored the northern territory and traded with the Indigenous peoples.

Now see how a few specific details can bring the facts to life:

> The French voyageurs paddled their way along the river systems of the north, trading their blankets and copper kettles for the Iroquois peoples' furs.

Suggesting that you add concreteness doesn't mean getting rid of all abstractions. Balance the abstractions you use with accurate details. Additional information, if concrete and accurate, can improve your writing.

Make important ideas stand out

Experienced writers know how to manipulate sentences in order to emphasize certain points. Here are some of their techniques:

Place key words in strategic positions

The positions of emphasis in a sentence are the beginning and, above all, the end. If you want to bring your point home with force, don't put the key words in the middle of the sentence. Save them for the last:

> *orig.* People are less concerned with efficient and equitable use of resources than they are with getting what they want in this consumption-oriented society.

> *rev.* In this consumption-oriented society, people are less concerned with efficient and equitable use of resources than with getting what they want.

Subordinate minor ideas

People sometimes connect incidents with a string of *and*s, as if everything were of equal importance:

> We went to the study site and we saw a bear and John spilled his drink.

Remember to subordinate; that is, to make one part of a sentence less important in order to emphasize another point:

> Because of the flooding river, students couldn't get to their field study site.

Major ideas stand out more and connections become clearer when minor ideas are subordinated:

orig.   The oil well blew out and a repair crew was called in.

rev.   When the oil well blew out, a repair crew was called in.

Make your most important idea the subject of the main clause, and try to put it at the end, where it will be most emphatic:

orig.   I was relieved when I saw my marks.

rev.   When I saw my marks, I was relieved.

Vary sentence structure

As with anything else, variety adds spice to writing. One way to add variety, which also will make an important idea stand out, is to use a periodic rather than a simple sentence structure.

Most sentences follow the simple pattern of **s**ubject-**v**erb-**o**bject (plus modifiers):

The <u>dog</u> <u>bit</u> the <u>man</u> on the ankle.

       S   V   O

A *simple sentence* such as the one above gives the main idea at the beginning of the sentence, making it straightforward and easy to read. A *periodic sentence*, on the other hand, does not give the main clause until the end, following one or more subordinate clauses:

Since he had failed to keep his promises or to inspire the voters, in the next election <u>he</u> <u>was defeated</u>.

                S   V

The longer the periodic sentence is, the greater the suspense and the more emphatic the final part. Because this high-tension structure is more difficult to read than the simple sentence, your readers would be exhausted if you used it too often. Save it for those times when you want to create a special effect or play on emotions.

Vary sentence length

A short sentence can add punch to an important point, especially when it comes as a surprise. This technique can be used particularly effectively for conclusions. Don't overdo it, though. A string of long sentences may be monotonous, but a string of short ones has a staccato effect that can make your writing sound like a child's reader: "This is my turtle. See him swim." Still, academic papers are more likely to have too many long sentences than too many short ones. Because short sentences are easier to read, try breaking up clusters of long ones. Aim for variety.

Use contrast

Just as a jeweller will highlight a diamond by displaying it against dark velvet, so you can highlight an idea by placing it against a contrasting background:

> *orig.* Most employees in industry do not have indexed pensions.
>
> *rev.* Unlike civil servants, most employees in industry do not have indexed pensions.

Using parallel phrasing will increase the effect of the contrast:

> Although he often spoke to university audiences, he seldom spoke to business groups.

Use a well-placed adverb or correlative construction

Adding an adverb or two sometimes can help you to dramatize a concept:

> *orig.* Although I dislike the proposal, I must accept it as the practical answer.
>
> *rev.* Although emotionally I dislike the concept, intellectually I must accept it as the practical answer.

Correlatives such as *both . . . and* or *not only . . . but also* can be used to emphasize combinations as well:

> *orig.* Smith was a good lecturer and a good friend.
>
> *rev.* Smith was both a good lecturer and a good friend.
>
> *rev.* Smith was not only a good lecturer but also a good friend.

Use repetition

Repetition is a highly effective emphatic device. It helps to stir the emotions:

> He fought injustice and corruption. He fought complacent politicians and inept policies. He fought hard, but he always fought fairly.

Of course, you would use such a dramatic technique on rare occasions only.

Use your ears

Your ears are probably your best critics: make good use of them. Before producing a final copy of any piece of writing, read it out loud, in a clear voice. The difference between cumbersome and fluent passages will be unmistakable.

Some Final Advice: Write Before You Revise

No one would expect you to sit down and put all this advice into practice as soon as you start to write. You would feel so constrained that it would be hard to get anything down on paper at all. You will be better off if you begin practising these techniques during the editing process, when you are looking critically at what you have already written. Some experienced writers can combine the creative and critical functions, but most of us find it easier to write a rough draft first, before starting the detailed task of revising.

Chapter Summary

People use many techniques in their efforts to write clearly, accurately, concisely, and effectively. Yet, in an academic context, the importance of thinking clearly in advance—about what it is that you want to say, about the words that will help you say what you mean—is fundamental. The suggestions that have been made in this chapter highlight some of the methods you can practise as you learn to write in an impactful manner.

15 Grammar and Usage

In this chapter, we examine

- the basics of grammar;
- well-constructed sentences and how to write them; and
- problems to avoid when you write your course work.

Introduction

This chapter is not a comprehensive grammar lesson: it's simply a survey of those areas where students most often make mistakes. It will help you to keep a lookout for weaknesses as you are editing your work. Once you get into the habit of checking, it won't be long before you are correcting potential problems as you write. The grammatical terms used here are the most simple and familiar ones; if you need to review some of them, see pages 310–28.

Troubles with Sentence Unity

Sentence fragments

To be complete, a sentence must have both a subject and a verb in an independent clause; if it does not, it is a fragment. Occasionally a sentence fragment is acceptable, as in

> Will the government try to privatize national parks? <u>Not likely</u>.

Here the sentence fragment *not likely* is clearly intended to be understood as a short form of *It is not likely that it will try.* Unintentional sentence fragments, on the other hand, usually seem incomplete rather than shortened:

> ✗   I enjoy studying geography. Being a person who is interested in the world around me.

The last "sentence" is incomplete: where are the subject and verb? (Remember that a participle such as *being* is not a verb; "-ing" words by themselves are only verbals or part-verbs.) The fragment can be made into a complete sentence by adding a subject and a verb:

> ✔ <u>I am</u> a person who is interested in the world around me.

Alternatively, you could join the fragment to the preceding sentence:

> ✔ Being interested in the world around me, I enjoy studying geography.
> ✔ I enjoy studying geography, because I am interested in the world around me.

Run-on sentences

A run-on sentence is one that continues beyond the point where it should have stopped:

> ✘ Mosquitoes and blackflies are annoying, but they don't stop tourists from coming to spend their holidays in Canada and such is the case in Ontario's northland.

The *and* should be dropped and a period or semicolon added after *Canada*.

Another kind of run-on sentence is one in which two independent clauses (phrases that could stand by themselves as sentences) are wrongly joined by a comma:

> ✘ Jason Waterman has won international acclaim as a specialist on soil erosion, he is a geography professor at Waitsfield University.

This error is known as a *comma splice*. There are three ways of correcting it:

1. by putting a period after *erosion* and starting a new sentence:

   > . . . on soil erosion. He . . .

2. by replacing the comma with a semicolon:

   > . . . on soil erosion; he . . .

3. by making one of the independent clauses subordinate to the other:

   > Jason Waterman, who has won international acclaim as a specialist on soil erosion, is a geography professor at Waitsfield University.

The one exception to the rule that independent clauses cannot be joined by a comma arises when the clauses are very short and arranged in a tight sequence:

I opened the door, I saw the skunk, I shut the door.

Such instances are uncommon, obviously.

Contrary to what many people think, words such as *however*, *therefore*, and *thus* cannot be used to join independent clauses:

✗ Two of my friends started out in commerce, however, they quickly decided they didn't like accounting.

The mistake can be corrected by beginning a new sentence after *commerce* or (preferably) by putting a semicolon in the same place:

✔ Two of my friends started out in commerce; however, they quickly decided they didn't like accounting.

The only words that can be used to join independent clauses are the coordinating conjunctions—*and*, *or*, *nor*, *but*, *for*, *yet*, and *so*—and subordinating conjunctions such as *if*, *because*, *since*, *while*, *when*, *where*, *after*, *before*, and *until*.

Faulty predication

When the subject of a sentence is not connected grammatically to what follows (the predicate), the result is faulty predication:

✗ The <u>reason</u> for the failure of the IMF program was <u>because</u> it did not address the needs of the poor.

The problem here is that *because* means essentially the same thing as *the reason for*. The subject needs a noun clause to complete it:

✔ The <u>reason</u> for the failure of the IMF program was <u>that</u> it did not address the needs of the poor.

Another solution would be to rephrase the sentence:

✔ The IMF program failed because it did not address the needs of the poor.

Faulty predication also occurs with *is when* and *is where* constructions:

✗ The critical moment <u>is when</u> the researcher discovers the original source of the information.

You can correct this error in one of two ways:

1. Follow the *is* with a noun phrase to complete the sentence:

   ✔ The critical moment is <u>the discovery of the original source</u> by the researcher.

   (or)

   ✔ The critical moment is <u>the researcher's discovery</u> of the original source.

2. Change the verb:

   ✔ The critical moment <u>occurs</u> when the researcher discovers the original source.

Troubles with Subject–Verb Agreement

Identifying the subject

A verb should always agree in number with its subject. Sometimes, however, when the subject does not come at the beginning of the sentence, or when it is separated from the verb by other information, you may be tempted to use a verb form that does not agree:

   ✘ The <u>increase</u> in the rate for freight and passengers <u>were condemned</u> by the farmers.

The subject here is *increase*, not *freight and passengers*; therefore, the verb should be the singular *was condemned*:

   ✔ The <u>increase</u> in the rate for freight and passengers <u>was condemned</u> by the farmers.

"Either," "neither," "each"

The indefinite pronouns *either*, *neither*, and *each* always take singular verbs:

   ✘ <u>Neither</u> of those glaciers <u>have</u> a major crevasse.

   ✔ <u>Neither</u> of those glaciers <u>has</u> a major crevasse.

   ✔ <u>Each</u> of these glaciers <u>has</u> many crevasses.

Compound subjects

When *or, either . . . or*, or *neither . . . nor* is used to create a compound subject, the verb usually should agree with the last item in the subject:

✔ Neither the city planner nor the developers are going to the Municipal Board hearing.

If a singular item follows a plural item, however, a singular verb may sound awkward, and it's better to rephrase the sentence:

orig. Either my geography <u>books</u> or my biology <u>text is going</u> to gather dust this weekend.

rev. This weekend, I am going to read either my geography books or my biology text.

Unlike the word *and*, which creates a compound subject and therefore takes a plural verb, *as well as* or *in addition to* does not create a compound subject; therefore, the verb remains singular:

✔ Fertile soil <u>and</u> a good climate <u>are</u> important requirements for agriculture.

✔ Fertile soil <u>as well as</u> a good climate <u>is</u> an important requirement for agriculture.

Collective nouns

A collective noun is a singular noun, such as *family, class, army*, or *team*; each of these nouns includes a number of members. If the noun refers to the members as a unit, it takes a singular verb:

✔ The cultural geography <u>class goes</u> to the museum each year.

If the noun refers to the members as individuals, however, the verb becomes plural:

✔ The <u>team are receiving</u> their sweaters before the exhibition game.

✔ The <u>majority</u> of immigrants to North America <u>settle</u> in cities.

Titles

A title is singular even if it contains plural words; therefore, it takes a singular verb:

- ✔ *Tales of the South Pacific* was a bestseller.
- ✔ McCarthy and McCarthy is handling the court case.

Tense Troubles

Native speakers of English usually know the correct sequence of verb tense by ear, but a few tenses still can be confusing.

The past perfect

If the main verb is in the past tense and you want to refer to something before that time, use the past perfect (*had* plus the past participle). The time sequence will not be clear if you use the simple past in both clauses:

- ✗ He hoped that she <u>finished</u> reading the map.
- ✔ He hoped that she <u>had finished</u> reading the map.

Similarly, when you are reporting what someone said in the past—that is, when you are using past indirect discourse—you should use the past perfect tense in the clause describing what was said:

- ✗ He said that the tractor <u>caused</u> the soil compaction.
- ✔ He said that the tractor <u>had caused</u> the soil compaction.

Using "if"

When you are describing a possibility in the future, use the present tense in the condition (*if*) clause and the future tense in the consequence clause:

- ✔ If he <u>tests</u> us on Hägerstrand's diffusion model, I <u>will fail</u>.

When the possibility is unlikely, it is conventional—especially in formal writing—to use the subjunctive in the *if* clause, and *would* plus the base verb in the consequence clause:

✔ If she <u>were to cancel</u> the exam, <u>I would cheer</u>.

When you are describing a hypothetical instance in the past, use the past subjunctive (it has the same form as the past perfect) in the *if* clause, and *would have* plus the past participle for the consequence. A common error is to use *would have* in both clauses:

✘ If he <u>would have been</u> clearer, I <u>would have been</u> able to understand the question.

✔ If he <u>had been</u> clearer, I <u>would have been</u> able to understand the question.

Writing about literature

When you are describing a literary work in its historical context, use the past tense:

✔ Margaret Atwood <u>wrote</u> *Surfacing* at a time when George Grant's *Technology and Empire* <u>was persuading</u> people to reassess technocratic values.

To discuss what goes on *within* a work of literature, however, you should use the present tense:

✔ The narrator <u>retreats</u> to the woods and <u>tries</u> to escape the rationalism of her father's world.

When you are discussing an episode or incident in a literary work and want to refer to a prior incident or a future one, use past or future tenses accordingly:

✔ The narrator returns to Otago, where she <u>spent</u> her summers as a child; by the time she leaves, she <u>will have rediscovered</u> herself.

Be sure to return to the present tense when you have finished referring to events in the past or future.

Pronoun Troubles

Pronoun reference

The link between a pronoun and the noun it refers to must be clear. If the noun doesn't appear in the same sentence as the pronoun, it should appear in the preceding sentence:

✗   The textbook supply in the bookstore had run out, and so we borrowed <u>them</u> from the library.

Because *textbook* is used as an adjective rather than a noun, it cannot serve as referent or antecedent for the pronoun *them*. You must either replace *them* or change the phrase *textbook supply.*

✔   The <u>textbook supply</u> in the bookstore had run out, and so we borrowed the <u>texts</u> from the library.

✔   The <u>textbooks</u> in the bookstore had run out, and so we borrowed <u>them</u> from the library.

When a sentence contains more than one noun, make sure there is no ambiguity about which noun the pronoun refers to:

✗   The public wants increased social <u>services</u> as well as lower <u>taxes</u>, but the government does not advocate <u>them</u>.

What does the pronoun *them* refer to? The taxes, the social services, or both?

✔   The public wants <u>increased</u> social <u>services</u> as well as lower taxes, but the government does not advocate spending <u>increases</u>.

Using "it" and "this"

Using *it* and *this* without a clear referent can lead to confusion:

✗   Although the directors wanted to meet in January, <u>it</u> (<u>this</u>) didn't take place until May.

✔   Although the directors wanted to meet in January, <u>the conference</u> didn't take place until May.

Make sure that *it* or *this* clearly refers to a specific noun or pronoun.

Pronoun agreement and gender

A pronoun should agree in number and person with the noun that it refers to. Traditionally, the following sentence would have been considered incorrect:

> When a federal <u>employee</u> retires, <u>their</u> pension is indexed.

In the past, this sentence would have been revised as follows:

> When a federal <u>employee</u> retires, <u>his</u> pension is indexed.

The problem with this revision is that, in using the pronoun *his*, it appears to neglect the many female federal employees who also retire. Although some language experts still maintain that *he* has a dual meaning, one for an individual male and one for any human, today this usage is widely regarded as sexist. One solution is to use *his/her*, but this phrase is intrusive and awkward. For that reason, use of the plural *their* with reference to a singular noun, as in the first example above, is becoming increasingly common, and this trend appears to be gaining acceptance. Some people still object to it, however. To be on the safe side, you may prefer to rephrase the sentence—for example, by changing the singular noun to a plural:

> When federal <u>employees</u> retire, <u>their pensions are</u> indexed.

Whatever form you choose, check for agreement between subjects and verbs. Use neutral nouns whenever possible (see pp. 229–31). And, where appropriate, at least try to make clear in your examples and illustrations that you are referring to females as well as males—unless there is a clear need to differentiate.

Using "one"

People often use the word *one* to avoid overusing *I* or *you* in their writing. Although in Britain this is common, in Canada and the United States frequent use of *one* may seem too formal and even a bit pompous:

> If <u>one</u> were to apply for the grant, <u>one</u> would find oneself engulfed in so many bureaucratic forms that <u>one's</u> patience would be stretched thin.

In the past, a common way around this problem was to use the third person *his* or *her* as the adjectival form of *one*. Yet today this usage is increasingly regarded as unacceptable. As we saw in the preceding section, in some cases you may be able to substitute the plural *their*; just remember that some people still object to this usage as well.

In any case, try to use *one* sparingly, and don't be afraid of the occasional *I*. The one serious error is to mix the third person *one* with the second person *you*:

✘ When <u>one</u> visits the Rockies, <u>you</u> are impressed by the grandeur of the scenery.

Solutions include:

✔ When <u>you</u> visit the Rockies, <u>you</u> are impressed by the grandeur of the scenery.

✔ When visiting the Rockies, <u>you</u> are impressed by the grandeur of the scenery.

In formal academic writing generally, *you* is not an appropriate substitute for *one*.

Using "me" and other objective pronouns

Remembering that it is wrong to say "Ahmed and *me* were invited to speak to the planning committee" rather than "Ahmed and *I* were invited," many people use the subjective form of the pronoun even when the objective form is correct:

✘ The planning committee invited Ahmed and <u>I</u> to speak.

✔ The planning committee invited Ahmed and <u>me</u> to speak.

The verb *invited* requires an object, and *me* is the objective case. Here is a simple hint: read the sentence with only the problem pronoun ("... committee invited ... I to speak"). You will know by ear which form is correct:

✔ The planning committee invited <u>me</u> to speak.

Prepositions should also be followed by the objective case:

✘ <u>Between</u> you and <u>I</u>, Brown is a bore.

✔ <u>Between</u> you and <u>me</u>, Brown is a bore.

✘ Eating well is a problem <u>for we</u> students.

✔ Eating well is a problem <u>for us</u> students.

There are times, however, when the correct case can sound stiff or awkward:

> To whom was the award given?

Rather than keep to a correct but awkward form, try to reword the sentence:

> Who received the award?

Exceptions for pronouns following prepositions

The rule that a pronoun following a preposition takes the objective case has exceptions. When the preposition is followed by a clause, the pronoun should take the case required by its position in the clause:

> ✗ The students showed some concern over <u>whom would be selected</u> as spokesperson.

Although the pronoun follows the preposition *over*, it is also the subject of the verb *would be selected* and therefore requires the subjective case:

> ✔ The students showed some concern over <u>who would be selected</u> as spokesperson.

Similarly, when a gerund (a word that acts partly as a noun and partly as a verb) is the subject of a clause, the pronoun that modifies it takes the possessive case:

> ✗ The professor was impressed by <u>him presenting</u> both sides of the issue.

> ✔ The professor was impressed by <u>his presenting</u> both sides of the issue.

> ✗ He was tired of <u>me reminding</u> him.

> ✔ He was tired of <u>my reminding</u> him.

Troubles with Modifying

Adjectives modify nouns; adverbs modify verbs, adjectives, and other adverbs. Do not use an adjective to modify a verb:

> ✗ He played <u>good</u>. (Adjective with verb)

> ✔ He played <u>well</u>. (Adverb modifying verb)

> ✔ He played <u>really well</u>. (Adverb modifying adverb)

✔ He had a <u>good style</u>. (Adjective modifying noun)

✔ He had a <u>really good style</u>. (Adverb modifying adjective)

Squinting modifiers

Remember that clarity largely depends on word order: to avoid confusion, the relations between the different parts of a sentence must be clear. Modifiers should be as close as possible to the words they modify. A *squinting modifier* is one that, because of its position, seems to look in two directions at once:

✗ She expected <u>in the spring</u> the river to flood the valley.

Was *spring* the time of expectation or the time of the flood? To make the logical relation clear, try changing the order of the sentence, or rephrasing:

✔ <u>In the spring</u> she <u>expected</u> the river to flood the valley.

✔ She expected the river <u>to flood</u> the valley <u>in the spring</u>.

✔ She expected a <u>spring flood</u> in the valley.

Other squinting modifiers can be corrected in the same way:

✗ Our professor gave a lecture on rock slides in Mellon Hall, <u>which was well illustrated</u>.

✔ Our professor gave a <u>well-illustrated lecture</u> in Mellon Hall on <u>rock slides</u>.

Often the modifier works best when it is placed immediately in front of the element it modifies. Notice the difference that this placement makes:

<u>Only</u> she guessed the source of the error.

She <u>only</u> guessed the source of the error.

She guessed <u>only</u> the source of the error.

Dangling modifiers

Modifiers that have no grammatical connection with anything else in the sentence are said to be *dangling*:

✗ <u>Walking</u> around the campus in July, the river and trees made a picturesque scene.

Who is doing the walking? Here's another example:

✗ <u>Reflecting</u> on the results of the referendum, it was decided not to press for independence for a while.

Who is doing the reflecting? Clarify the meaning by connecting the dangling modifier to a new subject:

✔ <u>Walking</u> around the campus in July, <u>she</u> thought the river and trees made a picturesque scene.

✔ <u>Reflecting</u> on the results of the referendum, <u>the government</u> decided not to press for independence for a while.

Troubles with Pairs (and More)

Comparisons

Make sure that your comparisons are complete. The second element in a comparison should be equivalent to the first, whether the equivalence is stated or merely implied:

✗ Today's students have a greater understanding of calculus than their parents.

This sentence suggests that the two things being compared are *calculus* and *parents*. Adding a second verb (*have*) equivalent to the first one shows that the two things being compared are *parents' understanding* and *students' understanding*:

✔ Today's students <u>have</u> a greater understanding of calculus than their parents <u>have</u>.

A similar problem arises in the following comparison:

✗ That politician is <u>a tiresome man</u> and so are his press conferences.

Press conferences may be tiresome, but they are not a tiresome man. To make sense, the two parts of the comparison must be parallel:

✔ That politician is <u>tiresome</u>, and so are his press conferences.

Correlatives (coordinate constructions)

Constructions such as *both . . . and*, *not only . . . but*, and *neither . . . nor* are especially tricky. The coordinating term must not come too early, or else one of the parts that follows will not connect with the common element. For the implied comparison to work, the two parts that come after the coordinating term must be grammatically equivalent:

- ✘ He <u>not only</u> bakes cakes <u>but also</u> bread.

- ✔ He bakes <u>not only</u> cakes <u>but also</u> bread.

Parallel phrasing

A series of items in a sentence should be phrased in parallel wording. Make sure that all the parts of a parallel construction are in fact equal:

- ✘ Mackenzie King loved <u>his</u> job, <u>his</u> dogs, and mother.

- ✔ Mackenzie King loved <u>his</u> job, <u>his</u> dogs, and <u>his</u> mother.

Once you have decided to include the pronoun *his* in the first two elements, the third must have it too.

For clarity as well as stylistic grace, keep similar ideas in similar form:

- ✘ He <u>failed</u> Economics and <u>barely passed</u> Statistics, but Periglacial Geomorphology <u>was</u> a subject he did well in.

- ✔ He <u>failed</u> Economics and <u>barely passed</u> Statistics but <u>did well</u> in Periglacial Geomorphology.

Chapter Summary

While many students think that studying grammar is the most boring thing possible, learning the syntax (rules) of sentence construction in English (or any language) can improve your writing style and help you think and write more clearly and creatively. Using language correctly is essential to writing effectively; if you write well, your train of thought and your ideas will be clear to your instructor (and may result in higher grades). Applying grammatical rules appropriately, and becoming an effective communicator as a result, is important to your academic achievement, for your career success, and in your professional and personal communications.

16 Punctuation

In this chapter, we examine
- rules of punctuation and why you need to know them;
- how to use commas, periods, semicolons, and colons; and
- ways to use punctuation marks in sentences of varying complexity.

Introduction

Punctuation causes students so many problems that it deserves a chapter of its own. If your punctuation is faulty, your readers will be confused and may have to backtrack; worse still, they may be tempted to skip over the rough spots. Punctuation marks are the traffic signals of writing; use them with precision to keep readers moving smoothly through your work. Topics in this chapter are arranged alphabetically: *apostrophe, brackets, colon, comma, dash, ellipsis, exclamation mark, hyphen, italics or underlining, parentheses, period, quotation marks, quotation marks with punctuation, semicolon,* and *underlining.*

Apostrophe [']

The apostrophe forms the possessive case for nouns and some pronouns. (Remember that possession also may be shown without an apostrophe if the possessor is preceded by *of,* as in *the work of Harvey,* or *the end of the day.*)

1. **Add an apostrophe followed by *s* to**
   - all singular and plural nouns not ending in *s: the cat's dish, women's studies.*
   - singular *proper* nouns ending in *s: Kates's article, Sis's birthday* (but note that the final *s* can be omitted if the word has a number

of them already and would sound awkward, as in *Jesus'* or certain classical names such as *Eratosthenes'*.

   • indefinite pronouns: *someone's, anybody's,* etc.

2. **Add an apostrophe to plural nouns ending in** *s*: *our families' houses, the players' uniforms.*

3. **Use an apostrophe to show contractions of words**: *isn't, can't, winter of '97.* Caution: don't confuse *it's* (the contraction of *it is*) with the possessive of *it* (*its*), which has no apostrophe.

Brackets, or Square Brackets [ ]

Brackets are square enclosures, not to be confused with parentheses (which are round). Brackets are often referred to as square brackets.

Use brackets to set off a remark of your own within a quotation. Brackets show that the words enclosed are not those of the person quoted:

> Cowan maintains, "Obstacles to western unification [in the next decade] are as many as they are serious."

Brackets are sometimes used to enclose *sic* (Latin for *thus*), which is used after an error, such as a misspelling, to show that the mistake was in the original. *Sic* may be italicized or underlined:

> The politician, in his letter to constituents, wrote about "these parlouse [*sic*] times of economic difficulty."

Colon [:]

A colon indicates that something is to follow.

1. **Use a colon before a formal statement or series:**

   ✔ The winners are the following: Alain, Vladimir, and Sonia.

   Don't use a colon if the words preceding it do not form a complete sentence:

   ✘ The winners are: Alain, Vladimir, and Sonia.

   ✔ The winners are Alain, Vladimir, and Sonia.

Occasionally, however, a colon is used if the list is arranged vertically:

✔ The winners are: Alain

Vladimir

Sonia

2. **Use a colon for formality before a direct quotation:**

The leaders of the anti-nuclear group repeated their message: "The world needs bread before bombs."

3. **Use a colon between numbers or groups of numbers expressing time and ratios:**

5:46 p.m.

1:100 (as in "1 cm equals 100 m," or "1 inch equals 100 feet")

Comma [,]

Commas are the trickiest of all punctuation marks; even the experts differ on when to use them. Most agree, however, that too many commas are as bad as too few, since they make writing choppy and awkward to read. Certainly recent writers use fewer commas than earlier stylists did. Whenever you are in doubt, let clarity be your guide. The most widely accepted conventions are these:

1. **Use a comma to separate two independent clauses joined by a coordinating conjunction** (*and, but, for, or, nor, yet, so*). By signalling that there are two clauses, the comma will prevent readers from confusing the beginning of the second clause with the end of the first:

✘ He went out for dinner with his sister and his roommate joined them later.

✔ He went out for dinner with his sister, and his roommate joined them later.

When the second clause has the same subject as the first, you have the option of omitting both the second subject and the comma:

✔ He can construct a stem and leaf plot, but he cannot calculate the mean.

✔ He can construct a stem and leaf plot but cannot calculate the mean.

If you mistakenly punctuate two sentences as if they were one, the result will be a *run-on sentence*; if you use a comma but forget the coordinating conjunction, the result will be a *comma splice*:

✗ She went to the library, it was closed.

✔ She went to the library, but it was closed.

Remember that words such as *however, therefore,* and *thus* are conjunctive adverbs, not conjunctions: if you use one of them the way you would use a conjunction, the result will again be a *comma splice*:

✗ She was accepted into graduate school, however, she took a year off to earn her tuition.

✔ She was accepted into graduate school; however, she took a year off to earn her tuition.

Conjunctive adverbs often are confused with conjunctions. You can distinguish between the two if you remember that a conjunctive adverb's position in a sentence can be changed:

✔ She was accepted into graduate school; she took a year off, however, to earn her tuition.

The position of a conjunction, on the other hand, is invariable; it must be placed between the two clauses:

✔ She was accepted into graduate school, but she took a year off to earn her tuition.

When, in rare cases, the independent clauses are short and closely related, they may be joined by a comma alone:

✔ I came, I saw, I conquered.

A *fused sentence* is a run-on sentence in which independent clauses are slapped together with no punctuation at all:

✗ He watched the wave tank all afternoon the only exercise he got was going to the cafeteria for an occasional break.

A fused sentence sounds like breathless babbling—and it is a serious error.

2. **Use a comma between items in a series.** Place a coordinating conjunction before the last item:

   ✔ The landscape had nucleated villages, houses with mansard roofs, and "French" church architecture.

   ✔ Continuing agricultural expansion in frontier areas is a reflection of economic factors, technological change, available labour, and government policies.

   The comma before the conjunction is optional:

   ✔ She kept a cat, a dog and a budgie.

   Sometimes, however, the final comma can help to prevent confusion:

   ✔ When we set out to do our field work, we were warned about muddy fields, angry farmers, trespassing on private property, and bears.

   In this case, the comma prevents the reader from thinking that *we* might trespass on *bears* as well as on *private property*.

3. **Use a comma to separate adjectives preceding a noun when they modify the same element:**

   > It was a rainy, windy night.

   When the adjectives do *not* modify the same element, you should *not* use a comma:

   > It was a pleasant winter outing.

   Here *winter* modifies *outing*, but *pleasant* modifies the total phrase *winter outing*. A good way of determining whether or not you need a comma is to see whether you can reverse the order of the adjectives. If you can reverse it (*rainy, windy night* or *windy, rainy night*), use a comma; if you cannot (*winter pleasant outing*), omit the comma.

4. **Use commas to set off an interruption (or "parenthetical element"):**

   ✔ The film, I hear, isn't nearly as good as the book.

   ✔ My tutor, however, couldn't answer the question.

   Remember to put commas on both sides of the interruption:

   ✘ The model, they say was adapted from a model in biology.

   ✔ The model, they say, was adapted from a model in biology.

5. **Use commas to set off words or phrases that provide additional but non-essential information:**

✔ Our president, Sue Stephens, does her job well.

✔ The black retriever, his closest companion, went with him everywhere.

Sue Stephens and *his closest companion* are *appositives*: they give additional information about the nouns they refer to (*president* and *retriever*), but the sentences would be understandable without them. Here is another example:

✔ The Minister of Environment, who represents Edmonton South, was in Paris last week.

The phrase *who represents Edmonton South* is called a *non-restrictive* modifier, because it does not limit the meaning of the phrase it modifies (*Minister of Environment*). Without that modifying clause the sentence would still specify who was in Paris last week. Since the information the clause provides is not necessary to the meaning of the sentence, you must use commas on both sides to set it off.

By contrast, a *restrictive* modifier is one that provides essential information; it must not be set apart from the element it modifies, and commas should not be used:

✔ The Six Nations people who live near Brantford do not yet hold title to land along the entire Grand River.

Without the clause *who live near Brantford*, the reader might not know where the people live.

To avoid confusion, be sure to distinguish carefully between essential and additional information. The difference can be important:

Students, who are not willing to work, should not receive grants.

Students who are not willing to work should not receive grants.

6. **Use a comma after an introductory phrase when omitting it would cause confusion:**

✘ On the river bank above the happy fluvial geomorphologist stood.

✔ On the river bank above, the happy fluvial geomorphologist stood.

✘ When he turned away some students quietly left the room.

✔ When he turned away, some students quietly left the room.

7. **Use a comma to separate elements in dates and addresses:**

> February 2, 2011 (commas often are omitted if the day comes first: "2 February 2011")

> 117 Hudson Drive, Edmonton, Alberta.

> They lived in Dartmouth, Nova Scotia.

Note that in Britain a comma is placed after the number in an address: "117, Hudson Drive."

8. **Use a comma before a quotation in a sentence:**

> He said, "Life is too short to worry."

> "The children's safety," he warned, "is in your hands."

For more formality, you may use a colon (see pp. 269–70).

9. **Use a comma with a name followed by a title:**

> D. Gunn, Ph.D.

> Alice Smith, President

10. **Do not use a comma between a subject and its verb:**

> ✘ The editor of the book, is Miriam Stoyanovich.
> ✔ The editor of the book is Miriam Stoyanovich.

11. **Do not use a comma between a verb and its object:**

> ✘ Felber said, that the soil sample was large enough for the experiment.
> ✔ Felber said that the soil sample was large enough for the experiment.

12. **Do not use a comma between a coordinating conjunction and the following clause:**

> ✘ Go to the lab now or, once you complete the test.
> ✔ Go to the lab now or once you complete the test.

Dash [— or --]

A dash creates an abrupt pause, emphasizing the words that follow. (Most word-processing packages offer dashes in their special character sets. If yours doesn't, type two hyphens together, with no space on either side. Both

forms are shown here.) Never use dashes as casual substitutes for other punctuation: overuse can detract from the calm, well-reasoned effect you want.

1. **An *em dash* is the long (or double) dash. It is used to stress a word or phrase:**

    The British--as a matter of honour--vowed to retake the islands.

    Foster was well received in the office—at first.

2. **Use a dash in interrupted or unfinished dialogue:**

    "It's a matter—to put it delicately—of personal hygiene."

    "But I thought—" Donald tried to explain, but Mario cut him off: "You were wrong."

3. **An *en dash* is like a hyphen because it connects words.** The en dash is specifically used to denote a *range* between two things. The en dash is slightly larger than a hyphen; on your computer you can insert the en dash from the symbols menu or learn the keyboard shortcut. Note the difference between an en dash [–] and a hyphen [-] (see pp. 276–7).

    the Toronto–Calgary route

    the April–May season

    pages 162–169

Ellipsis [. . .]

1. **Use an ellipsis (three spaced dots) to show the location of any omission from a quotation:**

    - If you start a quotation in the middle of a sentence, indicate the omission of the earlier material by inserting an ellipsis (*three* dots):

      . . . a wood stove does not burn efficiently at very low temperatures.

    - If you quote two parts of one sentence, link them with *three* dots. Leave one space after the last word before the ellipsis and another before the word following it:

      A wood stove . . . creates good heat when used carefully.

- If you omit the end of the sentence, indicate this by using *four* dots. The first one represents the period at the end of the sentence, so you should not leave a space between the last letter and the first dot:

  A wood stove made from cast iron creates good heat. . . .

- Four dots followed by a new sentence indicate only that some material has been omitted, whether the end of the first sentence or one or more complete sentences following it. Don't forget to leave a space between the last dot and the new sentence:

  A cast iron wood stove creates good heat. . . . Oak has high heat value.

2. **Use an ellipsis to show that a series of numbers continues indefinitely:**

   1, 3, 5, 7, 9. . . .

Exclamation Mark [!]

An exclamation mark helps to show emotion or feeling. It usually is found in dialogue:

"Woe is me!" she mourned.

In academic writing, you should use an exclamation mark only in those rare cases when you want to give a point an emotional emphasis:

He concluded that inflation would decrease in 2018. Some forecast!

Hyphen [-]

1. **Use a hyphen to separate the parts of certain compound words:**
   - compound nouns:
        sister-in-law, Lieutenant-Governor, vice-president
   - compound verbs:
        test-drive, freeze-dry
   - compound adjectives used as modifiers preceding nouns:
        well-considered plan, twentieth-century attitudes

When you are not using such expressions as adjectives, do not hyphenate them:

> The plan was <u>well considered</u>.

> These are attitudes of the <u>twentieth century</u>.

After long-time use, some compound nouns drop the hyphen. When in doubt, check a dictionary.

2. **Use a hyphen with certain prefixes** (*all-*, *self-*, *ex-*, and those prefixes preceding a proper name):

   > all-party, self-imposed, ex-jockey, anti-nuclear, pro-Trinidad

3. **Use a hyphen to emphasize contrasting prefixes:**

   > The coach agreed to give both <u>pre-</u> and <u>post-game</u> interviews.

4. **Use a hyphen to separate written-out compound numbers from one to ninety-nine and compound fractions used as modifiers:**

   > eighty-one years ago

   > seven-tenths full

5. **If your computer isn't capable of creating an en dash (see "Dash"), use a hyphen to separate parts of inclusive numbers or dates:**

   > the years 1890-1914

   > pp. 3-40

Italics [*Italics*] or Underlining

Italics are slanted (cursive) letters. Most instructors will expect you to use italics for book and journal titles; however, some may ask that you underline them. If you are writing something in long-hand, remember to underline where necessary, as free-hand italics are usually indistinguishable in handwriting.

1. **Use italics (or underlining) for the titles of books, long poems that are complete books, plays, films, and lengthy musical pieces (e.g., a symphony):**

   > Yi-Fu Tuan's *Space and Place* is one of my favourite books.

For articles, essays, and short poems or musical pieces, use quotation marks. If the title contains another title, be sure to set it off in the correct style:

- When both titles are books, use quotation marks for the internal one:

  Her latest book is *An Interpretation of "Space and Place."*

- When the internal title is a book but the main title is not, use italics (or underlining):

  For more detail see Joseph Thrill's essay "Lawrence Kaplan's *Street Kids and Political Reaction* as a Primer for Understanding Poverty and Despair," in Agard Sinclair's edited book *Humanistic Geography of the City.*

- Do not use italics when neither title is a book. Instead, use the alternative form of quotation marks. 'Whale Song' here refers to a short choral work:

  My essay is entitled "Imagery in 'Whale Song' by Evans."

2. **Use italics (or underlining) to emphasize an idea:**

   It is important that all equipment be washed *immediately*.

   Be sparing with this use of italics. For less intrusive ways of creating emphasis see pages 250–3.

3. **Use italics (or underlining) to emphasize a word (or phrase):**

   The term *areal differentiation* is an example of geographical jargon.

   Quotation marks may be used for the same purpose.

4. **Use italics (or underlining) for scientific names:**

   Cape May warbler (*Dendroica tigrina*)
   Black-throated green warbler (*Dendroica virens*)
   Pinus radiata (a species of pine)

Parentheses [( )]

1. **Use parentheses to enclose an explanation, example, or qualification.** Parentheses show that the enclosed material is of incidental

importance to the main idea. They make a less pronounced interruption than a dash, but a more pronounced one than a comma:

My wife (who is the mother of our two children) is a great plumber.

His latest plan (according to neighbours) is to dam the creek.

Remember that although punctuation should not precede parentheses, it may follow them if required by the sense of the sentence:

I like coffee in the morning (if it's not instant), but she prefers tea.

If the parenthetical statement comes between two complete sentences, it should be punctuated as a sentence, with the period inside the parentheses:

I finished my last essay on April 30. (It was on Christaller's Central Place Theory.) Fortunately, I had three weeks free to study for the exam.

2. **Use parentheses to enclose references.** See Chapter 7 for details.

Period [.]

1. **Use a period at the end of a sentence.** A period indicates a full stop, not just a pause.
2. **Use a period with abbreviations.** Whereas British style omits the period in certain cases (UK, USA, BSc, MA, PhD, Dr, Rev, etc.), North American style usually requires it for abbreviated titles (B.Sc., M.A., Ph.D., Dr., Rev., etc.) and expressions of time (6:30 p.m.). In Canada, there is a trend away from the use of periods in many abbreviations. State and provincial abbreviations do not require periods (BC, NT, NY, DC). While the acronyms and initialisms for some organizations include periods, the most common ones generally do not (BBC, CIA, CIDA, FAO, IDRC, MIT, RCMP, UNESCO, etc.). Some (e.g., UN [or U.N.]) appear with and without periods. Whichever format you use, be consistent.
3. Use a period at the end of an indirect question. Do not use a question mark:

    ✘ He asked if I wanted a substitute?

    ✔ He asked if I wanted a substitute.

4. **Use a period for questions that are really polite orders:**

> Will you please send him the report by Friday.

Quotation Marks [" " or ' ']

Quotation marks are usually double in American style and single in British. In Canada either is accepted—just be consistent.

1. **Use quotation marks to signify direct discourse (the actual words of a speaker):**

> I asked, "What is the matter?"
>
> He said, "I have a pain in my big toe."

2. **Use quotation marks to show that words themselves are the issue:**

> The term "love" in tennis may be derived from the French expression for "the egg."

Alternatively, you may italicize or underline the terms in question.
Sometimes quotation marks are used to mark a slang word or an inappropriate usage, to show that the writer is aware of the difficulty:

> The "experts" were wrong.

Use this device only when necessary. In general, it is better to let the context show your attitude, or to choose another term.

3. **Use quotation marks to enclose the titles of poems, short stories, songs, and articles in books or journals.** By contrast, titles of books, films, paintings, or longer musical works are italicized or underlined:

> The essay I liked best in James Smith's *Agricultural Land: A Compendium* is "The Rural-Urban Fringe" by Z. Oseia.

4. **Use quotation marks to enclose quotations within quotations** (single or double, depending on your primary style):

> He said, "Several of the 'expert witnesses' knew nothing about the topic."

5. **Do not use quotation marks for indented, single-spaced block quotations.** When the material being quoted is *four lines or longer*, it

should be indented (usually with a double indent) and single spaced. No quotation marks should be used. If the block quotation is from the beginning of a paragraph, the normal indentation of the first word should be included:

> If the isolated village of Bytown ever becomes the capital of the country, it is clear that thereafter not only will Bytown grow but all the occupied lands will speedily be settled by a sturdy and industrious people. Hamlets will spring, as if by magic, into villages, villages into towns, and towns into cities.

If the material is not from the beginning of a paragraph, no extra indentation is required.

Quotation marks with punctuation

Both the British and the American practices are accepted in Canada. British style usually places punctuation outside the quotation marks, unless it is actually part of the quotation. The American practice, followed in this book, is increasingly common in Canada:

1. **A comma or period always goes inside the quotation marks:**

   > He said, "Give me another chance," but I replied, "You've had enough chances."

2. **A semicolon or colon always goes outside the quotation marks:**

   > Some have called the simulation "realistic"; I disagree.

3. **A question mark, dash, or exclamation mark goes inside quotation marks if it is part of the quotation, but outside if it is not:**

   > He asked, "What's for dinner?"

   > Did he really call the boss a "lily-livered hypocrite"?

   > His speech was hardly an appeal for "blood, sweat, and tears"!

   > I was just whispering to Mark, "That instructor is—" when suddenly she glanced at me.

4. **When a reference is given parenthetically (in round brackets) at the end of a quotation, the quotation marks precede the parentheses**

and the sentence punctuation follows them, and there is no period before the source information:

> Riverton suggests that we should "abandon spring burning as a means for fertilizing soils" (*Daily Rag*, 12 April 2011).

Semicolon [;]

A semicolon indicates a degree of separation intermediate in value between a comma and a period.

1. **Use a semicolon to join independent clauses (complete sentences) that are closely related:**

   > For five days he worked non-stop; by Saturday he was exhausted.
   >
   > His lecture was confusing; no one could understand the terminology.

   A semicolon is especially useful when the second independent clause begins with a conjunctive adverb such as *however, moreover, consequently, nevertheless, in addition,* or *therefore* (usually followed by a comma):

   > He bought a bag of doughnuts; however, none of the group was hungry.

   Some grammarians may disagree, but usually it is acceptable to follow a semicolon with a coordinating conjunction if the second clause would be complicated by other commas:

   > Blair, my cousin, is a keen jogger in all weather; but sometimes, especially in winter, I think it does him more harm than good.

2. **Use a semicolon to mark the divisions in a complicated series when individual items themselves need commas.** Using a comma to mark the subdivisions and a semicolon to mark the main divisions will help to prevent mix-ups:

   > ✘ He invited Shiraz Habib, the vice-principal, Jane Hunter, and John Jenkins.

Is the vice-principal a separate person? If so, changing all the commas to semicolons will make that clear. On the other hand, if either Habib or Hunter is the vice-principal, one comma should remain; its location will depend on which of the two the title refers to:

✔ He invited Shiraz Habib, the vice-principal; Jane Hunter; and John Jenkins.

✔ He invited Shiraz Habib; the vice-principal, Jane Hunter; and John Jenkins.

In a case such as this, the elements separated by the semicolon need not be independent clauses.

Underlining

See "Italics," pages 277–8.

Chapter Summary

The correct use of punctuation is one of the components of good writing. While many students think that studying punctuation is pointless, a single error in punctuation (such as a misplaced comma) can completely change the meaning of your written words or result in ambiguity. In either case, the sentences you write will be hard to understand and could be misinterpreted, perhaps with costly outcomes. Even if you use shortcuts in e-mails and text messages, academic and professional writing requires attention to the details of punctuation. The time you spend to learn and apply the rules of punctuation will "pay off" in clear, emphatic writing.

Misused Words and Phrases

In this chapter, we examine

- numerous words and phrases that are misused frequently; and
- correctly using troublesome words and phrases.

Introduction

Here are some words and phrases that often are misused. A periodic read-through will refresh your memory and help you avoid needless mistakes.

accept, except. Accept is a verb meaning to *receive affirmatively*; **except**, when used as a verb, means to exclude:

> I accept your offer.

> The teacher excepted him from the general punishment.

accompanied by, accompanied with. Use accompanied by for people; accompanied with for objects:

> He was accompanied by his wife.

> The brochure arrived, accompanied with a discount coupon.

advice, advise. Advice is a noun, advise a verb:

> He was advised to ignore the others' advice.

affect, effect. Affect is a verb meaning to *influence*; **effect** can be either a noun meaning *result* or a verb meaning to *bring about*.

> The eye drops affect his vision.

> The effect of higher government spending is higher inflation.

all ready, already. To be **all ready** is simply to be ready for something; **already** means *beforehand* or *earlier*:

> The students were <u>all ready</u> for the lecture to begin.

> The professor had <u>already</u> left her office by the time Blair arrived.

all right. Write as two separate words: all right. This can mean safe and sound, in good condition, okay; correct; satisfactory; or I agree.

> Are you <u>all right</u>?

> The professor's directions to us were <u>all right</u> but I was still confused about the experiment.

> The student's answers were <u>all right</u>.

all together, altogether. **All together** means *in a group*; **altogether** is an adverb meaning *entirely*:

> He was <u>altogether</u> certain that the field trip students were <u>all together</u>.

allusion, illusion. An **allusion** is an indirect reference to something; an **illusion** is a false perception:

> The rock image is an <u>allusion</u> to the myth of Sisyphus.

> He thought he saw a sea monster, but it was an <u>illusion</u>.

alot. Write as two separate words: *a lot*.

alternate, alternative. **Alternate** means *every other* or *every second* thing in a series; **alternative** refers to a *choice* between options:

> The two sections of the class attended discussion groups on <u>alternate</u> weeks.

> Is there an <u>alternative</u> route to the park?

among, between. Use **among** for three or more persons or objects, **between** for two:

> <u>Between</u> you and me, there's trouble <u>among</u> the team members.

amount, number. **Amount** indicates quantity when units are not discrete and not absolute; **number** indicates quantity when units are discrete and absolute:

> A large <u>amount</u> of timber.

> A large <u>number</u> of students.

See also **less, fewer.**

analysis. The plural is **analyses**.

anyone, any one. Anyone is written as two words to give numerical emphasis; otherwise it is written as one word:

> Any one of us could do that.
>
> Anyone could do that.

anyways. Non-standard English: use *anyway*.

aqueduct. Note that the fourth letter in this word is **e**. Some similar words use an **a**, as in **aquamarine**, or an **i**, as in **aquifer**.

as, because. As is a weaker conjunction than **because** and may be confused with *when*:

> ✗ As I was working, I ate at my desk.
>
> ✔ Because I was working, I ate at my desk.
>
> ✗ He arrived as I was leaving.
>
> ✔ He arrived when I was leaving.

as to. A common feature of bureaucratese. Replace it with a single-word preposition such as *about* or *on*:

> ✗ They were concerned as to the range of disagreement.
>
> ✔ They were concerned about the range of disagreement.
>
> ✗ They recorded his comments as to the treaty.
>
> ✔ They recorded his comments on the treaty.

bad, badly. Bad is an adjective meaning *not good*:

> The meat tastes bad.
>
> He felt bad about forgetting the dinner party.

badly is an adverb meaning *not well*; when used with the verbs **want** or **need**, it means *very much*:

> She thought he played the villain's part badly.
>
> I badly need a new suit.

beside, besides. Beside is a preposition meaning *next to*:

> She worked beside her assistant.

besides has two uses: as a preposition it means *in addition to*; as a conjunctive adverb it means *moreover*:

> Besides recommending the changes, the consultants are implementing them.

> Besides, it was hot and we wanted to rest.

between. See **among**.

bite, byte. To **bite** is to *cut into* with the teeth; a **byte** is a single unit of information stored in a computer.

bring, take. One **brings** something to a closer place and **takes** it to a farther one:

> Take it with you when you go.

> Next time you come to visit, bring your friend along.

can, may. Can means to *be able*; **may** means to *have permission*:

> Can you fix the lock?

> May I have another piece of cake, please?

In speech, **can** is used to cover both meanings: in formal writing, however, you should observe the distinction.

can't hardly. A faulty combination of the phrases **can't** and **can hardly**. Use one or the other of them instead:

> He can't swim.

> He can hardly swim.

capital, capitol. As a noun **capital** may refer to a seat of government, the top of a pillar, an upper-case letter, or accumulated wealth. **Capitol** refers only to a specific American—or ancient Roman—legislative building.

cite, sight, site. To **cite** something is to *quote* or *mention* it as an example or authority; **sight** can be used in many ways, all of which relate to the ability to *see*; **site** refers to a specific *location*, a particular place at which something is located.

clayey. Because *clay* ends in a y, add *ey*—and not just *y*—to make it into an adjective:

> The soils on his farm are very clayey.

climatic, climactic. Similar-sounding adjectives with entirely different meanings. **Climatic** refers to the *climate* of an area; **climactic** refers to the *climax* of something (for instance, the climactic scene in a play).

complement, compliment. The verb to **complement** means to *complete something else, or to make it better*; to **compliment** means to *praise*.

> His engineering skill <u>complements</u> the skills of the designers.

> I <u>complimented</u> her on her outstanding report.

compose, comprise. Both words mean *to constitute* or *make up*, but **compose** is preferred. **Comprise** is correctly used to mean *consist of*, or *be composed of*. Using **comprise** in the passive ("is comprised of")—as you might be tempted to do in the second example below—is usually frowned on in formal writing:

> These students <u>compose</u> the group that will go overseas.

> Base camp <u>comprised</u> a sleeping tent, a dining tent, and a latrine.

continual, continuous. Continual means *repeated over a period of time*; **continuous** means *constant* or *without interruption*:

> The strikes caused <u>continual</u> delays in building the road.

> In August, it rained <u>continuously</u> for five days.

could of. Incorrect, as are **might of**, **should of**, and **would of**. Replace **of** with **have**.

- ✗ He <u>could of</u> done it.
- ✔ He <u>could have</u> done it.
- ✔ They <u>might have</u> been there.
- ✔ I <u>should have</u> known.
- ✔ We <u>would have</u> left earlier.

council, counsel. Council is a noun meaning an *advisory* or *deliberative assembly*. **Counsel** as a noun means *advice* or *lawyer*; as a verb it means to *give advice*.

> The college <u>council</u> meets on Tuesday.

> We respect his <u>counsel</u>, because he's seldom wrong.

> As a camp <u>counsellor</u>, you may need to <u>counsel</u> parents as well as children.

criterion, criteria. A **criterion** is a standard for judging something. **Criteria** is the plural of **criterion** and thus requires a plural verb:

> These are my criteria for selecting the paintings.

data. The plural of **datum**. The set of information, usually in numerical form, that is used for analysis as the basis for a study. Informally, **data** is often used as a singular noun, but in formal contexts it should be treated as a plural:

> These data were gathered in an unsystematic fashion. Therefore they are inconclusive.

> John reported that his data are exactly what he needs.

deduce, deduct. To **deduce** something is to *work it out by reasoning*; to **deduct** means to *subtract* or *take away* from something. The noun form of both words is **deduction**.

defence, defense. Both spellings are correct: **defence** is common in Britain and Canada, **defense** in the United States.

delusion, illusion. A delusion is a belief or perception that is distorted; an **illusion** is a false belief:

> He had delusions that he could pass the exam without studying.

> He thought he saw a sea monster, but it was an illusion.

dependent, dependant. **Dependent** is an adjective meaning *contingent on* or *subject to*; **dependant** is a noun.

> Andrew's graduation is dependent upon his passing cartography.

> Andrew is a dependant of his father.

depletion, depression, deprivation. **Depletion** means *using up* (as with a non-renewable resource) or *reducing* the amount or quality of a (renewable) resource to the point where it cannot easily recover. **Depression** literally means *pressing down*. Thus in economic terms it refers to a marked downturn or trough in the business cycle, which can cause extreme economic hardship; in physical terms it refers to a marked trough, as in a *cyclonic depression*, with associated violent weather conditions. **Deprivation** is the denial of access to basic human requirements.

device, devise. The word ending in -**ice** is the noun; that ending in -**ise** is the verb.

> A ground penetrating radar (GPR) is a useful <u>device</u>.

> She is working to <u>devise</u> a model of eco-industrial development.

different than, different from. Use **different from** to compare two persons or things; use **different than** with a full clause:

> You are different from me.

> This city is different than it used to be.

diminish, minimize. To **diminish** means to *make* or *become smaller*; to **minimize** is to *reduce* something to the smallest possible amount or size.

disinterested, uninterested. Disinterested implies impartiality or neutrality; **uninterested** implies a lack of interest:

> As a <u>disinterested</u> observer, he was in a good position to judge the issue fairly.

> <u>Uninterested</u> in the proceedings, he yawned repeatedly.

due to. Although increasingly used to mean *because of,* **due** is an adjective and therefore needs to modify something:

> ✘ <u>Due to</u> his impatience, we lost the contract. [Due is dangling.]

> ✔ The loss was <u>due to</u> his impatience.

e.g., i.e. E.g. means *for example*; **i.e.** means *that is.* The two are *incorrectly* used interchangeably. See **Latin abbreviations** (p. 320).

entomology, etymology. Entomology is the study of insects; **etymology** is the study of the derivation and history of words.

exceptional, exceptionable. Exceptional means *unusual* or *outstanding,* whereas **exceptionable** means *open to objection* and it is generally used in negative contexts.

> His accomplishments are <u>exceptional</u>.

> There is nothing <u>exceptionable</u> in his behaviour.

farther, further. Farther refers to distance, **further** to extent; more:

> He paddled <u>farther</u> than his friends.

> He explained the plan <u>further</u>.

focus (noun). The plural may be either **focuses** (also spelled **focusses**) or **foci**.

good, well. Good is an adjective that modifies a noun; **well** is an adverb that modifies a verb.

> He is a good rugby player.

> The experiment went well.

hanged, hung. Hanged means *executed by hanging*. **Hung** means *suspended* or *clung to*:

> He was hanged at dawn for the murder.

> He hung the picture.

> He hung on to the boat when it capsized.

hereditary, heredity. Heredity is a noun; **hereditary** is an adjective. **Heredity** is the biological process whereby characteristics are passed from one generation to the next; **hereditary** describes those characteristics.

> Heredity has determined that you have brown hair.

> Your short legs must be hereditary.

hopefully. Use **hopefully** as an adverb meaning *full of hope*:

> She scanned the horizon hopefully, waiting for her friend's ship to appear.

In formal writing, using **hopefully** to mean *I hope* is still frowned upon, although increasingly common; it's better to use *I hope*:

> ✗ Hopefully the experiment will go off without a hitch.

> ✔ I hope the experiment will go off without a hitch.

i.e. *Not* the same as **e.g.**! See **e.g.**

illusion. See **allusion**; **delusion**.

incite, insight. Incite is a verb meaning to *stir up*; **insight** is a noun meaning (often sudden) *understanding*.

infer, imply. To **infer** means to *deduce* or *conclude by reasoning*. It is often confused with **imply**, which means to *suggest* or *insinuate*.

> We can infer from the high population density that there is a large demand for services.

> The high population density implies that there is a large demand for services.

inflammable, flammable, non-flammable. Despite its **in-** prefix, **inflamma-ble** means the same as **flammable**: it describes things that are *easily* set on fire; **non-flammable** means the opposite. To prevent any possibility of confusion, it's best to avoid **inflammable** altogether.

irregardless. Redundant; use *regardless*.

its, it's. Its is a possessive pronoun; **it's** is a contraction of *it is.* Many people mistakenly put an apostrophe in **its** in order to show possession.

✗ The cub wanted <u>it's</u> mother.

✔ The cub wanted <u>its</u> mother.

✔ <u>It's</u> time to leave.

less, fewer. Less is used when units are *not* discrete and *not* absolute ("less wood-land"). **Fewer** is used when the units *are* discrete and absolute ("fewer people").

lie, lay. To **lie** means to *assume a horizontal position*; to **lay** means to *put down*. The changes of tense often cause confusion:

Present	Past	Past participle
lie	lay	lain
lay	laid	laid

like, as. Like is a preposition, but it is often wrongly used as a conjunction. To join two independent clauses, use the conjunction **as**:

✗ I want to progress <u>like</u> you have this year.

✔ I want to progress <u>as</u> you have this year.

✔ Prof. Dodd is <u>like</u> my old school principal.

might of. See **could of**.

minimize. See **diminish**.

mitigate, militate. To **mitigate** means to *reduce the severity* of something; to **militate** against something means to *oppose* it.

myself, me. Myself is an intensifier of, not a substitute for, *I* or *me*:

✗ He gave it to John and <u>myself</u>.

✔ He gave it to John and <u>me</u>.

✗ Jane and <u>myself</u> are invited.

✔ Jane and <u>I</u> are invited.

✔ <u>Myself</u>, <u>I</u> would prefer a swivel chair.

nor, or. Use **nor** with **neither** and **or** by itself or with **either**:

He is <u>neither</u> overworked <u>nor</u> underfed.

The plant is <u>either</u> diseased <u>or</u> dried out.

off of. Remove the unnecessary **of**:

✗ The fence kept the children <u>off of</u> the premises.

✔ The fence kept the children <u>off</u> the premises.

phenomenon. A singular noun: the plural is **phenomena**.

plaintiff, plaintive. A **plaintiff** is a person who brings a case against someone else to court; **plaintive** is an adjective meaning sorrowful.

populace, populous. **Populace** is a noun meaning the *people* of a place; **populous** is an adjective meaning *densely inhabited*.

The <u>populace</u> of Hilltop village is not well educated.

With so many people in such a small area, Hilltop village is a <u>populous</u> place.

practice, practise. **Practice** can be a noun or an adjective; **practise** is always a verb. Note, however, that in the United States and sometimes in Canada, the spelling of the verb is **practice**:

The soccer players need <u>practice</u>. (noun)

That was a <u>practice</u> game. (adjective)

The players need to <u>practise</u> (or <u>practice</u>) their skills. (verb)

precede, proceed. To **precede** is to *go before* (earlier) or *in front of* others; to **proceed** is to *go on* or *ahead*:

The faculty will <u>precede</u> the students into the hall.

The medal winners will <u>proceed</u> to the front of the hall.

prescribe, proscribe. These words are sometimes confused, although they have quite different meanings. **Prescribe** means *to advise the* *use of* or *impose authoritatively*. **Proscribe** means to *reject, denounce, or ban*:

> The professor <u>prescribed</u> the conditions under which the equipment could be used.

> The student government <u>proscribed</u> the publication of unsigned editorials in the newspaper.

principle, principal. Principle is a noun meaning a *general truth* or *law*; **principal** can be used as either a noun or an adjective, meaning *first in rank or importance*.

rational, rationale. Rational is an adjective meaning *logical* or *able to reason*. **Rationale** is a noun meaning *explanation*:

> That was not a <u>rational</u> decision.

> The president sent around a memo with a <u>rationale</u> for her proposal.

real, really. Real, an adjective, means *true* or *genuine;* **really**, an adverb, means *actually, truly, very*, or *extremely*.

> The nugget was <u>real</u> gold.

> The nugget was <u>really</u> shiny and <u>really</u> worth a lot.

sceptic, septic, septic tank. A **sceptic** is one who *doubts* or who *critically questions;* **septic** means *infected* with harmful micro-organisms that cause pus to form, as in a septic wound; a **septic tank** is a container into which sewage is conveyed and in which it remains until the activity of bacteria makes it liquid enough to drain away.

Scots, Scottish, Scotch. Scots and **Scottish** mean the same thing: *of Scotland* (e.g., people, accents, etc.). **Scotch** is used in various compound nouns, such as *Scotch mist, terrier*, and of course, *whiskey*. Never refer to a *Scotsman* or *Scotswoman* as a Scotchman or Scotchwoman.

seasonable, seasonal. Seasonable means *usual* or *suitable for the season;* **seasonal** means *of, depending on*, or *varying with the season*:

> The temperature is <u>seasonably</u> high.

> The clothes you pack must take into account <u>seasonal</u> changes in the weather.

should of. See **could of.**

stratum. A singular noun. The plural is **strata**.

their, there. Their is the possessive form of the third person plural pronoun. **There** is usually an adverb, meaning *at that place* or *at that point*; sometimes it is used as an expletive (an introductory word in a sentence):

> They parked <u>their</u> bikes <u>there</u>.
>
> <u>There</u> is no point in arguing with you.
>
> <u>There</u>, look at the whales!

tortuous, torturous. The adjective **tortuous** means *full of twists and turns* or *circuitous*. **Torturous**, derived from *torture*, means *involving torture* or *excruciating*:

> To avoid heavy traffic, they took a <u>tortuous</u> route home.
>
> The band concert was a <u>torturous</u> experience for the audience.

toward, towards. Toward is the preferred spelling in Canada and the United States; towards is more common in the United Kingdom and Australia.

translucent, transparent. A **translucent** substance permits light to pass through, but not enough for a person to see through it; a **transparent** substance permits light to pass unobstructed, so that objects can be seen clearly through it.

turbid, turgid. Turbid, with respect to a liquid or colour, means *muddy, not clear*, or (with respect to literary style) *confused*. **Turgid** means *swollen, inflated*, or *enlarged*, or (again with reference to literary style) *pompous* or *bombastic*.

unique. This word, which means *of which there is only one* or *unequalled,* is both overused and misused. Because there are no degrees of comparison—one thing cannot be more unique than another—expressions such as **very unique** are incorrect.

while. To avoid misreading, use **while** only when you mean *at the same time that*. Do not use *while* as a substitute for *although*, *whereas*, or *but*:

> ✗   <u>While</u> he's getting fair marks, he'd like to do better.
>
> ✔   I headed for home, <u>while</u> she decided to stay.
>
> ✔   He fell asleep <u>while</u> he was reading.

-wise. Never use **-wise** as a suffix to form new words when you mean *with regard to*:

✗   Sales-<u>wise</u>, the company did better last year.

✔   The company's sales increased last year.

would have, would of. When people are describing a hypothetical instance in the past, they often mistakenly use **would have** in both the condition (*if*) clause and the consequence clause: see pages 259–60. For **would of**, see **could of**.

your, you're. Your is a pronominal adjective used to show possession; **you're** is a contraction of *you are*:

<u>Your</u> sleeping bag is warmer than mine.

<u>You're</u> likely to miss your train.

Chapter Summary

In this chapter, the focus on misused words and phrases is intended to illustrate not only some of the common errors that people make in their use of English, but also how to correctly use these problematic words and phrases. Paying attention to grammar (syntax) and avoiding common errors is important, both so your writing will not appear sloppy or unprofessional and so your readers will concentrate on what you have to say (not your errors).

18 Important Definitions

In this chapter, we examine

- definitions of essential words and concepts for students in geography, sustainability studies, and environmental sciences; and
- definitions of basic words and concepts pertaining to writing.

Introduction

This chapter offers definitions of numerous terms you will encounter in your studies, many of which do not appear in standard dictionaries. First, we cover terms commonly used by geographers, sustainability scholars, and other environmental scientists. Get to know them so you can use them carefully and correctly in your own work. This chapter also examines definitions of language fundamentals. Take note of the examples provided in order to improve your writing skills.

Definitions in Geography, Sustainability Studies, and the Environmental Sciences

accessibility. The relative opportunity for interaction and contact; the (lack of) ease with which a place or thing can be reached from other places. Also, writing that is easily understood without specialist knowledge.

acculturation. The process of adopting a culture; generally used in reference to an immigrant group's acceptance of the culture of the host society over a period of time. See also **assimilation** and **integration**.

adaptation. The process whereby a living organism changes in order to adjust to and thrive in a particular environment.

appropriate technology. Generally, the simplest and most effective technology to achieve the intended purpose in less developed areas as well as technologies that are socially and environmentally acceptable in more developed locations—technology that is appropriate in the context of its use. Appropriate technologies are affordable, easy to maintain using local skills and materials, sustainable (require fewer natural resources, produce less pollution), small scale (to give power to the local users), and appropriate (in terms of environmental, ethical, social, cultural, political, and economic contexts).

areal differentiation. The differences in and between various areas on the surface of the earth from the perspectives of the *interrelations* between phenomena, the *differential character* of the phenomena and the complexes they form, and their *areal* expression.

assimilation. In *sociology*, the process whereby a minority becomes increasingly like the dominant society; **assimilation** implies that the minority will lose its cultural distinctiveness. See **integration**. In *science*, the term refers to conversion into a similar substance (e.g., the conversion by an animal or plant of extraneous material into fluids and tissues identical with its own).

average, mean, median. An **average** is obtained by adding several quantities together and dividing the total by the number of quantities. The **mean** is between the first and last of an arithmetical or geometrical progression; thus 2 and 8 have arithmetic mean 5, and geometric mean 4. **Mean** also refers to the midpoint between two extremes (e.g., **mean sea level** is the halfway point between high and low water). The **median** is the middle number in a given set of numbers (e.g., the median of 3, 5, 7, 12, 65 is 7, but the median of 3, 5, 7, 10 is 6—halfway between the two middle numbers).

BC, BCE. BC means *before Christ* and is paired with the term AD, *Anno Domini*; **BCE** means *before the Common Era*. BCE is the more commonly accepted term in academic writing. It is paired with the term CE, meaning *Common Era*.

biocapacity. The biological capacity of an ecosystem to generate an ongoing supply of biological materials used by people and to absorb the waste materials produced by humans.

bioenergetics. The study of energy production and flow within and between organisms.

biofuel. Abbreviation of **biomass fuel,** which is fuel derived from renewable organic sources.

biography, autobiography. A **biography** is a written account of another person's life that generally adheres to facts; an **autobiography** is a biography of oneself.

biomass. The total weight of organic substances found in a defined area; a renewable source of energy.

biome. See **ecosystem**.

boundary, frontier. A **boundary** is a *line* denoting the limit of any territorial unit, whether physical, social, political, or economic. A boundary that is *delimited* or *delineated* is merely agreed to on paper; one that is *demarcated* is marked on the ground also. A **boundary** also can be a dividing line between contrasting cultural and political systems, with competing constructions of socio-spatial consciousness that in turn are related to core notions of nationalism.[1] A **frontier** is an *area* at the margins of a territorial unit into which expansion can take place. See **territory**.

carrying capacity. Originally an ecological term used to refer to the maximum number of organisms that can be sustained in a particular area. Now often used to refer to the maximum number of users (animals and people) that can be sustained by the land and water resources in a particular area (such as a national park).

centrifugal, centripetal. Centrifugal means *moving away from* the centre or axis; **centripetal** means *moving toward* the centre or axis. The former is used literally in reference to a *centrifuge*. In addition, human geographers use both terms to refer to the counteracting processes that produce certain conditions within states, or that produce certain patterns of population and land use at more local levels, as in cities.

circulation. Used in human geography to refer to the myriad ways in which **spatial** movement (of ideas, people, and things) can occur. The term implies overcoming difficulties caused by distance and the geographical nature of the intervening space.

classification, regionalization. Classification is the differentiation of things (objects, people, places, ideas, etc.) into set groups according to predetermined criteria; **regionalization** is a particular type of classification, in which places or areas and their contents are grouped according to selected criteria.

climax. Point of greatest intensity; culmination; the final, self-sustaining, stable plant community that is formed after a series of developments, with the changes coming more slowly as the climax stage is approached. See also **equilibrium**.

complementarity. Used in economic geography to refer to the relation between two regions wherein one region produces goods that the other region does not have but wants. **Complementarity** is the basis for spatial interaction (see **spatial**).

culture. Derived from the Latin *colere*, to cultivate. Used in biology and medicine with reference to *tissue culture*: the propagation of micro-organisms (plant or animal) or of living tissue cells in special media that are conducive to their growth. **Culture** also is used widely in the social sciences, where it generally refers to a wide range of characteristics that help to define a population as a distinctive unit. *Elements* of **culture** are universally shared categories (including language, religion, politics, and family), but the particular *traits* or characteristics differ from group to group (hence a particular language, particular ways of doing things, particular social structures, etc.). **Culture** is *not* synonymous with **race**. See also the next entry.

culture area, culture history, cultural ecology, cultural landscape. Terms used in cultural geography, anthropology, and, selectively, other disciplines. **Culture area** refers to the distributional aspect of culture, with emphasis on regions; **culture history** refers to the historical dimension, especially from the perspective of origins and dispersals; **cultural ecology** is the study of the relationships between a group and its physical surroundings; **cultural landscape** is the physical environment as moulded and modified by human action. The study of any one of these themes necessarily involves consideration of the others.

cycle, recycle. A **cycle** is a series of events that recurs regularly, returning to a similar starting position or state after a particular period of time. There are many cycles, including the birth, death, decay, and rebirth of plants; diurnal (daily) and seasonal cycles; the hydrologic cycle; the flows of elements and nutrients in the biosphere; the lunar cycle; and the cycle of agricultural livelihood patterns. To **recycle** means to *reclaim* materials for further use that would otherwise be wasted; the recycling process is not a true cycle.

developed economy, economies in transition, developing economies. The United Nations Department of Economic and Social Affairs classifies all countries of the world into one of these three broad categories that reflect basic economic conditions in each country. Currently, human geographers examine measures of economic growth, social welfare, and modernization processes whereby an area continually grows bigger economically and more mature socially. However, a focus on *sustainable* development processes would identify how an area becomes "better" for everyone (i.e., reduction in poverty and disease). Accounting for the role of spatial inequalities in economic benefits, or the difficult environmental conditions that some countries face, is part of the challenge in defining development. See **sustainability**; **sustainable development**.

eco-. A prefix that has gained favour to qualify things related—directly or even vaguely—to environmental issues. Examples include *ecoaccident*, *ecoactivist*, *ecocrisis*, *eco-efficiency*, *ecoethics*, *eco-innovation*, *ecotourism*, and *econut*.

ecology. The study of relationships among living organisms with due concern for their interactions with the physical environment. **Political ecology**

refers to the study of environmental change as a result of power relations (that cause differences in access to resources).

ecological footprint. A metric that compares how fast humans consume resources (Earth's biocapacity) and generate waste in relation to how fast nature can absorb our waste and generate new resources.[2] See **biocapacity**.

ecosystem. A distinct community of interdependent organisms together with their environment. For instance, a pond inhabited by a particular species of frog may function as an ecosystem that is distinct from the fauna functioning as an ecosystem in an adjacent environment. An especially large ecosystem, such as the southern African savannah grasslands, may be referred to as a **biome**.

emigrate, immigrate, migrate, migratory, migration. To **emigrate** is to *leave* one country for another; to **immigrate** is to *come to* one country from another. Both terms imply a person's permanent relocation from one country to another. Birds and some mammals **migrate** by changing their place of living from one season to another; **migratory** birds are the ones that **migrate**. In each case, the act of moving is **migration**.

enclave, exclave. In political geography, both words refer to the same thing—a small territory belonging to one state that is surrounded by territory of another state (or states). However, the two terms reflect two different points of view: **enclave**, that of the surrounding territory; **exclave**, that of the home state.

environment. Often misspelled by students (e.g., "enviroment," "environement," "envirionment"). A useful, often abused word that means different things to different people. Disciplines, too, define **environment** in different ways. For example, the term means something quite different to (1) a nurse concerned with an individual's "environment"—meaning the total set of stressors that impinge upon that person's system, together with the resources available to cope with those stressors; (2) a soil scientist concerned with local chemical and physical factors in a surface or near-surface environment; (3) a biologist concerned with the ecological environs of a lake shore; (4) an urban geographer concerned with the physical environment and, in particular, the built environment in and on which people have an impact; (5) a planner concerned with the built environment as the place that can be purposefully and effectively changed to reflect some planned outcome; (6) a social or cultural geographer concerned with how people react to their surroundings and attribute meaning to those surroundings; and so on. Thus, **environment** can refer to the physical characteristics of places or the cultural settings of places and people, and may be qualified as necessary: *behavioural* environment, *phenomenal* environment, *social* environment, *economic* environment, *urban* environment, and so on. In the broadest sense, **environment** also is used to mean **nature**.

environmental sciences. The many disciplines that study the biological, geo-graphical, and physical world, with varying concern for the functioning of organisms, the physical environment, and the interaction between the two. The disciplines and areas of interdisciplinary focus include agri-culture, architecture, biology, botany, chemistry, earth and atmospheric science, ecology, environmental economics, environmental engineering, environmental monitoring and analysis, environmental protection, for-estry, **geography**, geology, horticulture, land economics, land resources, natural resources management, political ecology, physics, sustainability, toxicology, water resources, and zoology. Although common core require-ments for students in the environmental sciences may suggest close links between the various disciplines, too often disciplinary parochialism and differences in the scales of research foci serve to discourage collaboration.

environmental studies. Interdisciplinary programs that seek to study en-vironmental issues in an integrative manner, drawing from the biological, geographical, physical, and social sciences, and the humanities. See **sustainability**.

equilibrium. Balance; in ecological terms, refers to a system in which inputs and outputs are finely, though not statically, balanced; hence *dynamic equilibrium*.

frontier. See **boundary.**

Gaia. Concept that refers to the living "being" of the biosphere. Formulated by James Lovelock in the 1970s, the **Gaia hypothesis** (**theory** or **principle**) postulates that living matter on the earth forms a complex, self-regulating entity that keeps our planet healthy by controlling the chemical and physical environment.

geography, geographers. Widely used terms with numerous meanings. **Geography** is from the Greek *geo*, the earth, and *graphein*, to write; **geographers** "do" geography. Geography is commonly defined as the study of the earth's surface and the people who inhabit it, or "the study of the earth as the home of people."[3] The study of locations and place names is to geography as the study of the skeleton is to medicine: simply the basic framework. **Geographers** focus on **spatial** distributions, patterns, processes, and relationships between human societies, the physical **environment**, **nature**, the **cultural landscape**, **locations**, **circulation**, and **regional** structures. **Geographers** who stress physical properties and processes are more aligned with the physical sciences; those who stress societal organization and human behaviour set within particular places are more aligned with the social sciences and, in some cases, the humanities. Bridging the "pure" or "hard" sciences, the social sciences, and, at times, the arts, geography is a correlative discipline.[4] Geographers are uncomfortable with single perspective explanations, because they tend to see patterns and interrelationships that students and practitioners in other disciplines may miss. The **scale** of approach varies from the personal to small groups to large groups, from the laboratory to small areas to larger regions and to the world itself. All geographers share the goal of making "sense of that vast panorama of fact and fiction, pattern and event, on the surface of the earth."[5] Areas of study range from integrative regional geography through many systematic specializations, including physical, political, cultural, economic, social, feminist, historical, urban, climatological, geomorphological, soils, fluvial, environmental perception, tourism, sport, and more.[6] Much of the work is of an applied nature, including electoral redistricting, natural disaster recovery, river sedimentation, resource analysis and management, locational analysis for siting commercial and industrial functions, and working with people with disabilities. Some work highlights public policy issues, whether domestic or international, including climate change and terrorism.[7] Both qualitative and quantitative techniques are used, the former by cultural and humanistic geographers, the latter by physical and economic geographers. Air photo interpretation, traditional cartographic methods, computer-assisted cartographic techniques, GIS (geographic information systems) and remote sensing techniques also are used.

globalization. Accelerating notably since about 1980, globalization reflects the complex combination of economic, political, and cultural changes that have brought about not only an increasing interconnectedness of people and places, but also a loss of diversity. Debate continues regarding both positive and negative consequences of these changes. See **restructuring**.

greenwashing. False information knowingly disseminated by an organization in order to present an environmentally responsible public image.

habitat. The dwelling area of a species or community; in biology and biogeography, **habitat** generally refers to a specific type of habitat and its location, such as a forest floor, a wetland, or a seashore; in human geography **habitat** can refer to physical structures (e.g., farm dwellings) and their local environmental settings.

holism, holistic. In philosophy, **holism** is the theory that the whole is greater than the sum of its parts. Biologists use the term in the context of characteristics of organisms that are not functions of their individual components. Geographers attempt to be **holistic** in their approach, whether to the analysis of regions or to the interrelated physical and human dimensions of problems.

integration. Used in the social sciences, including human geography, to refer to the process or situation in which subgroups within a society mix with the broader group while retaining their distinctive identity and cultural separateness; **integration** contrasts with **assimilation**. **Integration** also is used to refer to economic unions resulting from trade agreements (e.g., those between Canada, the United States, and Mexico, or Australia and New Zealand), and, more broadly, instances of overall social, political, and economic union (such as in the European Union).

landscape. A term used widely to refer to the characteristics of the earth's surface resulting from the interplay of myriad physical and human processes. Physical geography focuses on the processes (fluvial, wind-blown, etc.) that shape the landscape. Human geography considers landscape from many perspectives: as *scenery* (with emphasis on aesthetic aspects), as **nature**, as **habitat**, as *artifact* (i.e., the product of human activity), as *place* (wherein people interact), and as **territory**. The term **landscape** is sometimes used as shorthand for **cultural landscape**. There is an extensive interdisciplinary literature on landscapes, stressing thematic concerns (e.g., woodlands, agricultural clearances, drainage systems, rural settlements, landscapes of leisure, landscapes of political and ideological conflict) at world, regional, and more local scales. Geographers learn to *read* landscapes as if they were paintings or texts, and seek to reveal and interpret symbolic meanings that are imbedded in them.[8] The value of historical landscapes as *heritage* has proven to be a contentious subject.[9]

limits to growth; beyond the limits. The 1972 *The Limits to Growth*[10] book, and the 1991 follow-up book *Beyond the Limits*,[11] identified how human use of many essential resources and the generation of pollutants had surpassed rates that were physically sustainable. The authors concluded that policy revisions (to reduce consumption and population growth), and drastic increases in the efficiency of energy and material use, could make a sustainable society technically and economically possible. However, they noted the psychological and political challenges in modifying the premise of perpetual material growth on which both personal identities and modern industrial culture has been built.

local state. The set of institutions that provide for the maintenance and protection of social, political, and economic relations at the subnational level; confusingly applied to a number of subnational forms of government, from township, county, or municipality to province or state (here meaning a state within the United States).

location. Where something is. **Locations** are identified in two ways: **site** (specific location) and **situation** (relative location).

mean, median. See **average**.

model, paradigm. Model refers to a simplified, idealized, and structured representation of a system (e.g., weather, freezing and thawing, traffic flows, or agricultural system). **Paradigm** refers to the working assumptions, procedures, and findings of scholars that collectively define particular patterns of scientific activity. Some people use the terms interchangeably, but **model** is more specific than **paradigm**. **Paradigm** has been used—and misused—ever since Thomas Kuhn popularized the term in his book *The Structure of Scientific Revolutions* (1962).

nature. The phenomena of the physical world as a whole. A basic methodological question for geographers also is a fundamental philosophical problem: "to what extent is it proper to regard Man [humans] as a part of Nature or as standing apart from it?"[12] Another much debated issue is how "natural" the "nature" is that many environmentalists seek to preserve. These concerns reflect an awareness that nature is as much a human creation, or social entity, as a physical one.[13]

objectivity. A disinterested stance; a position taken without personal bias or prejudice. See **subjectivity**.

orient, orientate. From the Latin *oriens*, the east or sunrise, one meaning of both verbs is to place something so that it faces eastward. More commonly, **orient** and **orientate** mean either to *adjust* or *adapt*, or to *aim at* or *direct*. See also **Orientalism**.

Orientalism. In the *social sciences*, literary criticism, and history, **Orientalism** refers to Western "constructions" of the "East" (or, more generally, "others") and the use of Western assumptions and "findings" as the justification for control, manipulation, and incorporation. Writers such as Edward Said, Amilcar Cabral, and Joan Cocks declare that it is imperative for all subjected people to negate "Orientalism"—the colonial misrepresentations of their reality—by producing and creating their own narratives.[14]

paradigm. See **model**.

place. A particular portion of the earth's surface occupied or recognized by humans who give meaning to it and derive meaning from it.

process. Put most simply, the term **process** refers to the way something changes from one state to another. The physical, biological, and social sciences all study processes, of widely varying kinds.

race, racism, racist. Race is associated with biology, where races are genetically distinct populations within the same species. All humans belong to the same human species and sub-species, and are not genetically divisible into races. The outcomes of inappropriately dividing humans into "races" have included **racism**, a particular form of prejudice that attaches characteristics of superiority or inferiority to a group of people who share some physically inherited characteristics, hence **racist** attitudes and behaviour. See also **culture** and Chapter 13.

region, regionalism. Region refers to an area defined according to a particular set of criteria; all regions are human creations in the sense that the criteria people select determine the areal extent of the region. A distinction is made between formal and functional regions. Formal regions are defined according to distribution (e.g., of loess soil in Europe, or milk production in Ontario), while functional regions are defined according to the **areal** extent of the linkages within a system (e.g., a settlement system, with reference to the area that is functionally linked to a large central place—such as Halifax's "urban field"). The concept of region is used in geography and in urban and regional planning. **Regionalism** reflects a sense of togetherness among the people of a relatively large area. It is recognizable only in the context of that area's being only a part of an even larger area (for instance, "southern" regionalism within the United States). When a regionalism finds political expression within the larger state and its leaders give primacy to the interests of their region, thus undercutting the role and, perhaps, the legitimacy of the state, the result is **sectionalism. Sectionalism** may lead to *self-determination* and *secession*.[15] Thus sectionalism operates as a centrifugal force within a state. (See also **classification** and **territory**.)

resilience. The ability of a community to recover (quickly) after a disaster (natural or man-made), conflict, or other shock. Sustainable practices help enhance **resilience** (e.g., growing food locally can reduce dependence on fuel for transport, reduce application of fertilizers, pesticides and herbicides, and reduce volume of plastic packaging used).

restructuring. The wide range of fundamental economic and social changes made as national societies seek to come to terms with global economic changes. See **globalization**.

scale. The level of representation of reality; an important concept in cartography. Confusingly, large-scale maps depict small areas (but can include considerable detail), whereas small-scale maps depict large areas (and thus include less detail). In geography, the scale selected for any study will help to determine the degree of focus and, thus, the conclusions that can be drawn from the analysis.

sectionalism. See **region.**

sewer, sewage, sewerage. A **sewer** is an artificial conduit, usually underground, used to carry waste matter. **Sewage** is waste matter which goes down the sewer. **Sewerage** refers to the process whereby waste material or sewage is removed by means of sewers; also, sewerage may mean a system of sewers.

site. The *specific* aspect of **location**. A specific site cannot change, although its internal characteristics can be altered. See **situation.**

situation. The *relative* aspect of **location**. The relative location of a site will change if alterations are made to external linkages. See **site.**

space. The continual expanse in which things exist and move; a portion of that continual expanse; the interval between locations. Space is a central concept for geographers, who are concerned with the absolute, relative, and relational nature of space over the surface of the earth. See **location**, **place**, **region**, **spatial**, and **territory**.

spatial. The adjectival form of **space**, as in *spatial analysis*, *spatial structure*, *spatial interaction*, *spatial preference*. Note that it is spelled with a *t*, not a *c*. **Spatial interaction** is the movement of goods, people, and ideas between interdependent regions. See **complementarity.**

stalactite, stalagmite. Both are deposits formed by dripping water in limestone caves: a **stalactite** hangs like an icicle from the roof of a cave; a **stalagmite** builds up from the floor.

sustainability; sustainable development. **Sustainable development** was defined in the 1992 Brundtland Commission Report as "development that meets the needs of the present without compromising the ability of future generations to meet their own needs." International challenges to the premise of "sustainable development" (meaning continued growth, getting bigger) led to a broader appreciation of the importance of environmental protection, social responsibility, and revised economic practices as part of enabling a sustainable, healthy global society (getting better, not bigger). **Sustainability** is an integrated, holistic approach to living that considers ecological, social, and economic dimensions together in decision making to create a better future for everyone.

territoriality. The attempt by an individual or group to influence or establish control over a particular **territory**. See **region** and **regionalism**.

territory. A particular portion of the surface of the earth. The term implies bounding, either formally or informally, by people who either hold or covet the area. Territory is both a physical and a psychological phenomenon, for people "see" meaning in and "obtain" meaning from it, perceiving the territory and its landscape as living entities that are filled with meaning. Such perceptions reflect cultural beliefs that exist only within the "geographies of the mind"; yet any group's **cultural ecology** and spatial patterning are powerfully influenced by their beliefs. The link between a people and "their" territory is complex. Having a territory offers a people security (to look inward to preserve the integrity of the society against outside forces) and opportunity (from which to reach out to other societies).[16] See **boundary**, **cultural landscape**, **space**, and **territoriality**. (See mental maps, Chapter 12.)

Definitions in Grammar and Writing

abbreviations. Shortened forms of words. There are two types: (a) true abbreviations, in which only the first few letters of the full word are used: e.g., *vol.* for *volume, cont.* for *continued*; and (b) suspensions, which include the last letter of the full word: e.g., *figs.* for *figures, Dr.* for *doctor*. This book follows the most common North American style, which uses a period after suspensions as well as contractions. However, some writers omit the period after suspensions, since these include the final letter. See also **acronyms, contractions, Latin abbreviations**. Common abbreviations include:

abbr.	abbreviation, abbreviate
abr.	abridged
acad.	academy
adapt.	adapted from (or by), adaptation
Amer.	American
assn.	association
attrib.	attributed to
bibliog.	bibliography, bibliographer, bibliographic
biog.	biography, biographer, biographic
bull.	bulletin
(c)	copyright
cf.	compare
colloq.	colloquial
comp.	compiler, compiled by
conf.	conference
diss.	dissertation
div.	division
doc.	document
ed.	editor, edited by, edition
ex.	example
fwd.	foreword
geog.	geography
geol.	geology
illus.	illustration
inst.	institute, institution
intr., introd.	introduction
jour.	journal
misc.	miscellaneous
ms., mss.	manuscript, manuscripts
n., nn.	note, notes (e.g., "64, nn. 8–19": "page 64, notes 8 to 19")
n.d.	no date
no.	number
n.p.	no place of publication cited, no publisher
n.pag.	no pagination
n.s.	new series (of a journal or monograph series)

orig.	original
o.s.	old (original) series (of a journal or monograph series)
proc.	proceedings
publ.	publisher, publication, published by
qtd.	quoted
rept.	report
rev.	review, revised, revision
ser.	series (e.g., of books on a given theme)
supp.	supplement
trans., tr.	translator, translation, translated by
UP	University Press (e.g., Oxford UP)
var.	variant
vers.	version

abstract. An **abstract** is a *brief statement* summarizing the main points of a work. Abstracts usually are required for formal scientific reports or papers, and upper-level undergraduate and graduate theses. The adjective **abstract** means *theoretical* rather than concrete.

abstract language. Language that deals with theoretical, intangible concepts or details, e.g., justice, goodness, truth. (Compare **concrete language**.)

acronyms, initialisms. Words formed by joining together the first letters from a set of words. Periods are generally not used in acronyms: e.g., *NATO* from *North Atlantic Treaty Organization*. Names in which each letter is pronounced separately (e.g., *CBC: Canadian Broadcasting Corporation*) are called **initialisms**. A few acronyms have been accepted as words in their own right: e.g., *laser*, from *light amplification* (by) *stimulated emission* (of) *radiation*.

adjective. A word that modifies or describes a noun or pronoun; hence a kind of noun marker: e.g., *red, beautiful, solemn*. An **adjectival phrase** or **adjectival clause** is a group of words modifying a noun or pronoun: e.g., *deep blue sky*.

adverb. A word that modifies or qualifies a verb, adjective, or adverb, often answering a question such as *how? why? when?* or *where?*:

e.g., *slowly, fortunately, early, abroad*. An **adverbial phrase** or **adverbial clause** is a group of words modifying a verb, adjective, or adverb: e.g., *by force, in revenge*. See also **conjunctive adverb**.

agreement. Consistency in tense, number, or person between related parts of a sentence: e.g., between subject and verb, or noun and related pronoun.

allegory. A story in which the characters and events stand for someone or something else.

alliteration. The repetition of the first letter of one word in the word or words that follow, a stylistic technique that, used sparingly, can have a good effect: e.g., *rushing river*.

ambiguity. Vague or equivocal language; a statement with more than one meaning.

ampersand (&). The character *&*, meaning *and*.

analogy. An argument in which one thing is likened to another; often the parallel is between something that is little understood and something more familiar: e.g., *Insulation is to a house as clothes are to the human body*.

antecedent (referent). The noun for which a following pronoun stands: e.g., *David* is the antecedent of *him* in this sentence: *Please give this essay to **David** when you see **him***.

antonyms. Pairs of words with opposite meanings: e.g., *quick* and *slow*; *hot* and *cold*. See **synonyms**.

appendix. An additional section following the main body of a work, containing material that contributes to but is not essential to the completeness of the work.

appositive. A word or phrase that identifies a preceding noun or pronoun: e.g., *Mrs. Jones*, **my aunt**, *is sick*. The second phrase is said to be *in apposition* to the first.

article. A word that precedes a noun and shows whether the noun is definite or indefinite; a kind of determiner or noun-maker. **Indefinite article**: *a (an)*. **Definite article**: *the*.

assertion. A positive statement or claim: e.g., *These findings are irrefutable*.

assonance. Repetition of the same vowel sound in a series of words for a special effect: e.g., *He drove home so slowly*.

auxiliary. A verb used in combination with another verb to create a verb phrase; a helping verb used to create certain tenses and emphases: e.g., *could, do, may, will, have*.

bibliography. (a) A list of works referred to or found useful in the preparation of an essay or report (see p. 133); (b) a reference book listing works available on a particular subject.

case. The inflected form of pronouns (see **inflection**). **Subjective case**: *I, we, he, she, it, the*. **Objective case**: *me, us, him, her, it, them*. **Possessive case**: *my, our, his, her, its, their*.

circumlocution. A roundabout or circuitous expression: e.g., *in the family way* for *pregnant*; *at this point in time* for *now*.

clause. A group of words containing a subject and predicate. An **independent clause** can stand by itself as a complete sentence: e.g., *I bought a hamburger*. A **subordinate** or **dependent clause** cannot stand by itself but must be connected to another clause: e.g., **Since I was hungry**, *I bought a hamburger*.

cliché. A trite or well-worn expression that has lost its impact through overuse: e.g., *slept like a log, sunny disposition, tried and true*.

collective noun. A noun that is singular in form but refers to a group: e.g., *family, team, jury*. It may take either a singular or a plural verb, depending on whether it refers to individual members or to the group as a whole.

colloquialisms. Expressions that are used in speech but generally not in writing, unless the writing style is informal or the phrase is used in written dialogue, as in a novel or play: e.g., *Let's grab a pizza.*

comma splice. See **run-on sentence**.

complement. A completing word or phrase that usually follows a linking verb to form a **subjective complement**: e.g., (1) He is **my father**. (2) *That cigar smells* **terrible**. If the complement is an adjective it is sometimes called a **predicate adjective**. An **objective complement** completes the direct object rather than the subject: e.g., *We found him* **honest and trustworthy**.

complex sentence. A sentence containing a dependent clause as well as an independent one: e.g., *I bought the ring, although it was expensive.*

compound sentence. A sentence containing two or more independent clauses: e.g., *I saw the oil spill and I reported it.* A sentence is called **compound-complex** if it contains a dependent clause as well as two independent ones: e.g., *When the fog lifted, I saw the oil spill and I reported it.*

conclusion. The part of an essay in which the findings are pulled together or the implications are revealed so that the reader has a sense of closure or completion.

concrete language. Specific language, giving particular details (often details of sense): e.g., *red corduroy dress, three long-stemmed roses.* See **abstract language**.

conditional. The conditional form of the verb expresses what may happen if a particular condition applies: e.g., **If it rains**, *the field trip will be cancelled.*

conjunction. An uninflected word used to link words, phrases, or clauses. A **coordinating conjunction** (e.g., *and, or, but, for, yet*) links two equal parts of a sentence. A **subordinating conjunction**, placed at the beginning of a subordinate clause, shows the logical dependence of that clause on another: e.g., (1) **Although** *I am poor, I am happy.* (2) **While** *others* *slept, he studied.* **Correlative conjunctions** are pairs of coordinating conjunctions (see **correlatives**).

conjunctive adverb. A type of adverb that shows the logical relation between the phrase or clause that it modifies and a preceding one: e.g., (1) *I sent the letter; it never arrived,* **however.** (2) *The battery died;* **therefore** *the car wouldn't start.*

connotation. Associative meaning; the range of suggestion called up by a certain word. Apparent synonyms, such as *poor* and *underprivileged,* may have different connotations. See **denotation**.

consistency. Use of the same style (of spelling, punctuation, documentation) throughout a given piece of work.

context. The framework provided by others' research, within which a given study is situated; the text surrounding a particular passage that helps to establish its meaning.

contractions. Words formed by combining and shortening two words: e.g., *isn't, can't, we're.* Contractions are permissible in informal writing.

coordinate construction. See **correlatives**.

coordinating conjunction. See **conjunction**.

correlatives (coordinates). Pairs of coordinating conjunctions: e.g., *either/ or, neither/nor, not only/but.*

dangling modifier. A modifying word or phrase (often a participial phrase) that is not connected grammatically to any part of the sentence: e.g., **Walking to school**, *the street was slippery.*

demonstrative pronoun. A pronoun that points out something: e.g., (1) **This** *is his reason.* (2) **That** *looks like my lost earring.* When used to modify a noun or pronoun, a demonstrative pronoun becomes a kind of **pronominal adjective**: e.g., *this hat, those people.*

denotation. The literal or dictionary meaning of a word. See **connotation**.

dependent clause. See **clause**.

diction. The choice of words with regard to their tone, degree of formality, or register. Formal diction is the language of orations and serious essays. The informal diction of everyday speech or conversational writing can, at its extreme, become slang.

direct/indirect speech (discourse). Direct speech (or **discourse**) consists of the actual words a person spoke or wrote. In writing, these words are enclosed in quotation marks: *The politician said, "Environmental issues are of prime importance to this government."* **Indirect speech** (or **discourse**) gives the meaning of the speech rather than the actual words. In writing, indirect discourse is not enclosed in quotation marks: *He said that environmental issues were very important to the government.*

discourse. Talk, either oral or written. **Discourse** may be **direct** or **indirect**; see the preceding entry.

editing. The process of checking what you have written for problems with spelling, grammar, expression, and content; an essential step in the writing process.

ellipsis marks. Spaced dots indicating an omission from a quoted passage (see pp. 275–6).

endnote. A footnote or citation placed at the end of an essay or report.

equi-. The prefix meaning *equal*; hence *equiangular, equidistant, equilateral, equilibrate,* **equilibrium** (see p. 303).

essay. A literary composition on any subject. Some essays are descriptive or narrative, but in an academic setting most are expository (explanatory) or argumentative.

euphemism. A word or phrase used to avoid some other word or phrase that might be considered offensive in some way: e.g., instead of saying *I have to pee*, someone might say *I have to see a man about a dog.*

expletive. Grammatically, a meaningless exclamation or phrase. The most common expletives are the sentence beginning with *It is* and *There is (are)*. In speech, an interjectory word or expression, frequently profane.

exploratory writing. The informal writing done to help generate ideas before formal planning begins.

figurative. The opposite of **literal**. **Figurative meaning** is abstract or imaginative; words used **figuratively** are given an abstract or imaginative meaning rather than their literal or face-value meaning.

figure of speech. A **figurative** expression used to create a special effect. See **hyperbole**, **imagery**, **metaphor**, and **simile**.

footnote. A citation placed at the bottom of a page or the end of the composition. See **endnote**.

foreword, preface. A brief section at the beginning of a book in which the author or editor explains his or her intentions and how the book came to be written; often includes acknowledgements, although these may be presented separately.

fused sentence. See **run-on sentence**.

general language. Language lacking specific details; abstract language.

gerund. A verbal (part-verb) or verb form that functions as a noun and is marked by an -ing ending: e.g., **Swimming** *can help you become fit.*

grammar. The study of the forms and relations of words, and of the rules governing their use in speech and writing.

headings. The titles given to chapters in a work, or sections and subsections, indicating to readers the topics which are about to be discussed.

homonyms. Sets of words with different meanings that have the same sound or spelling: e.g., *site, sight, cite*; (*tent*) *pole*, (*magnetic*) *pole*.

hyperbole. Exaggeration for emphasis: e.g., *You've been told a million times to tie your shoelaces!*

hypothesis. A supposition or trial proposition made as a starting point for further investigation. The plural is *hypotheses*.

hypothetical instance. A supposed occurrence; often shown by a clause beginning with *if*.

imagery. Language that creates pictures in the reader's mind; see **metaphor** and **simile**. Cultural geographers writing about landscape often examine imagery.

impersonal writing. Writing that does not express the character of the writer. Scientific writing is impersonal.

independent clause. See **clause**.

indirect discourse. See **direct/indirect speech**.

infinitive. A type of verbal (or verb form) not connected to any grammatical **subject**: e.g., *to ask*. The **base infinitive** omits the *to*: e.g., *ask*.

inflection. The change in the form of a word to indicate number, person, case, tense, or degree.

informal language. Language, written or spoken, with many **colloquial** words and phrases. Not used in essays—unless for a creative writing class—or other formal writing.

initialisms. See **acronyms**.

intensifier (qualifier). A word that modifies and adds emphasis to another word or phrase: e.g., **very** *tired*, **quite** *happy*, *I* **myself**.

interjection. A remark or exclamation interposed or thrown into a speech, usually accompanied by an exclamation mark: e.g., *Oh dear! Help!*

interrogative sentence. A sentence that asks a question: e.g., *What is the time?*

intransitive verb. A verb that does not take a direct object: e.g., *fall, sleep, talk.*

introduction. A section at the start of an essay that tells the reader what is going to be discussed and why; an extremely important element of any essay.

italics. Slanting type used for emphasis, sometimes replaced in typescript by underlining.

jargon. Technical terms used unnecessarily or in inappropriate places: e.g., *peer-group interaction* for *friendship.*

Latin abbreviations and terms. Many common abbreviations are derived from Latin words and phrases. Note where periods appear in these examples: *cf.* (from *confer,* "compare"); *e.g.* (from *exempli gratia,* "for example"); *etc.* (from *et cetera,* "and the rest"); *i.e.* (from *id est,* "that is"). One Latin term that is not abbreviated is *idem,* meaning "the same author" or "the same place." Today these terms usually are not italicized (but see p. 269 on *sic*). Be careful not to confuse *e.g.* and *i.e.*

linking verb (copula verb). The verb *to be* used to join subject to complement: e.g., *The apples* **were** *ripe.*

linking words. Words that connect and develop ideas. See **conjunction** and **conjunctive adverb**.

literal meaning. The primary, or denotative, meaning of a word. See **figurative**.

logical indicator. A word or phrase—usually a conjunction or conjunctive adverb—that shows the logical relation between sentences or clauses: e.g., *since, furthermore, therefore.*

metaphor. A word picture that makes an implicit comparison without using the words *like* or *as.* A metaphor is created by replacing one element with another that is not literally applicable, but is imaginatively appropriate: e.g., *The car* **rocketed** *off the ramp.* (By implicitly comparing the car to a rocket, this sentence becomes more vivid than *The car* **drove** *off the ramp.*)

modifier. A word or group of words that describes or limits another element in the sentence. A **misplaced modifier** causes confusion because it is not placed next to the element it should modify: e.g., *I* **only** *ate the pie.* [Revised: *I ate only the pie.*]

mood. (a) As a grammatical term, the form that shows a verb's function (indicative, imperative, interrogative, or subjunctive); (b) when applied to literature generally, the state of mind or feeling shown.

narrative. The story or account of something, whether true or imaginary. In a novel, the narrative generally is distinguished from the dialogue.

negatives. Words that are used to convey a negative meaning: e.g., *never, no, not, nothing.* Some words can be made negative by the addition of the prefixes *dis* (dislike), *in* (insecure), *non* (non-appearance), *un* (unlikely).

non-restrictive element. See **restrictive element**.

noun. An inflected part of speech marking a person, place, thing, idea, action, or feeling, and usually serving as subject, object, or complement. A **common noun** is a general term: e.g., *dog, paper, automobile.* A **proper noun** is a specific name: e.g., *Mary, Ottawa, Ski-Doo.*

numbers, cardinal, and ordinal. Cardinal numbers such as 1, 2, 3, etc., indicate how many of an item there are: e.g., *the town has 2,341 inhabitants.* **Ordinal numbers** such as 1st, 2nd, 3rd, etc., indicate rank: e.g., *the city is the 5th largest in the country.*

object. (a) a noun or pronoun that, when it completes the action of a verb, is called a **direct object**: e.g., *He passed the* **puck**. An **indirect object** is the person or thing receiving the direct object: e.g., *He passed the* **puck** (direct object) *to* **Richard** (indirect object). (b) The noun or pronoun in a group of words beginning with a preposition; pronouns take the objective case: e.g., *at the* **house**, *about* **her**, *for* **me**.

objective complement. See **complement**.

onomatopoeia. From the Greek for *word-making*; refers to words whose sounds echo their meaning: e.g., cats *meow*, thunder *booms*, grilling meat *sizzles*.

outline. With regard to an essay or report, a brief sketch of the main parts; a written plan.

paragraph. A unit of sentences arranged logically to explain or describe an idea, event, or object; usually marked by indentation of the first line.

parallel wording. Wording in which a series of items has a similar grammatical form: e.g., *At her marriage my great-grandmother promised* **to love**, **to honour**, **and to obey** *her husband.*

paraphrase. Restate in different words.

parentheses. Curved lines, enclosing and setting off a passage; not to be confused with square brackets (see pp. 269 and 278).

parenthetical element. An interrupting word or phrase: e.g., *My musical career,* **if it can be called that**, *consisted of playing the triangle in kindergarten.*

participle. A verbal (part-verb) or verb form that functions as an adjective. Participles can be either **present**, usually marked by an *-ing* ending (e.g., *taking)*, or **past** (*having taken*); they also can be passive (*having been taken*).

parts of speech. The major classes of words. Some grammarians include only function words (nouns, verbs, adjectives, and adverbs); others also include pronouns, prepositions, conjunctions, and interjections.

passive voice. See **voice**.

past participle. See **participle**.

periodic sentence. A sentence in which the normal order is inverted or an essential element suspended until the very end: e.g., *Out of the house, past the* *grocery store, through the school yard, and down the railroad tracks* **raced the frightened boy**.

person. In grammar, the three classes of personal pronouns refer to the person speaking (first person), person spoken to (second person), and person spoken about (third person). With verbs, only the third person singular has a distinctive form.

personal pronoun. See **pronoun**.

personification. A stylistic technique in which objects are treated as if they were persons.

phrase. A unit of words lacking a subject-predicate combination. The most common kind is the **prepositional phrase**—a unit comprising preposition plus object. Some modern grammarians also refer to the **single-word phrase**.

plagiarism. Using someone else's words as your own, without attribution. (See pp. 15–17.)

plural. Indicating two or more in number. Nouns, pronouns, and verbs all have plural forms.

possessive case. See **case**.

précis. A brief summary of a piece of writing, usually using different words.

preface. See **foreword**.

prefix. An element placed in front of the root form of a word to make a new word: e.g., *pro-, in-, neo-, sub-*. See **suffix**.

preposition. A short word heading a unit of words containing an object, thus forming a prepositional phrase: e.g., **under** *the tree*, **before** *my time*.

pronoun. A word that stands in for a noun. A **personal pronoun** stands in for the name of a person: *I, he, she, we, they*, etc.

proofreading. The critically important process of checking written work (whether an essay, a lab report, or whatever else) for mistakes of any kind before handing it in.

punctuation. A conventional system of signs used to indicate stops or divisions in a sentence and to make meaning clearer: e.g., comma, period, semicolon, etc. (see Chapter 16).

qualifier. A word that intensifies or reinforces other words: e.g., *These soils are* **very** *good for potatoes.*

quotation. The exact replication of someone else's words. See **quotation marks** in Chapter 7 for when and when not to use quotation marks.

redundancy. The use of more words than are necessary: e.g., *The* **three triplets** *are all in my class.* See **tautology**.

reference works. Material consulted when preparing an essay or report.

referent (antecedent). The noun for which a pronoun stands.

reflexive pronoun. A pronoun that ends in *-self* or *-selves* and so refers to the subject: e.g., *The professor cut* **himself** *on the beaker.* Don't make the mistake of saying things like, "Send the material to myself" (when you should say ". . . to me").

reflexive verb. A verb that has the same person as subject and object: e.g., *The student taught himself how to use the computer.*

register. The degree of formality in word choice and sentence structure.

relative clause. A clause headed by a relative pronoun: e.g., *the man* **who came to dinner** *is my uncle.*

relative pronoun. *Who, which, what, that*, or their compounds beginning an adjective or noun clause: e.g., *the house* **that** *Jack built;* **whatever** *you say.*

restrictive element. A phrase or clause that identifies or is essential to the meaning of a term: e.g., *The book* **that I need** *is lost.* Such a phrase should not be set off by commas. A non-restrictive element is not needed to iden-tify the term and is usually set off by commas: e.g., *This book,* **which I got from my aunt,** *is one of my favourites.*

rhetoric/oratory. Language that is intended to persuade listeners; **oratory** re-fers only to spoken language.

rhetorical questions. Questions posed and answered by a speaker (or writer) for stylistic effect, to draw attention to a point; no audience response is needed or expected: e.g., *"What am I to you?" asked the Minister of the Environment. "I am the person in government who cares most about envi-ronmental issues."*

root. The part of a word that carries its essential meaning: e.g., *spac* is the root of *spacious* because it carries the meaning "space."

run-on sentence. A sentence that goes on beyond the point where it should have stopped. The term covers both the **comma splice** (two sentences joined by a comma) and the **fused sentence** (two sentences joined with-out any punctuation between them).

sentence. A grammatical unit that includes both a subject and a predicate. The end of a sentence is marked by a period.

sentence fragment. A group of words lacking either a subject or a verb; an incomplete sentence.

sexist language. Language that excludes or demeans one sex or the other. See Chapter 13.

simile. A figure of speech in which one thing is explicitly likened to something else: e.g., *The lawn is* **as** *smooth* **as** *a billiard table; The lake is* **like** *glass.* Similes are neither as direct nor as vivid as **metaphors**.

simple sentence. A sentence made up of only one clause: e.g., *Joan climbed the tree.*

slang. Colloquial speech, inappropriate for academic writing; often used in a special sense by a particular group: e.g., *gross* for *disgusting; gig* as a musi-cian's term.

split infinitive. A construction in which a word is placed between *to* and the base verb: e.g., *to completely finish*. Many people object to this kind of construction, but splitting infinitives is sometimes necessary when the alternatives are awkward or ambiguous.

squinting modifier. A kind of misplaced modifier; one that could be connected to elements on either side, making meaning ambiguous: e.g., *When he wrote the letter* **finally** *his boss thanked him*.

standard English. The English spoken and written by literate people; or, the set of words, grammar, and basic linguistic sounds that are used by them. There are no set rules for governing what is accepted as the English language develops. (In contrast, the *Académie française* decides what, and what not, to accept as appropriate French.) Two broadly based forms of English are recognized: British-English and American-English. British-English is sometimes referred to as International English, since it extends from Britain throughout the Commonwealth, and more widely. "Non-standard" English (some of it class-based) can be found in numerous locales as well as broad regional settings (with some unique words) within Britain and the United States and also in Canada, New Zealand, Australia, South Africa, India, the West Indies, and so on. In addition, of course, there are different accents everywhere!

stem. The basic word to which prefixes and suffixes are added. The stem remains unchanged: e.g., *agriculture, agricultural, agriculturist, monoagriculture*.

subject. In grammar, the noun or noun equivalent about which something is predicated; that part of a clause with which the verb agrees: e.g., **They** *swim every day*; *the* **tortoise** *laid her eggs*.

subjective complement. See **complement**.

subjectivity. A personal stance, not impartial. See **objectivity**.

subordinate clause. See **clause**.

subordinating conjunction. See **conjunction**.

subordination. Making one clause in a sentence dependent on another.

suffix. An addition placed at the end of a word to form a derivative: e.g., *prepare—preparation*; *sing—singing*. See **prefix**.

symbol (in science). Shortened form of a term: e.g., *CO*$_2$ stands for *carbon dioxide*; *Hz* stands for *hertz*. See also **symbolism**.

symbolism. The use of one thing to represent or suggest something other than itself: e.g., in some cultures, white is a symbol of innocence; the maple leaf is a symbol of Canada.

synonyms. Words with the same dictionary meaning: e.g., *begin* and *commence*.

syntax. Sentence construction; the grammatical relations of words.

tautology. Repetition using different words, usually unnecessarily: e.g., *The tractor* **returned back** *to the shed*.

technical writing. Writing by a specialist for other specialists—as in soils engineering or fluvial geography—using technical words and phrases that may not be familiar to outside readers.

tense. The time reference of verbs.

theme. A recurring or dominant idea.

thesis statement. A one-sentence assertion that gives the central argument of an essay or thesis.

topic sentence. The sentence in a paragraph (usually at the beginning) that expresses the main or controlling idea.

transition word. A word that shows the logical relation between sentences or parts of a sentence and thus helps to signal the change from one idea to another: e.g., *therefore, also, accordingly*.

transitive verb. One that takes an object: e.g., *hit, bring, cover*.

usage. Accepted practice.

verb. That part of a predicate expressing an action, state of being, or condition, telling what a subject is or does. Verbs inflect to show tense (time). The principal parts of a verb are the three basic forms from which all tenses are made: the base infinitive, the past tense, and the past participle.

verbal. A word that is similar in form to a verb but does not function as one: a participle, a gerund, or an infinitive. Also, oral or spoken words, rather than written words.

voice. The form of a verb that shows whether the subject acted (active voice) or was acted upon (passive voice): e.g., *He* **hit** *the ball* (active). *The ball* **was hit** *by him* (passive). Only transitive verbs (verbs taking objects) can be passive.

Chapter Summary

In this final chapter we have provided definitions of numerous terms you likely will encounter and need to use in your geography, sustainability, and environmental courses. In addition, we have included definitions of basic words and concepts related to writing. If you take the time to learn these and other terms, you should become more adept in their use and, once again, improve the quality of your written work and enhance your ability to communicate effectively.

Notes

1. Anssi Paasi, *Territories, Boundaries and Consciousness* (Chichester: Wiley, 1996).
2. "Ecological Footprint," Global Footprint Network, accessed July 10, 2018, https://www.footprintnetwork.org/our-work/ecological-footprint/.
3. Yi-Fu Tuan, "A View of Geography," *Geographical Review*, 81 (1991): 99; the full article is on pp. 99–107. See also Geoffrey J. Martin, *All Possible Worlds: A History of Geographical Ideas*, 4th ed. (New York: Oxford University Press, 2005).
4. John E. Chappell, Jr., "Relations Between Geography and Other Disciplines," in *On Becoming a Professional Geographer*, M.S. Kenzer, ed. (Columbus: Merrill, 1989), pp. 17–31.
5. Anne Buttimer, *The Practice of Geography* (London: Methuen, 1983), p. 12.
6. For discussions of the full array of specialties, methods, techniques, and applications see the references listed in note 1 in Chapter 2.

7. Harm J. de Blij, *Why Geography Matters: Three Challenges Facing America* (New York: Oxford University Press, 2005).

8. Denis Cosgrove and Stephen Daniels, *The Iconography of Landscape* (Cambridge: Cambridge University Press, 1998); Peter Atkins, I. Simmons, and B. Roberts, *People, Land and Time: An Historical Introduction to the Relations Between Landscape, Culture and Environment* (London: Arnold, 1998); and Brett Wallach, *Understanding the Cultural Landscape* (New York: Guilford, 2005).

9. David Lowenthal, *The Heritage Crusade and the Spoils of History* (Cambridge: Cambridge University Press, 1998).

10. Donella H. Meadows, Dennis L. Meadows, Jorgen Randers, and William W. Behrens III. *The Limits to Growth: A Report of the Club of Rome's Project on the Predicament of Mankind* (New York: Universe Books, 1972).

11. Donella H. Meadows, Dennis L. Meadows, and Jorgen Randers. *Beyond the Limits: Confronting Global Collapse, Envisioning a Sustainable Future* (White River Junction, VT: Chelsea Green Publishing Co., 1992).

12. R.J. Chorley, "Geography as Human Ecology," in *Directions in Geography*, R.J. Chorley, ed. (London: Methuen; New York: Barnes and Noble, 1973), p. 158.

13. Neil Evernden, *The Social Creation of Nature* (Baltimore: Johns Hopkins University Press, 1992).

14. Edward W. Said, *Orientalism* (New York: Vintage Books, 1979), and Anne Godlewska and Neil Smith, eds., *Geography and Empire* (Oxford: Blackwell, 1994).

15. David B. Knight, "People Together, Yet Apart: Rethinking Territory, Sovereignty, and Identities," in *Reordering the World: Geopolitical Perspectives on the 21st Century*, 2nd ed., George J. Demko and William B. Wood, eds. (Boulder, CO: Westview, 1999), pp. 209–26.

16. Jean Gottmann, *The Significance of Territory* (Charlottesville: University Press of Virginia, 1973), and Robert David Sack, *Human Territoriality: Its Theory and History* (Cambridge: Cambridge University Press, 1986).

Appendix I
Weights, Measures, and Notation

The conversion factors are not exact unless so marked. They are given only to the accuracy likely to be needed in everyday calculations. Imperial measurements are used in Canada. You may not know the following: *are*, as a noun, refers to a surface measure equal to 100 square metres (100 ares = 1 hectare, the principal unit of land measurement for most of the world); *cwt* means a hundredweight (*c* being Latin for 100), commonly equivalent to 100 pounds, or 45.359 kilograms.

1. METRIC PREFIXES

	Abbr. or symbol	Factor
deca-	da	10
hecto-	h	10^2
kilo-	k	10^3
mega-	M	10^6
giga-	G	10^9
tera-	T	10^{12}
peta-	P	10^{15}
exa-	E	10^{18}
deci-	d	10^{-1}
centi-	c	10^{-2}
milli-	m	10^{-3}
micro-	μ	10^{-6}
nano-	n	10^{-9}
pico-	p	10^{-12}
femto-	f	10^{-15}
atto-	a	10^{-18}

These prefixes may be applied to any units of the metric system, such as: hectogram (hg) = 100 grams; kilowatt (kW) = 1,000 watts; megahertz (MHz) = 1 million hertz; centimetre (cm) = 1/100 metre; microvolt (μV) = one-millionth of a volt; picofarad (pF) = 10^{-12} one trillionth of a farad; and are sometimes applied to other units (megabit).

2. IMPERIAL AND AMERICAN, WITH METRIC EQUIVALENTS

Linear measure

1 inch	= 25.4 millimetres exactly
1 foot = 12 inches	= 0.3048 metre exactly
1 yard = 3 feet	= 0.9144 metre exactly
1 (statute) mile = 1,760 yards	= 1.609 kilometres
1 int. nautical mile = 1.150779 miles	= 1.852 km exactly

Square measure

1 square inch	= 6.45 sq. centimetres
1 square foot = 144 sq. in.	= 9.29 sq. decimetres
1 square yard = 9 sq. ft.	= 0.836 sq. metre
1 acre = 4,840 sq. yd.	= 0.405 hectare
1 square mile = 640 acres	= 259 hectares

Cubic measure

1 cubic inch		= 16.4 cu. centimetres
1 cubic foot = 1,728 cu. in.		= 0.0283 cu. metre
1 cubic yard = 27 cu. fl.		= 0.765 cu. metre

Capacity measure

Name	System	Equal to	Metric
fluid oz.	Imperial	1/20 imp. pint	28.41 ml
	US (liquid)	1/16 US pint	29.57 ml
gill	Imperial	1/4 pint	142.07 ml
	US (liquid)	1/4 pint	118.29 ml
pint	Imperial	20 fl.oz.(imp.)	568.26 ml
	US (liquid)	16 fl.oz.(US)	473.18 ml
	US (dry)	1/2 quart	550.61 ml
quart	Imperial	2 pints	1.1365 litres
	US (liquid)	2 pints	0.9464 litre
	US (dry)	2 pints	1.1012 litres
gallon	Imperial	4 quarts	4.546 litres
	US (liquid)	4 quarts	3.785 litres
peck	Imperial	2 gallons	9.092 litres
	US (dry)	8 quarts	8.810 litres
bushel	Imperial	4 pecks	36.369 litres
	US (dry)	4 pecks	35.239 litres

Avoirdupois weight

1 grain	= 0.065 gram
1 dram	= 1.772 grams
1 ounce =16 drams	= 28.35 grams
1 pound =16 ounces = 7,000 grains	= 0.45359237 kilogram exactly
1 stone = 14 pounds	= 6.35 kilograms
1 quarter = 2 stones	= 12.70 kilograms
1 hundredweight = 4 quarters = 112 lb.	= 50.80 kilograms
1 (long) ton = 20 cwt. = 2,240 lb.	= 1.016 tonnes
1 short ton = 2,000 pounds	= 0.907 tonne

3. METRIC, WITH IMPERIAL EQUIVALENTS

Linear measure

1 millimetre	= 0.039 inch
1 centimetre = 10 mm	= 0.394 inch
1 decimetre = 10 cm	= 3.94 inches
1 metre = 100 cm	= 1.094 yards
1 decametre = 10 m	= 10.94 yards
1 hectometre = 100 m	= 109.4 yards
1 kilometre = 1,000 m	= 0.6214 mile

Square measure

1 square centimetre	= 0.155 sq. inch
1 square metre = 10,000 sq. cm	= 1.196 sq. yards
1 are = 100 sq. metres	= 119.6 sq. yards

1 hectare = 100 ares	= 2.471 acres
1 square kilometre = 100 ha	= 0.386 sq. mile

Cubic measure

1 cubic centimetre	= 0.061 cu. inch
1 cubic metre = one million cu. cm	= 1.308 cu. yards

Capacity measure

1 millilitre	= 0.002 pint (Imperial)
1 centilitre = 10 ml	= 0.018 pint
1 decilitre = 100 ml	= 0.176 pint
1 litre = 1,000 ml	= 1.76 pints
1 decalitre = 10 l	= 2.20 gallons (Imperial)
1 hectolitre = 100 l	= 2.75 bushels (Imperial)

Weight

1 milligram	= 0.015 grain
1 centigram = 10 mg	= 0.154 grain
1 decigram = 100 mg	= 1.543 grain
1 gram = 1,000 mg	= 15.43 grain
1 decagram = 10 g	= 5.64 drams
1 hectogram = 100 g	= 3.527 ounces
1 kilogram = 1,000 g	= 2.205 pounds
1 tonne (metric ton) = 1,000 kg	= 0.984 (long) ton

4. SI UNITS (INTERNATIONAL SYSTEM OF UNITS)

Base units

Physical quantity	Name	Abbr. or symbol
length	metre	m
mass	kilogram	kg
time	second	s
electric current	ampere	A
temperature	kelvin	K
amount of substance	mole	mol
luminous intensity	candela	cd

Supplementary units

Physical quantity	Name	Abbr. or symbol
plane angle	radian	rad
solid angle	steradian	sr

Derived units with special names

Physical quantity	Name	Abbr. or symbol
frequency	hertz	Hz
energy	joule	J
force	newton	N
power	watt	W
pressure	pascal	Pa
electric charge	coulomb	C
electromotive force	volt	V
electric resistance	ohm	O
electric conductance	siemens	S
electric capacitance	farad	F
magnetic flux	weber	Wb
inductance	henry	H
magnetic flux density	tesla	T
luminous flux	lumen	lm
illumination	lux	lx

TEMPERATURE

Celsius (or Centigrade): Water boils (under standard conditions) at 100° and freezes at 0°

Fahrenheit: Water boils at 212° and freezes at 32°

Kelvin: Water boils at 373.15 kelvins and freezes at 273.15 kelvins

Celsius	Fahrenheit
−17.8°	0°
−10°	14°
0°	32°
10°	50°
20°	68°
30°	86°
40°	104°
50°	122°
60°	140°
70°	158°
80°	176°
90°	194°
100°	212°

To convert Celsius into Fahrenheit: multiply by 9, divide by 5, and add 32.

To convert Fahrenheit to Celsius: subtract 32, multiply by 5, and divide by 9.

POWER NOTATION

This expresses concisely any power of ten (any number that is composed of factors of 10). 10^2 or ten squared = $10 \times 10 = 100$; 10^3 or ten cubed = $10 \times 10 \times 10 = 1,000$. Similarly, $10^4 = 10,000$ and $10^{10} =$ one followed by ten zeros = 10,000,000,000. Proceeding in the opposite direction, dividing by ten and subtracting one from the index, we have $10^2 = 100$, $10^1 = 10$, $10^0 = 1$, $10^{-1} = 1/10$, $10^{-2} = 1/100$, and so on; $10^{-10} = 1/10,000,000,000$.

BINARY SYSTEM

Only two units (0 and 1) are used, and the position of each unit indicates a power of two. One to ten written in binary form:

	eights (2^3)	fours (2^2)	twos (2^1)	one
1				1
2			1	0
3			1	1
4	1	0	0	
5		1	0	1
6		1	1	0
7		1	1	1
8	1	0	0	0
9	1	0	0	1
10	1	0	1	0

Ten is written as 1010 ($2^3 + 0 + 2^1 + 0$); one hundred is written as 1100100 ($2^6 + 2^5 + 0 + 0 + 2^2 + 0 + 0$).

Appendix II

Selected Websites of Interest to Geographers, Sustainability Scholars, and Environmental Scientists

The following (selective) URL list includes websites of special interest to geographers and others concerned with environmental issues. Some offer access to specific agencies and their publications, and many offer links to other useful sites.

American Association of Geographers (AAG): www.aag.org
American Association of Geographers: My Community, Our Earth: www.aag.org/sustainable
American Geographical Portal: www.amergeog.org
Association for the Advancement of Sustainability in Higher Education: www.aashe.org
Australian Government – Department of the Environment and Energy: environment.gov.au
BBC Online: www.bbc.co.uk
Bioline International: www.bioline.org.br
Botany, Internet Directory for: www.botany.net/IDB/
British Library, The: www.bl.uk
Canada—Agriculture and Agri-Food Canada: www.agr.gc.ca
Canada—Archives Canada: www.archivescanada.ca
Canada—Atlas of Canada: atlas.nrcan.gc.ca
Canada—Auditor General of Canada, Office of: www.oag-bvg.gc.ca
Canada—Canadian Environmental Assessment Agency: https://www.canada.ca/en/environmental-assessment-agency
Canada—Committee on the Status of Endangered Wildlife in Canada: https://www.canada.ca/en/environment-climate-change/services/committee-status-endangered-wildlife.html
Canada—Environment and Climate Change Canada: https://www.canada.ca/en/environment-climate-change.html
Canada—Fisheries and Oceans Canada: www.dfo-mpo.gc.ca
Canada—Indigenous and North Affairs Canada: http://www.aadnc-aandc.gc.ca
Canada—Library and Archives Canada: www.nlc-bnc.ca
Canada—National Energy Board: www.neb.gc.ca
Canada—Natural Resources Canada – Earth Sciences: www.nrcan.gc.ca/earth-sciences
Canada—Natural Resources Canada – Energy Efficiency: www.nrcan.gc.ca/energy/offices-labs/office-energy-efficiency
Canada—Natural Resources Canada: www.nrcan.gc.ca
Canada—Natural Resources Canada: www.nrcan.gc.ca/forests
Canada—Parks Canada: www.pc.gc.ca
Canada—Polar Continental Shelf Program: www.nrcan.gc.ca/the-north/polar-continental-shelf-program
Canada—Statistics Canada: www.statcan.gc.ca
Canada—Sustainable Development: www.canada.ca/en/environment-climate-change/services/sustainable-development.html
Canadian Association of Geographers (CAG): www.cag-acg.ca
Canadian Broadcasting Corporation (CBC): www.cbc.ca
Canadian Environmental Law Association: www.cela.ca

Canadian Geographic Education: http://www.cangeoeducation.ca/
Canadian Legal Information Institute: www.canlii.org
Canadian Society of Soil Science: www.csss.ca
Canadian Water Network: www.cwn-rce.ca
Canadian Water Resources Association: www.cwra.org
Center for International Earth Science Information Network (CIESIN): www.ciesin.org
Directory of Open Access Journals: www.doaj.org
Earthweek—a diary of the planet: www.earthweek.com
Encyclopaedia Britannica Online: www.britannica.com
EnviroLink: www.envirolink.org
Environmental Activism (incl. international): www.ecomall.com/activism
Environmental Science.org: https://www.environmentalscience.org/sustainability
ESRI—What is GIS?: https://www.esri.com/en-us/what-is-gis/overview
Federation of Canadian Municipalities: www.fcm.ca
Geograph (Ordnance Survey), photos and maps of the UK: www.geograph.org.uk
Geographical Association (UK): www.geography.org.uk
Geography Departments Worldwide: univ.cc/geolinks
GeoHive (Global Population Statistics): www.geohive.com
Global Change International Geosphere-Biosphere Programme: www.igbp.net
Global Change Master Directory: gcmd.nasa.gov
Home of Geography: www.homeofgeography.org
Human Rights Watch: hrw.org
Humanities and Social Sciences Online: H-Net Discussion Networks: www.h-net.org/lists/
Intergovernmental Panel on Climate Change: www.ipcc.ch
International Boundaries Research Unit, Durham University: www.dur.ac.uk/ibru/
International Council for Science (ICSU): www.icsu.org
International Geographical Union: igu-online.org
International Geography Olympiad (iGeo): www.geoolympiad.org
International Joint Commission (Canada and the US): www.ijc.org
International Labour Organization: www.ilo.org
International Organizations, Disasters & Humanitarian Relief: www.lib.berkeley.edu/
    doemoff/govinfo/intl/gov_humane.html
ipl2: information you can trust: www.ipl.org
Library of Congress: Cultural Landscapes: memory.loc.gov/ammem/gmdhtml/setlhome.html
Library of Congress: Geography & Map Reading Room: www.loc.gov/rr/geogmap/
Local Governments for Sustainability (Canada): http://www.icleicanada.org/
Major International Health Organizations, The: www.imva.org/Pages/orgfrm.htm
NASA: www.nasa.gov
NASA's Earth Observing System: eospso.gsfc.nasa.gov
National Council for Geographic Education (US): www.ncge.org
National Geographic Society (US): www.nationalgeographic.com
*NationMaster (a massive central data source on myriad topics for numerous countries; you
    can generate maps and graphs on all kinds of statistics)*: www.nationmaster.com
New Zealand—Environment and Conservation Organizations: www.eco.org.nz/about-us/
    ECO-networks.html
New Zealand—Ministry for the Environment: www.mfe.govt.nz
Newspapers: www.onlinenewspapers.com *and* www.newspapers.com
NGO links: www.ngo.org/links/index.htm
*Northwestern University Libraries – Government & Geographic Information
    Collection*: www.library.northwestern.edu/libraries-collections/evanston-campus/
    government-information/international-documents

Ontario Association for Geographic and Environmental Education: www.oagee.org
Pembina Institute: www.pembina.org
Program on Water Issues: www.powi.ca
Resources for Economists on the Internet: rfe.org
Resources for the Future: www.rff.org
Royal Canadian Geographical Society: www.rcgs.org
Royal Geographical Society, (UK): www.rgs.org
Smithsonian (US): www.si.edu
Smithsonian Museum of Natural History: www.mnh.si.edu
Society for Human Ecology: www.societyforhumanecology.org
Soil Conservation Council of Canada: www.soilcc.ca
Soil Science Society of America: www.soils.org
Sustainability International: https://www.sustainability-international.org/
Sustainability Network: https://sustainabilitynetwork.ca/
Sustainable Development: www.ulb.ac.be/ceese/meta/sustvl.html
ThoughtCo – Geography: https://www.thoughtco.com/geography-4133035
UN Cartographic Section: www.un.org/Depts/Cartographic/english/htmain.htm
UN Development Programme: www.undp.org
UN Environment Programme: www.unep.org
UN Framework Convention on Climate Change: unfccc.int/2860.php
UN Office for Sustainable Development: www.unosd.org
UN Refugee Agency: www.unhcr.org
UN Sustainable Development Knowledge Platform: sustainabledevelopment.un.org/
    index.html
UNESCO World Heritage List: whc.unesco.org
UNESCO: www.unesco.org/new/en/unesco/
UNICEF (for country stats): www.unicef.org
Union of Concerned Scientists: www.ucsusa.org
United Nations: www.un.org
United States—Census, numerous sites including: www.census.gov *and* www.census.gov/
    geo/www/maps/
United States—CIA World Factbook: www.cia.gov/library/publications/
    the-world-factbook/
United States—Department of State, Background Notes: www.state.gov/r/pa/ei/bgn
United States—Environmental Protection Agency: www.epa.gov
United States—Geological Survey, numerous sites, including: www.usgs.gov *and*
    nationalmap.gov *and* geography.usgs.gov *and* www.usgs.gov/science/ *and* www.usgs
    .gov/envirohealth/
United States—National Atlas: www.nationalatlas.gov
United States—State and Local Government on the Net: www.statelocalgov.net
United States—USGS Earthshots: Satellite Images of Environmental Change: earthshots.
    usgs.gov
World Bank: www.worldbank.org
World Health Organization: www.who.int/en/
World Meteorological Organization: www.wmo.int/pages/index_en.html
World Trade Organization: www.wto.org
Worldwatch Institute: www.worldwatch.org
WWW Virtual Library, The: www.vlib.org

Index

Note: Some terms not found in the index may be found in the "Important Definitions" section.

The Making Sense Series

Margot Northey
MAKING SENSE
A Student's Guide to Research and Writing
Ninth Edition

Margot Northey, Dianne Draper, and David B. Knight
MAKING SENSE IN GEOGRAPHY AND ENVIRONMENTAL SCIENCES
A Student's Guide to Research and Writing
Seventh Edition

Margot Northey, Lorne Tepperman, and Patrizia Albanese
MAKING SENSE IN THE SOCIAL SCIENCES
A Student's Guide to Research and Writing
Seventh Edition

Margot Northey and Judi Jewinski
MAKING SENSE IN ENGINEERING AND THE PHYSICAL SCIENCES
A Student's Guide to Research and Writing
Sixth Edition

Margot Northey and Patrick von Aderkas
MAKING SENSE IN THE LIFE SCIENCES
A Student's Guide to Research and Writing
Third Edition

Margot Northey, Bradford A. Anderson, and Joel N. Lohr
MAKING SENSE IN RELIGIOUS STUDIES
A Student's Guide to Research and Writing
Third Edition

Margot Northey and Brian Timney
MAKING SENSE IN PSYCHOLOGY
A Student's Guide to Research and Writing
Third Edition